UNITING STATES

Uniting States

VOLUNTARY UNION IN WORLD POLITICS

Joseph M. Parent

OXFORD
UNIVERSITY PRESS

OXFORD
UNIVERSITY PRESS

Oxford University Press, Inc., publishes works that further
Oxford University's objective of excellence
in research, scholarship, and education.

Oxford   New York
Auckland   Cape Town   Dar es Salaam   Hong Kong   Karachi
Kuala Lumpur   Madrid   Melbourne   Mexico City   Nairobi
New Delhi   Shanghai   Taipei   Toronto

With offices in
Argentina   Austria   Brazil   Chile   Czech Republic   France   Greece
Guatemala   Hungary   Italy   Japan Poland   Portugal   Singapore
South Korea   Switzerland   Thailand   Turkey   Ukraine   Vietnam

Published by Oxford University Press, Inc.
198 Madison Avenue, New York, New York 10016

www.oup.com

Oxford is a registered trademark of Oxford University Press

Library of Congress Cataloging-in-Publication Data
Parent, Joseph M.
Uniting States : voluntary union in world politics / Joseph M. Parent.
   p.   cm.
Includes bibliographical references.
ISBN 978-0-19-978219-2 (hardback : alk. paper)—ISBN 978-0-19-978220-8 (pbk. : alk. paper)
1. Federal government. 2. Confederation of states. 3. Constitutional history—United States.
4. European federation. 5. Latin American federation. I. Title.
JC355.P33   2011
327.1'16—dc22   2010053178

9 7 8 6 5 4 3 2 1

Printed in the United States of America
on acid-free paper

For Kate and Jerry Parent

Contents

Acknowledgments

YOU MAY BE tempted to skip ahead to the work proper, dedications not having the significance they once held. But books ask a lot from readers, and readers have a right to know up front at whom the work is aimed, who had a hand in its production, and who their tour guide is. Content is no doubt more important than the carrier; nonetheless, the intended audience and the author's debts may be of use to you.

This book is intended to provoke political scientists, irritate historians, challenge scholars of American politics, educate general interest readers, and entertain undergraduates. It is written for intelligent non-specialists and presumes little prior background.

What follows should dispel any illusions about this being the work of a lone gunman, if the notes—once delightfully described as "promiscuous overcitation"— do not. I would be remiss to extend my gratitude only to those kind souls who helped me along the last stretch of road. Driving a moving donkey is one thing, moving an inert ass is another. In Milwaukee, Jack Bleier, the late Muriel Bukant, Suzanne Kessler, Kathy Kupfer, Barbara Netzow, the late Mary Ellen Ladogiannis, the late Raffaele Sacripanti, and Mike Sweeney deserve paeans for overcoming my stubborn indolence.

At Chicago, Jasen Castillo, the late Chee-Jun Chan, James Fearon, Michael Freeman, Hyung-Min Joo, John Mearsheimer, Bart Schultz, Nathan Tarcov, Lynn

Tesser, and Steve Walt exceeded their charge. Without their tolerant instruction I would not have produced this and would, presumably, have met a reverse fate: stuck at a hateful job (or worse), and quarantined for authority problems. I cannot prove it, but I am pretty sure that I would never have been admitted to Columbia University unless Richard Betts took a chance on me, which made a large difference in my life. At different times, Tom Bernstein, Bob Legvold, and Andy Nathan's active forbearance kept me in the field.

Many eyes read earlier drafts, and the most buoyant glutton for punishment was Josh Baron, a friend good and true, who loyally told me what I did not want to hear. This work would have been vastly inferior without his years of bellyaching. My advisors, Bob Jervis, Jack Snyder, and Ken Waltz—all living proof that political realists are lovable—acted as if liberally paroled from their incentive structures. They were unsurpassable in their advice, candor, courtesy, and efficiency. Consuelo Cruz, Page Fortna, and Erik Gartzke helped in the early drafts, and Alex Cooley, Bruce Cronin, Daniel Deudney, Andrew Moravcsik, and Jeff Staton aided in the end stages.

For help on the hypotheses chapter, my appreciation to Bernd Beber, Tanisha Fazal, Suzanne Katzenstein, and Alex Weisiger; Akhil Amar, Brian Barry, Marc Dodge, Stacie Goddard, Paul MacDonald, Jon Monten, and Rich Robinson made the American chapter better; and Reidar Maliks was a Greek chorus in the Sweden-Norway chapter. For aid with the appendix, thanks to Adam Branch, Hanna Gray, Alison Kennedy, Frank Lovett, Zane Mackin, Stefan Pedatella, Panos Papadopoulos, Fritz Stern, and Nadia Urbinati. Chris Robinson did the maps. The indefatigable Bob Art and intrepid Ken Waltz requested, endured, and commented on multiple drafts of several chapters. I owe an inordinate debt especially to Ken; he and his beloved wife Huddie showed great grace and kindness to my wife and I, for which we are unceasingly grateful.

The Saltzman Institute of War and Peace Studies funded fieldwork for constitutional research. Columbia University funded presentations at the Athens Institute for Education and Research in May 2004, the Columbia University International Politics Seminar, September 2005, and the Midwest Political Science Association Conference, April 2006. The Political Science Department's faculty workshop at the University of Miami afforded a constructive forum and a demanding gauntlet; my thanks to Merike Blofield, Louise Davidson-Schmich, George Gonzalez, Roger Kanet, Casey Klofstad, Greg Koger, Art Simon, Bill Smith, and Joe Uscinski. Given the work's pedigree, the fault can only lay with me if the progeny produced is a bastard.

Sebastian Rosato gregariously shared book manuscripts with me. Portions of this book first appeared as "Europe's Structural Idol: An American Federalist

Republic?" Reprinted by permission from *Political Science Quarterly*, vol. 124, no. 3 (Fall 2009), pp. 513–535. Much of the appendix first saw light as "Machiavelli's Missing Romulus and the Murderous Intent of *The Prince*," *History of Political Thought*, vol. 26, no. 4 (Winter 2005), pp. 625–645, and appears here also by permission. At Oxford, Caelyn Cobb, Dave McBride, Michael O'Connor, and an anonymous reviewer were patient, professional, and supportive.

My friends and family suffered me with good humor, and without them I would not have been compelled to write. My heroic partner Abby kept my head down on good days and up on bad ones. I am sorry I could not complete the project before the deaths of my grandparents, and hope it reflects the values they worked hard to instill. For their thoughtful support, I must also single out my uncles Jim, John, and Peter Morse, and my aunts Connie, Janet, and Marcia. The book is dedicated to my parents, Jerry and Kate. Whatever exertions and sacrifices I made to produce this, theirs were much greater. Profound thanks.

Coconut Grove, Florida

August 2010

UNITING STATES

In Theseus, however, they had a king of equal intelligence and power; and one of the chief features in his organization of the country was . . . to merge them in the single council chamber and town hall of the present capital. . . . so that when Theseus died he left a great state behind him.

—THUCYDIDES[1]

1

Introduction

ENVY GEORGE WASHINGTON. When he died in 1799, he had liberated and united thirteen sprawling and disparate states, founding a country that would rocket to great power status within a century, and within two centuries attain levels of power never seen in modern history. He died in his bed, wealthy and beloved, surrounded by adoring compatriots.

Contrast Washington's tranquil demise with the last throes of another great American. Simón Bolívar, also a heroic general and liberator, was consumed in a futile bid to unify five sprawling and disparate states. His lungs filled with green fluid, he died alone on the highway, abject, betrayed, exiled, and despised. He lit the flame for a unified, continental power, but his torch lies extinguished where he fell.

In the pantheon of fortune's favorites, what bestows brilliant success on some unifiers and crushing failure on others? What makes some states come together and others fall apart? Everyone knows that ruthless force is capable of enforcing unity at gunpoint; dictators and despots are amply understood. Yet Washington and Bolívar rise above ordinary leaders. They refused to degenerate into tyrants, their unions were voluntary, and their examples contain golden lessons on a fundamental issue in international politics: the problem of peaceful change.

Unification is uncommon, voluntary unions more so. We can see how dreaded a prospect political merger is by how seldom it happens and the lengths states go to avoid it. Fifty of 202 states have died since 1815; 35 have done so violently.[2] Like revolutions and wars, voluntary unions are quite rare, but rare events tell us a great deal about what orders societies in normal times.

Voluntary union is a potential solution for several persistent problems. Some see in voluntary union a remedy for environmental threats, as well as for conventional and nuclear war.[3] If we wish to have an informed debate on the European Union (EU) or other "ever closer unions," we would do well to put them in comparative perspective. Imagine how different history would look if Theseus's Athens or Washington's United States had not united. In short, understanding how weak, divided areas become strong, unified states is a challenge of the first order and sheds light on federalism, partition, identity formation, and how to escape anarchy.

Despite the need for a good explanation of voluntary union, no school of thought has come up with one. If realists are right, voluntary union should never happen. States value their sovereignty supremely and would never give it up to a state that could not conquer them. Yet the United States and Switzerland are glaring exceptions to this view. If liberals and constructivists are right, voluntary union should be much more common. Classic determinants of integration, like trade and communication, are stronger than they have ever been. Yet the number of states in the world has spiraled up, and the most favorable arena for unification, the EU, seems to be hitting a glass ceiling.

I argue that unification is an extreme alliance prompted by extreme circumstances. First, unification demands a peculiar set of background conditions. In order for union to occur, states must balance against an optimally intense, indefinite, symmetrically afflicting threat. Second, elites must exploit a security crisis to trigger rethinking of foreign policy. Third, elites must persuade the relevant domestic audiences of unification's necessity. Elites effect their drastic policy by influencing three pathways: the media, the military, and political procedures.

Running this logic in reverse helps explain why states disintegrate. I test the argument against the universe of cases: two successes, the United States and Switzerland, and two successes that later failed, Sweden-Norway and Gran Colombia, and then analyze the prospects of the EU. Having sketched some puzzles of voluntary union, my argument, and evidence, the next section details what this work is about, and the last section overviews the book.

GROUNDWORK: OVERCOMING ANARCHY THE EASY WAY

My central question is: What causes voluntary political union? This question prompts the issues of what a voluntary political union is and how we know one when we see it. Let us define what is intended by voluntary, political, and union,

respectively. Two factors make union less voluntary. The first is the power disparity between unifying states. When a large state annexes a small state, the outcome
cannot be called voluntary. Hitler absorbed Czechoslovakia peacefully, but few
scholars struggle to explain why. Equal states can threaten destabilizing war, but
they cannot credibly threaten conquest.[4]

The second factor is external aid; some powerful states wish to sponsor a
union but not join it. There is no satisfactory way to describe this set of unions,
but I refer to them as forced unions. No matter how benign, external intervention is a phenomenon different from up-by-the-bootstraps, self-help unification.
Any muscular, motivated matchmaker is also burly enough to change the security environment, effectively blunting the necessity to balance against threats.
These distinctions are broken down in table 1.1.

All these paths are worthy of study, but they lead in different directions. If the
battles must be fought, they should be fought sequentially. My primary interest
is explaining voluntary union. Why? Because these cases offer secrets to profound cooperation with minimal coercion but are badly served by existing theories. The rest of this work focuses on the upper left box of table 1.1: self-help,
equal unions. Thus, some cases are excluded from my purview either because
they are between unequals (e.g., the formation of the USSR, Germany, Italy,
Tanganyika-Zanzibar, Malaysia-Singapore, the United Arab Republic, and Yemen)
and/or because union was guided by outside powers (e.g., the Balkan League and
many postcolonial states).[5]

Next, political unions should be contrasted with monetary, economic, social, or
cultural unions. Politics is fundamentally about power, not money, status, or culture, although of course these things intertwine. For analytical clarity, this work
will concentrate on concentrations of power. Attempts to unify are essentially
wagers on the optimal strength of a state.[6]

Finally, union involves a transition from anarchy to hierarchy. Hierarchy is a
situation with reliable third-party enforcement; anarchy is a situation without it.

TABLE 1.1

Scope of the Work		
	Self-Help Unions	Forced Unions
Equal Unions	Switzerland, United States	Early EU, Australia
Unequal Unions	USSR, Italy, Germany	Many postcolonial states

The difference between the two turns on how centralized enforcement capability is. Naturally, anarchy and hierarchy need not be dichotomized (see figure 1.1). Why is it useful to do so here? Because crossing the midpoint threshold is the most grueling step. Unification compels a change in political supremacy; it marks a shift in the legitimate use of force in an area; it institutionalizes a new status quo that severely handicaps autonomy.

In practice, we know states have unified when: (1) they formally centralize the means to pursue a single foreign policy, and (2) they cannot legitimately resort to force to resolve disputes between each other.[7] The best hallmark of a unified state is an army that enforces national legal supremacy, but other hallmarks include international recognition and an independent revenue stream larger than any constituent unit.

Wrapping up, this book is about voluntary political unions. For the rest of the work, when I speak of unification or union, I am referring strictly to self-help mergers between equals. Unification is a transition from anarchy to hierarchy, and this phenomenon stands out because it is the most arresting movement along the anarchy-hierarchy spectrum.

THE BENEFITS OF READING ON

The organization of the rest of the work is as follows. Chapter 2 elaborates the logic of my argument, derives testable hypotheses from it, and compares them to alternate hypotheses. Chapter 3 takes a different look at the mysterious origins of the United States Constitution. Chapter 4 analyzes the sources of U.S. unity and evaluates the virtues of the main argument relative to rivals. Chapter 5 reviews the history of Switzerland, and investigates why it took the Swiss hundreds of years to unify while the Americans covered the same ground faster. Chapters 6 and 7 trace the initial successes followed by the failures of union in Sweden-Norway and Gran Colombia to probe why states do *not* unify. Chapter 8 examines the most promising present candidate for voluntary union, Europe, and what stands in its way. And chapter 9 summarizes the results and discusses implications of the work. Without further ado, we go on to chapter 2.

FIGURE 1.1 The Anarchy-Hierarchy Spectrum

[M]en enter upon no enterprise more dangerous or bold than this, for it is very difficult and very dangerous in every part of it.

—MACHIAVELLI[1]

2

Explaining Political Union

FROM THE BEGINNING, realists have looked at voluntary union with disbelief, when they looked at it at all. Thucydides alludes to a case of voluntary union, but does not investigate its causes. Hobbes speculates about states forming in primitive conditions, but only briefly. In terror of nuclear weapons, E. H. Carr, George Kennan, and Hans Morgenthau, among others, have expressed ambivalent interest in liberal ideas on integration, but never developed them. Modern realists, like Kenneth Waltz and Stephen Walt, have discussed unification, but fleetingly.[2] The only realist with detailed thought on unification between equals is Machiavelli, and his scheme entails appalling carnage and papal assassination (see appendix).

Realists down the line have reached similar conclusions for similar reasons: autonomy is too precious to give up without a fight; states seek friends, but never spouses. The patron saints of the realist canon assume that "voluntary unions" is an empty category. Nonetheless, this assumption is empirically false and not entirely consistent with realist logic. States do unify voluntarily, and not just minor states like Switzerland but great powers like the United States.

Other scholars, Akhil Amar and William Riker for instance, offer realist-flavored accounts of unification. They stress security or geopolitics as the root cause of union, and sometimes add that not just fear but greed can cause unification. States unify to fend off strong states or conquer weak ones.[3] Unfortunately, none of these explanations is helpful; they wildly overpredict. Any state at any time can point to something that tempts or threatens it. If a wide range in the degree and kind of threat can cause unification, then when would states *not* be unifying?

I argue that there is a good realist explanation of unification, and it is in fact better than its rivals. To make my case, the next section unpacks the logic of the argument. In the second section, I elaborate the logic of alternate arguments, and sum hypotheses in the third. Finally, the fourth section offers technical specifications of how the argument will be tested.

UNITING WITH LESS FIGHTING: THE LOGIC OF THE ARGUMENT

My main argument is that whether, when, and how states unify depend on opportunity, fortune, and virtue. First, unification will not have the opportunity to occur without a special set of background conditions. Security threats are the only menace capable of effecting such profound political change, and unifying threats must be of a distinct variety: optimally intense, indefinite, and symmetrically shared. Second, these conditions need a spark of fortune to light the flames of unification. This spark takes the form of a public crisis that showcases security deficiencies in the prevailing order. Third, political entrepreneurs persuade their audiences that unification will cure what ails them.[4] Their impact depends on the ability to influence three domestic spheres: the media, the military, and political procedures.

Opportunity: Background Conditions

We start with the basics of realism. States treasure their autonomy, but will cooperate with others when threats force them to. Small threats prompt small responses, but as threat increases, cooperation should increase until the threat

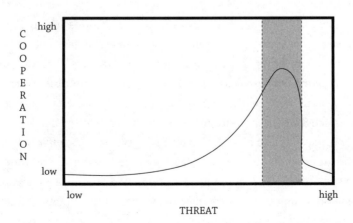

FIGURE 2.1 The Relationship between Cooperation and Threat

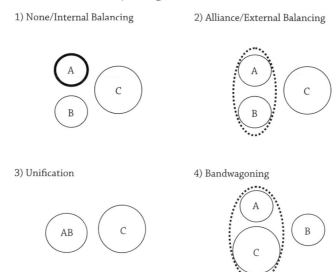

1) None/Internal Balancing

2) Alliance/External Balancing

3) Unification

4) Bandwagoning

FIGURE 2.2 Potential Alignments for a Threatened State

becomes so large that collaboration becomes pointless.[5] Between small and large threats exists a sweet spot, where threats are distant enough to promise rewards from cooperation but close enough to spur action and to discipline thought. The relationship is graphed in figure 2.1.

Within this optimal zone, cooperation is not as straightforward as it seems. Think of two small, contiguous states and a large, distant power; each small state is threatened by the other as well as by the large state. States may side with the stronger, which is bandwagoning, or side with the weaker, which is balancing. Scholars typically think of balancing as either internal—relying only on domestic efforts to manage a threat—or external—seeking outside help to address a threat.

From the perspective of a small state, there are at least four options open: (1) internally balance against the small state and the large state; (2) externally balance against the large state by an alliance of varying intimacy with the other small state; (3) balance against the large state by merging with the other small state; or (4) bandwagon with the large state.[6] These options are summarized in figure 2.2.

Unification is, I argue, the balancing coalition of last resort. Realism suggests that states prefer balancing over bandwagoning and internal balancing over external balancing so states prefer option (1) to option (2) to option (3) to option (4). Unifying states are decisively yielding self-defense capability to a collective, turning neighbors into intimates. Such a strategy is frightening because a number of things can go wrong: the collective might collapse in violence, oppress its members, or elicit attack. Nevertheless, if weak states are desperate, the risks may be worth it. Joining a union beats being at the beck and call of a bigger state or dying alone.

Before unification efforts stand a chance on realist logic, there must be an unusual combination of circumstances. Threat environments do not all look alike, and many, by their nature, suggest some responses over others. The threat environment most conducive to union possesses at once three necessary conditions: optimally intense, indefinite, and symmetrical.

Intensity

Union happens on a knife-edge. Threats need to be extremely intense to suggest unification, but threats that are too intense overwhelm balancing efforts and sterilize them. While unification's parameters are hard to sharply bookend, any threat that could be met with a regular alliance is too small, and any threat that could not be met with the most strenuous alliance is too large. Unification is a last ditch measure; if any other form of balancing will suffice, unification will not happen.

Threats must come from powerful outside states that can be balanced against in a timely manner—unions are designed to fight fire with fire. Still, unifying states will also feel threatened by each other; any state strong enough to be a valuable friend is strong enough to be a nasty enemy. Yet the fear of union partners does not cause unions; it is just a by-product of balancing in an unsafe neighborhood. If states unified to tie down their biggest threats, the balance of power would break down and a world state would result. Should threats inside a union outweigh threats outside a union, that union is headed for disunion.

Duration

Threats must extend to the time horizon for a radical action like unification to make sense. More accurately, union is alluring where states are optimally threatened indefinitely. On this view, duration measures expectations of relative power over one- to two-generation time spans (i.e., 25–50 years). When passing threats are very intense, they do not lead to unification, they lead to alliances. For example, in World War II, the Axis and Allied Powers felt highly threatened, yet states in the war formed strong alliances, not superstates. The threat was quelled, the alliances loosened and reassembled. When threats are less intense but enduring, an abiding alliance or confederation is adequate. Examples here include the lasting alignment of Austria with Germany from the late nineteenth century to the mid-twentieth and the Swiss Confederation prior to 1798. But when states live in the shadow of a persistent, optimal threat, "a constant state of tension places a value on stable leadership and dampening of within-group competition."[7]

On realist logic, unification must be an act of balancing against great power security threats; bandwagoning for profit or prestige are insufficient. Unification is not a short-term swap; it is surrendering the freedom to make war and peace indefinitely. If two states wanted to loot a third, they could simply form an alliance, despoil their opponent, and go their separate ways, as Germany and the Soviet Union did to Poland in 1939. Unification is totally superfluous to such a design, and downright damaging afterward. No booty in the world is great enough to lure states to unify to get it.

Unions are hard to enter into, but harder to leave. However, commitments to a union are not ratcheted in place, and what makes them endure is largely the stamina of common threats. The institutions of union perform the marginal but critical task of tamping down the probability of accidents that could snowball into costly defection. By agreeing to terms, unifying states are tying hands and burning bridges for the foreseeable future, but not forever. When the environment changes, it takes time and expense, but knots can be untied and bridges rebuilt. Union's institutions are no match for major temptations to cheat, but they drain the color from lesser enticements.

This answers Joseph Grieco's concern that realism "has not offered an explanation for the tendency of states to undertake their cooperation through institutionalized arrangements."[8] States use institutions to manage discount rate problems; institutions are successful to the extent that states invest enforcement power in them, and states invest enforcement power in them only as far as threats necessitate. Institutions are like levees of varying fortitude that, sooner or later, shifts in power will break.

Symmetry

Threats are symmetrical when states are mutually vulnerable to military threats, that is, security interdependence.[9] Asymmetric vulnerability acts as a wedge that splits potential partners; if there is a significant disparity in how threats afflict different states, some states will be tepid toward unification. States search for alliance partners when they face an intense threat; states search for unification partners when they face an optimally intense, indefinite threat; but states will not find responses to union overtures until others suffer similar anxieties. In brief, states will not merge unless backed into the same corner. Rather restrictive conditions, these.

Three corollaries follow. First, contiguity aids unity. Symmetry is more likely if unified boundaries would be territorially defensible or a strategic asset. Proximity makes force projection more efficient and perceived threat more uniform.[10] Second, states that grow apart can paradoxically highlight symmetry. If states are security interdependent, then decreases in cooperation will sharply accentuate the stakes. If two people are pushing a boulder uphill and one slacks off, the other will notice and appeal for more support, lest they both be crushed. Third, symmetry is more likely when the number of states is low. It is harder to find symmetrically threatened states and act collectively as numbers increase.[11] For example, the German principalities may have been slow unifiers after the Thirty Years' War because there were too many of them.

In a sense, unification is the result of negligence or ignorance. States seek security, and it would be counterproductive to foster a new and improved adversary. In this way, one person's successful union is another's failure to divide and conquer. When a state sees a union forming, it would require little intelligence or effort to interfere with unification attempts by playing some states off against others, diminishing balancing incentives through blandishments, or by conquering pivotal states. Opposing states should be quick to strangle unions in their cradle if they promise to become a threat. Peripheral states, however, are not worth the trouble. For these reasons, unions are prone to happen on the inner edge of the political periphery—too close to powerful territories invites intervention, too far away deprives unification of its security impetus.

In sum, unification demands that states be symmetrically and durably endangered by a threat grave enough to offset sacrificing sovereignty, but not so overwhelming that a union could not meet the peril. In fact, while there may be cases where union was effected without these conditions, I have not discovered any.

Fortune: Crisis Trigger

An action as extreme as union requires leaden evidence that all is not well. Citizens will not take on faith that drastic action must be done—they need some sort of proof. Causally, triggers are not very important; they are easily found and slightly less easily created.[12] Yet they cannot be conjured out of thin air, and they cannot be dispensed with. Unification can only proceed if some concrete current event or events highlight unification-worthy deficiencies. A critical number of skeptics will not be won over without a high profile setback or setbacks.

Essentially, unification is about security scarcity. Pro-union advocates need crises that signal what a perilous position a state is in. Crises are by their nature wasting assets, and for maximal effectiveness entrepreneurs must strike while the iron is hot. Although almost all of whether states unify is explained by background conditions and how they unify is explained by elite persuasion, some of the "when" is explained by crises.

Virtue: Elite Persuasion

States do not spearhead unification, people do. States are set up to provide stability and continuity; they are designed to protect themselves from radical change. Individuals are necessary to circumvent this conservatism. Is mine an argument exalting individuals, singling out state-making superheroes? That depends on one's expectations. Individuals have little power over whether unification will happen, but much of the when and how are explained by elite politics. Individuals' ideas and actions shape institutions in ways that circumstances do not predestine.[13]

Pro-union political entrepreneurs pitch breathtaking remedies, and gaining converts demands success in several endeavors. The best entrepreneurs are part Martin Luther King, Jr., part P. T. Barnum, and part Gandhi. That is, they must interpret the world in a manner that aids unification, publicize what they see as the problem and the solution, and catalyze policy.[14] Not all entrepreneurs are elites, but it sure helps to be one. When pro-unification entrepreneurs are elites, they have privileged access to three realms that are indispensable to unification drives: the media, the military, and political procedures.

Elite political entrepreneurs are not like common economic entrepreneurs. Very few economic entrepreneurs can reconfigure the market to make it more welcoming to their product, whereas some political elites are capable of slanting circumstances to favor their products. Such persuasion can take verbal and extra-verbal form. While a theory that predicts how elites will win acceptance of their policy is no more likely than a theory predicting how a war will unfold, we can outline critical battles that most contribute to success. Victory goes to elites who dominate at least two of three key tools: the pen, the sword, and the gavel.

Media

Propaganda plays a significant role in unification, since how people react to their environment depends on how they perceive it. Unification involves battles over ideas, and the winners tend to reflect underlying material factors. As Jack Snyder argues, the structure of the marketplace of ideas determines how elites control the sources of information, how segmented the media market is, and how independent journalists are from political elites.[15] Where elites have a strong grasp on the flow of information, they can prejudice audiences in favor of their policies. Where the media market is segmented, elites can better target friendly demographics, while not mobilizing hostile groups—so-called dog whistle politics. Where journalists are heavily dependent on elites, elites naturally possess a propaganda advantage.

Military

Paradoxically, unification is inherently biased against force, but simultaneously biased toward force. In matrimonial terms, union is an indefinite commitment, and states put a premium on their freedom. Without a neighborly nudge (read hefty shove) down the aisle, states are apt to get cold feet. Until they are forced to pick between marriage and losing a promising partner, states would prefer to keep their options open. In Thomas Schelling's apt metaphor, this is the manipulation of risk, like two people in a rowboat, neither of whom wants to fall in the water, but both of whom can influence each other by rocking the boat.[16]

This requires high-wire balancing acts on balancing acts: trying to balance against an outside threat by pushing one's neighbors to unify without pushing them into the arms of an adversary. Being too rough poisons relations between intimates; not being rough enough stalls unification. If an entrepreneur can configure her potential partner's incentives, she can credibly threaten certain war between neighbors now—with all the chaos and risk of outside intervention that would bring—versus union and its attendant uncertainty. Choosing between such unpalatable alternatives, leaders might find union relatively tolerable.

Political Procedures

In addition, powerful entrepreneurs could control the ground rules. With such power, proponents could influence who has a seat at the table, where the table is, what the timetable is, what is discussed, and whose rules prevail.[17] Possessed of an array of procedural powers, even small bands of elites can surprise, divide, and conquer opposition. Of course, one could claim that all politics is procedural manipulation, usually bending the rules to take from the many to give to the few. Yet, even though the lines are sometimes blurry, all is not permitted. When elites can fundamentally change the rules of the political game contrary to the prevailing ground rules, this is an instance of what I intend by procedural manipulation.

Influencing procedures is a delicate operation. Because union requires extraordinary politics—politics outside ordinary means—procedures must be manipulated to transition from anarchy to hierarchy. Nevertheless, the outcome must be viewed as legitimate, discouraging rampant manipulation and encouraging secrecy. Some degree of democracy may facilitate union by allowing enough flexibility to bend the rules to create unions but not break them irreparably, so parties can credibly commit to bargains. In short, if they are to succeed, elites cannot play by regular rules, but they cannot brazenly cheat either.

Extensions of the Argument

The argument has purchase on how state institutions evolve, what conditions encourage particular institutions, and how and why unions dissolve. First, the argument bears on institutional genesis, selection, and stamina. This chapter has argued that institutional innovation arises in the face of security threats, claiming unoriginally that necessity is the mother of invention. At the beginning of the process, threats prompt new thinking about state inadequacies, and, at the end, an institutional arrangement is selected in anticipation of what will answer future security threats. The nature of the threat narrows the range of possible responses, though within that range, competition between entrepreneurs in their idiosyncratic contexts determines what policy is chosen. If an institution is selected imprudently, the environment will punish it until entrepreneurs go back to the drawing board and devise an adequate solution.

International politics is a competitive system, though some periods feature fiercer competition than others, and there are selective pressures on all institutions. Institutional innovations are pruned back if they are not comparatively successful at addressing challenges. Negative feedback is not the only evolutionary mechanism; successful innovations tend to be copied and legitimized, proliferating slightly different adaptations of an innovation across the system to compete with each other. Therefore, from creation to duration, institutions tend to thrive in proportion to the skill of their founders.[18]

Second, the variables that explain unification may explain when other institutional forms will emerge and endure. When symmetry is high, institutions are likely to feature equal burden sharing, like the alliance between Britain and France in World War I. When symmetry is low, institutions are likely to display asymmetric relations, like the United States being an "associated power" during World War I. Holding symmetry constant, intensity and duration can fill in many of the gray areas in alignment behavior.

Table 2.1 simplifies why particular institutions are probable in particular circumstances.[19] Long-term threats yield long-term solutions, like confederations or unions; short-term threats yield briefer dalliances, like alliances and informal alignments. High intensity threats trigger intimate coalitions, like unions or alliances; low intensity threats spur more aloof groupings, like confederations and informal alignments. Very high and very low intensity threats cause bandwagoning, not balancing.

Third, the argument helps explain how unions come undone.[20] If we run the logic in reverse, we would expect unions to drift apart when there is no union-worthy threat on the horizon. Members may become more threatened by each other than foreign states, and the need to form a different balancing coalition may

TABLE 2.1

The Relationship between Threat Intensity, Threat Duration, and Institutional Form

DURATION

I		Long	Short
N			
T	High	Union	Alliance
E			
N			
S			
I	Low	Confederation	Alignment
T			
Y			

become appealing. Threats could grow too large, too small, too occasional, or too asymmetrical to justify union.

A security crisis would then reveal this institutional inadequacy, and that could take several forms. A crisis could show an overwhelming threat; it could highlight asymmetry of threat; it could demonstrate that deunification would increase autonomy without compromising security. Once the crisis has opened a window of opportunity, elites would compete in the media, with the military, and through political procedures to disentangle their states.

We would expect disunion to be slow in coming. Institutions have inertia, and they socialize people to cooperate in particular patterns. This is especially true of unions because the means of coercion are centralized. John Calhoun warned ante-bellum America: "How many bleeding [pores] must be taken up on passing the knife of separation through the body politic . . . . *We must remember, it is the most difficult process in the world to make two people of one.*"[21] When states detach themselves from unions, there is uncertainty about the balance of forces and incentives to use war to prevent former partners from becoming future threats. Extrication is painful and perilous, and it is reasonable to expect potential states to be reluctant to disturb such a hornet's nest. States come together because they foresee facing the same problems and come apart because they foresee a future of different problems. State divorce is a courtship dance done backward.

ALTERNATE EXPLANATIONS

This section collects and analyzes three groups of alternate explanations: constructivism, liberalism, and binding. No paradigm has a monopoly on wisdom, and below I detail what I have borrowed from, and how I dissent from, rival views. We all share a normative commitment to minimizing the amount of coercion in the world, but have reasonable disagreements about the best way to bring that about.

Although in general I focus on one to two high-profile exemplars of each view throughout the work, in the empirical chapters, to be more thorough and inclusive, I occasionally incorporate other authors whose work speaks directly to a particular case. The upshot of this section is that none of the rival factors inhibit integration, but are, I claim, too weak to bring about voluntary union, singly or jointly. But different readers have different needs, and this section sets out a menu of explanations and compares them for the reader to weigh and consider.

Constructivism

Like all paradigms, constructivism is a heterogeneous band of scholars united by a familial resemblance. The immense power of ideas is the tie that binds these thinkers—critical theorists, radical feminists, postmodernists—together. Ideas are, on this view, the prime movers in human affairs, and discourse is the primary causal mechanism. Behavior follows belief; if we thought about the world differently, the world would be a different place.[22]

Karl Deutsch is the grandfather of this school, and what I call union he called an "amalgamated security community."[23] Emmanuel Adler and Michael Barnett explicitly pick up Deutsch's baton, and present a state-of-the-art constructivist view on political integration. Alas, they have largely forgone discussing union, seeking instead to account for security communities where power is not unified. But why stop there? If their logic on integration is correct, it should apply to unions, a logical terminus of integration. Indeed, Alexander Wendt has done exactly this and boldly argued that a world state is inevitable.

For Adler and Barnett, unification would be the culmination of a three-tiered road. In the first tier, almost any precipitating condition could start closer alignment, such as changes in technology, demographics, economics, the environment, external threats, new interpretations of social reality, and the list goes on.[24] In tier two, states, peoples, and especially farsighted elites alter their environment by cultivating a "we-feeling" and redefining identities, through "cores of strength" (i.e., dominant state), transactions, organizations, and learning. Finally, in tier three, the once different peoples now share collective identity, which fosters trust and expectations of peaceful change.

I concur with constructivists that brute force is not the end-all-be-all of political power. My explanation too has a role for interpretation, farsighted elites, and persuasion. Nonetheless, our disagreements are fundamental. The main disagreement is that I believe constructivists have their causation backwards—material factors are more causes than consequences. Constructivists pay too little attention to how the distribution of power forges identities, polities, and resonant ideas. Their mechanisms for integration—identity change, social learning, and cores of strength—are ill-specified.

Take identity change. One of the main shortcomings of constructivist arguments is that they do not adequately specify when some characteristic will become the primary identity trait over others or how similar cultural traits must be to be compatible. There are only the notions that birds of a feather flock together and that plumage is a social construction. At bottom, constructivists are vague about how and when intimacy leads to political intertwining; "close ties demand efforts to confederate, but these same ties have brought about the familiarity that breeds mistrust."[25]

To illustrate, circa 1770 cultural DNA was nearly identical in the United Kingdom, the American colonies, several Caribbean islands, and parts of Canada. Within a decade, the American colonies would be at war with the mother country—instead of, say, neighboring Native Americans and Spaniards—and Canada and several Caribbean islands would refuse to join the revolution. Common culture may have helped the proto–United States cooperate, but it was a poor predictor of political conflict. Likewise, Switzerland and the United States look more culturally diverse than what was once the Incan Empire or Sweden-Norway. Yet the former two areas are unified and the latter two are not. Common culture may spark sympathy and some integration, but it is a weak reed for unification.

Social learning is a wooly concept in the best constructivist literature. Adler and Barnett believe that repeated social intercourse builds trust. Sometimes it does, sometimes not. But they fail to give a mechanism that causes one outcome over the other. For instance, it took the Swiss over 550 years from their first alliance to their final unification, whereas the same process in the United States took about a decade. Would constructivists conclude that the Swiss are 55 times slower learners than Americans? Or 55 times less trustworthy?

States unify, I argue, not because their identities change but because their environment does. People generally prefer autonomy and are equally sensible about their own interests across time; what changes is their incentive structure. Power shifts mean that the freedom of one group encroaches on the freedom of another, and those who can balance against such threats will. There is likely a constructivist element to this dynamic; group membership criteria are malleable, there is more than one way to define outsiders and insiders, and people become socialized to lasting status quos. But identity is not infinitely fluid, and the distribution of power curtly curtails the parameters of group formation. When the distribution of power changes, incentives change and that brings perceptions and behavior, eventually, to heel. Culture is more the horse than the rider in this process.[26]

As for cores of strength, it is true that larger states lead and offer inducements to join a union, but this is a realist explanation. When the material distribution of power is driving an outcome, it fits squarely on realist real estate. Cores of strength, such as Virginia and Sweden, behaved as realists describe they should, bullying and conceding where expedient, and reaping resulting profits.

The most damning criticism of constructivism is the evidence. Discourse, learning, farsighted elites, cores of strength, these are all commonplace in the world. Where are all the unions that should be happening? Communication and contact have never been easier, education has never been so widespread—so why does the number of states in the world keep growing?

Liberalism

Liberal theory has a long history, but the crux of it is that economic considerations pull states together, a process that could lead to union. David Mitrany took classical liberal theory and improved on it with his functionalist theory.[27] Functionalism argued that states should try to cooperate where they could, starting small and building trust for greater projects, which would dampen the probability of war.

Ernst Haas advanced functionalism by making it more systematic. He developed neofunctionalism to address how European cooperation over coal and steel would lead to greater integration among European states. Neofunctionalism asserts that self-interested experts create formal institutions to facilitate some sector of their trade. Once both sides see the mutual gains from trade, they are disposed to expand the scope of their cooperation to reap more gains. Depending on the extent of interdependence, positive feedback loops and spillover effects could lead to greater cooperation and political integration. Alas, greater scientific rigor made neofunctionalism easier to disconfirm, causing it to wilt.[28]

Dani Rodrik is the most prominent exponent of the updated liberal view, and he ambitiously suggests that economics is driving us toward a world federation. The nub of the matter is a trilemma: international economic integration, mass politics, and the nation-state cannot coexist. At best, two of the three are possible at once. Because mass politics are here to stay and markets are unmatched in their ability to supply needs, the nation-state will lose out. Where Haas saw technocratic government as the way of the future, Rodrik sees something more familiar: "Politics need not, and would not, shrink: it would relocate to the global level. The United States provides a useful way of thinking about this: the most contentious political battles in the United States are fought not at the state level, but at the federal level."[29]

To be sure, states enjoy the economic advantages of union where they are to be had, and liberal theory helps account for lower levels of integration. But these are

separate issues from the causes of union. Glossing over the distinction between
high politics (security) and low politics (everything else) is not helpful when
explaining unification.[30] Trade may explain why states join a customs union, but it
does not account for why they would surrender foreign policy autonomy and unify.
If Rodrik's logic held, it ought to work in North America. Canada and the United
States are each other's largest trading partner and Rodrik suggests they would
profit more if their borders were erased. Yet even in the most auspicious circumstances there are no proposals for union; in both countries that notion is stillborn.

Like constructivists, liberals have poor explanatory success. The world economy has never been richer, there have never been better economic incentives to
come together, yet the number of states in the world increases and the most
auspicious integration schemes seem stuck. Trade is more a consequence than a
cause of unification.[31]

Apart from Rodrik's economic liberalism, there are a number of other liberal
explanations of political integration, only one of which I can briefly address here.[32]
Most notably, liberal thinkers tend to emphasize domestic political factors, especially democracy.[33] Democratic institutions may make unification easier because
they allow for credible commitments with less risk of later exploitation. It could also
be that democracies socialize their citizens to be more pacific toward each other.

My argument inclines toward this view, but in a very hedged fashion. Like cultural compatibility, democratic compatibility appears to promote integration, but
is a poor predictor of union. Many states are democracies, few of them are voluntary unions, but the most successful unions are all democratic. These relationships
suggest that there is something to the democratic argument, but not much.

My position is similar to Charles Kupchan's: democracy is not necessary for
integration, but it has its advantages.[34] Democratic norms and institutions may
help calm the heady uncertainty of unification; they may make behavior more predictable and less exploitative. But this effect is hard to disentangle from the background conditions. The security environment that generates voluntary unification
(i.e., small, equal states on the political periphery) correlates with other decentral-
ized institutions, like capitalism and democracy. In addition, the great explosion
of democracies in history happened after 1945, an era that witnessed no voluntary
unions. In sum, democracy likely contributes to unification, but the causal priority
of power politics is much higher.

Binding

Some of the most promising work being done on integration are hybrid approaches that cross-pollinate paradigms.[35] The most interesting of the lot is Daniel
Deudney's republican security theory. Advancing sophisticated revisions of classic

thought, Deudney argues that increasingly destructive weapons have made traditional power politics progressively more perilous. War has grown so catastrophic that new institutions must rise to manage the dangers of anarchy without the excesses of too much hierarchy, a happy medium called negarchy. Like Wendt and Rodrik, Deudney suggests a federal world government but is short on specifics of how to achieve it. In short, unification is about states binding together to avert the cataclysm of war.[36]

Deudney's points are wonderfully argued and I am sympathetic to them. I agree that the dangers of hierarchy can loom as large as the dangers of anarchy, and unifying states are severely leery of centralizing too much authority. Unifying states do not go from full anarchy to full hierarchy, but partial anarchy to partial hierarchy. I also agree that security threats are the critical impetus to political integration. But the central difference between Deudney's arguments and mine is whether non-state threats can cause voluntary unification. My position is no, Deudney's is yes.

While Deudney focuses on nuclear weapons, others, who make similar arguments, cast a wider net. Amitai Etzioni asks: "Can there be a 'we' without a 'they'? My response is that the new 'they' could be a virus or a weapon of mass destruction or some other such 'enemy.' After all, we have long seen people uniting to fight a runaway fire or flooding rivers."[37] To be thorough, I discuss a broad range of non-state threats.

Let us start with war as a unifying threat. All states know that if they unified they would be much less likely to fight each other. And we do see evidence of alliances formed to manage tension between alliance partners. Yet there appear to be steep limits on how far states will bind themselves. Few states can be prodded, kicking and screaming, to unify, even fewer states make the leap to voluntarily unify, and there are no instances of poles in the international system politically uniting for any reason.

It could be that the nuclear revolution has reversed old dynamics of political integration—nuclear weapons will weld the world together. If we reframe the matter as states wishing to avoid highly destructive wars, then the obvious test cases are nuclear-armed adversaries and whether they make unification overtures to avert war. The track records of the USSR-U.S. and India-Pakistan rivalries are not encouraging. Even tentative plans for nuclear sharing and joint management between adversaries, like the Baruch Plan, have never gotten far.

In fact, the reverse is true: nuclear weapons have fragmented the world. As offensive weapons, nuclear arms have a long, lousy track record. As defensive weapons, they have, so far, seemed somewhat useful, and have made it safe for a variety of states, with or without them, to improve their autonomy. The invention of nuclear weaponry has correlated with increases in the number of states in the world (only some of which, of course, may be attributed to nuclear weaponry). Although political disintegration has not characterized America's backyard, it has manifested near other nuclear-capable states, like the United Kingdom and the former Soviet Union. Hence, there is a solid case to be made that a nuclear world is not hospitable to unification efforts. But in Deudney's defense, numerous nuclear detonations near cities, accidental or not, could negate my arguments. For the above reasons, I suspect they would not, but, given the dearth of data and Deudney's compelling logic, I cannot rule it out.

On similar grounds, terrorism is an improbable threat to cause unification. Terrorism is increasing in frequency but remains uncommon, and it certainly is not as lethal as interstate war. Further, it is not clear that union would be an appropriate counter to the threat that terrorism poses.[38] States have already boosted their counterterrorism cooperation, and while there has been conquest in response to terrorism, it has not led to annexation or unification. Over decades, powerful states like the United Kingdom, Israel, and the United States have not, in their collective wisdom, found in unification an answer to their problems with terrorism.

What about environmental, economic, or cultural threats? No modern states have unified in reaction to environmental pressures, and indeed areas with the most onerous environmental pressures are politically fractured.[39] If cultural and economic threats cause states to unify, we should expect to see unification in places like Africa and South America. Despite ample time and intelligent, charismatic leaders in charge of armies, like Simón Bolívar, Kwame Nkrumah, and Julius Nyerere, such unification drives have all derailed.

Non-state threats, like those listed above, are transient evils and lack the indefinite duration necessary for unification to be successful, no matter their intensity. For example, the 1918 influenza pandemic killed 50 million people worldwide, and it was not met through union—it was not a threat that union could have alleviated. Moreover, states, like people, are prone to viewing themselves as basically benign and competent and are therefore unlikely to have the will or ability to bind themselves. In addition, states, like people, are liable—paraphrasing Jacques Barzun—to the whirligig of boredom and fatigue.[40] Throughout history, attitudes toward war have inverted, swinging from horror to eagerness and back, sometimes within a generation.

But a simpler answer may be that states are generally rational and take calculated gambles. Millions of travelers each day decide that the freedom of planes, trains, and automobiles is worth the risk of a fatal crash; so, too, states are willing to take the chance of war as the price for greater freedom. Since 1945, great powers have avoided fighting each other for the longest period in history, and most of the world has prospered like never before. States regularly deplore war and could at any time unify to squelch the risk of fighting, which would, if carried to its logical conclusion, ultimately produce a world state. That we have never seen anything near a world state is not encouraging for the thesis under investigation. To close, binding arguments only work when they are consistent with balance of power theory, and balance of power theory holds regardless. Binding is helpful in alliances but gratuitous in unions.

Wrapping up this section, I distill what value my arguments add to the literature. There is nothing new in arguing that threat promotes unity—that might be the oldest explanation in politics.[41] There is also nothing new in claiming that crises facilitate change and that domestic machinations are the best way to radically restructure a state. What is new is a realist explanation for voluntary union, developed in more than cursory fashion, which does not require copious amounts of bloodshed. This work provides a realist argument in a field dominated by other paradigms and hybrid views. It also leads to different conclusions; Wendt, Rodrik, and Deudney all foresee some form of world government—I do not. The next section lays out these differences concisely.

HYPOTHESES ON UNIFICATION

This section condenses the core hypotheses that will be tested throughout the rest of the book. We begin with the hypotheses of the main argument:

The threat environment:

- While other advantages may be harvested from union, only security deficiency causes states to unify. Unification is extreme balancing behavior against other states.
- Threats cause union. There must be an optimally intense, indefinite external threat, symmetrically shared among states.

The crisis trigger:

- A security-related event must occur that can be seized as evidence that the status quo needs revision.

Elite persuasion:

- Elite persuasion is the main mechanism guiding unification attempts.
- Success depends on the structure of the marketplace of ideas, namely control over the flow of information, market segmentation, and journalistic independence.

- Success depends on the ability of political entrepreneurs to manipulate the decisional calculus of opponents, militarily or procedurally.

With regard to alternate explanations:

Constructivism:

- Almost any external shock may initiate unification: technology, demographics, etc.
- Social learning and discourse are the chief mechanisms driving unification.
- Farsighted elites are the agents of unification, promoting integration out of enlightened self-interest.

Liberalism:

- Changes in the world economy drive integration by converging economic preferences. Wealth is the goal of unification.
- Domestic groups are the prime agents propelling moves toward unification.
- Lobbying by economic interest groups is the mechanism by which integration occurs.

Binding:

- Changes in violence interdependence cause integration. Insecurity causes unification.
- Fear of major war causes union by pushing political elites toward a world federation of republics.
- Unions are more about accommodating mutual security concerns, from inside and outside the state, than balancing against state threats.

When the causes of unification disappear, deunification grows probable; reversing the above logics helps to explain state disintegration.

TECHNICAL SPECIFICATIONS: TESTING THE ARGUMENT

For those wishing to peer under the hood, this section walks through the social science fundamentals inside the work: the methods, case selection/universe of cases, potential problems, variable operationalization, and limits of the argument. The method is straightforward. I use process tracing to immerse myself in a case and evaluate the causal links within and between cases.[42] I then examine cases where union was attempted and compare successful outcomes to less successful outcomes, checking the hypotheses against the empirical record.

Cases were selected because: (1) they fit the scope conditions; (2) data richness; (3) within-case variation of independent variables; (4) they meet a minimum threshold of pooling sovereignty; and (5) to the best of my knowledge, they are the modern universe of cases. By a minimum threshold of pooling sovereignty, I mean cases where a policy is put forward to formally centralize the powers of war and peace, and impartial spectators believe the proposal's prospects to be about even odds. The cases are the modern universe of cases (i.e., since 1750), not the complete universe of cases. Union has been a major part of international politics since the beginning of political science. Alas, adequate evidence is not available until the last several centuries.

To enumerate the case studies: the United States, Switzerland, Sweden-Norway, and Gran Colombia. The United States and Switzerland are the two most successful cases. Sweden-Norway and Gran Colombia are instances where union is instituted but falls apart. They are critical cases because the conventional wisdom is that they unified for a number of reasons, but not power politics.

Of what are these cases an instance? At the broadest level, this work is about political integration and alliance formation. More precisely, it is about political unions, and within political unions, I am only examining the most voluntary examples. Another way to frame my main research question is: Why is voluntary union so rare? The central cases of this study all have a plausible claim to have unified; they are by no means representative of an average country or an average integrating country, and this exposes me to charges of selecting on the dependent variable. There are several replies to this.

First, while all the cases have some claim to have unified, there is variation in the strength of these unions; therefore, we can speak of variation in outcome. Moreover, half the cases unify and then dissolve, giving variation on the dependent variable. Second, studying extreme cases can give leverage on hard problems. Many memorable insights have been generated through immersion in rare events, for example Geoffrey Blainey's *Causes of War*, Theda Skocpol's *States and Social Revolutions*, and Evan Luard's *War and International Society*. Third, the scope conditions allow me to analyze all the relevant cases and assess necessary conditions.[43] In brief, the method's benefits outweigh its costs in a phenomenon as unusual as unification.

The dependent variable of this work is self-help unification among relative equals, which I operationalize as states formally centralizing the means of foreign policy and members cannot legitimately resort to force to resolve disputes with other members. The dependent variable is unfortunately not dichotomous. When there is a gray case of union, I lay out the ledger and make my accounting explicit for others to judge.

The causes of unification in the main argument can be classed in three groups: background conditions, crisis trigger, and elite persuasion. All are necessary but none sufficient conditions. My independent variables in more detail are as follows.

Whether, and to what extent, background conditions are conducive for extraordinary balancing coalitions depends on three factors: intensity, duration, and symmetry. Intensity of threat is based on geographic proximity, aggregate power, and offensive military capability. To make the uprights as clear, correct, and immobile as possible, an optimally intense threat is one that cannot be met through alliance or confederation but can be met through extreme balancing. Duration of threat may be accessed in two ways: whether or not elites perceive an optimal threat over 25- to 50-year time spans or, where primary sources are wanting, whether a rational actor would expect an optimal threat to persist indefinitely. For symmetry, I compare the congruence of states' abandonment fears; the more mutually vulnerable states are, the higher the symmetry. Symmetry is measured by the alignment preferences of governing elites, as indicated by how elites spend their political capital.

The next element is the presence or absence of a security-related crisis trigger, recorded through historical sources. Do participants feel they are in a dramatic political moment where security is unusually scarce? Who is the ultimate source of threat during a crisis?

Entrepreneurial persuasion I discuss qualitatively. Whether entrepreneurs are elites can be operationalized by examining social, economic, and political positions in domestic hierarchies. To avoid tautology, I track elites prior to the initiation of unification campaigns, then process trace how the domestic political competition plays out.[44] I analyze the degree of formal and informal influence over domestic institutions, specifically the media, military, and political procedures.

What would falsify my argument? Disconfirmation would take the form of unification without an optimally intense, indefinite, symmetrical security threat, or any alignment less than union in the face of such a threat. Non-contiguous and/or large numbers of states unifying are unlikely by my logic, as are cases where unification partners do not menace each other before they attempt to unify. When unification takes place in the absence of a security-related crisis, such an instance would not support my argument. Where unification is led by non-elites, or those with little power over the media, the military, or political procedures, my argument has failed.

Every analysis has its limitations, and this one is no different. Although the cases are geographically spread out, they are temporally bunched; all begin their unification attempts between 1785 and 1845. Without a more contemporary case, the findings may not be tailored for direct application to the present day, especially with the changing calculus of conflict.[45] States interact in different world historical moments and are socialized to different norms, and my explanation picks up poorly on that. While I attempt to cover the most important necessary conditions in my argument, I do not arrogate that they are exhaustive or cannot work in conjunction with other factors. Shifts in the balance of power are commonly gradual and their consequences hard to read. What explains how people perceive threat? Why do people react to objective conditions the way they do? I do not have an explanation of threat perception or rationality. In fact, I am not certain and do not assume that states and people are rational, but I believe with Waltz that states and elites are punished until they act that way.[46] Anyone working half as long would have created an explanation twice as good, but mine is as parsimonious as materials and abilities allow.

I should not be taken as favoring union in the abstract.[47] Unification is no panacea, and some states have found neither security nor unity in coming together. If we wish to avert the dangers of dysfunctional or unrealized unions, we are well advised to understand the causes of unification. But that says nothing about what the ideal size of states is or should be; size depends on conditions. If done competently, this study should be relevant whenever egalitarian unions are forming or dividing.

TABLE 2.2

Comparison of the Core Arguments

Explanation	Why	Whether	When	How
Realism	Threat → Union	Background conditions (3)	Security crisis	Elite persuasion
Constr'ism	Ideas → Union	Far-sighted elites	Almost any shock	Social learning
Liberalism	Trade → Union	Economic preferences align	Economic preferences converge	Interstate bargaining
Binding	War → Union	Increased violence interdependence	Security crisis	Federation of republics

CONCLUSION

As a final review of how the main hypotheses stack up against each other, see table 2.2. The table encapsulates why unification happens, what determines whether unification will be successful, when unification is likely to be attempted, and how unification is effected.

Summing up, this chapter has developed a realist explanation of unification with broad implications. For realists, outside threats drive unity, but for their chief opponents, constructivists, liberals, and binding theorists, ideas, trade, and war, respectively, cause unity. With the hypotheses presented, the empirical world beckons. We start with the most difficult case: the ratification of the United States Constitution.

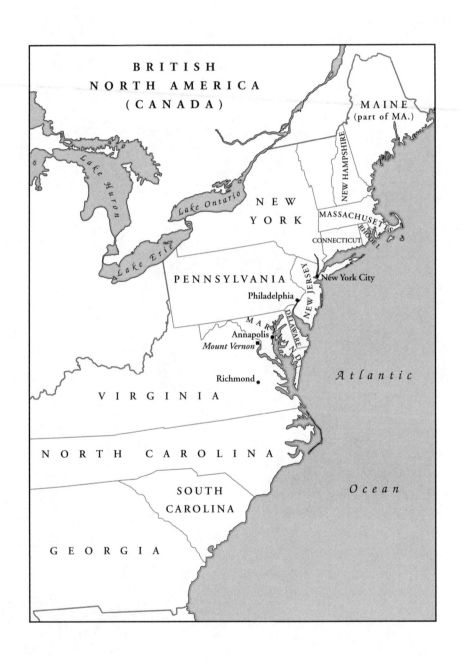

It . . . seems to have been reserved for the people of this country . . . to decide the important question, whether societies of men are really capable or not of establishing good government from reflection and choice, or whether they are forever destined to depend on their political constitutions on accident and force. . . . Happy will it be if our choice should be directed by a judicious estimate of our true interests. . . . But this is a thing more ardently to be wished than seriously to be expected.

—PUBLIUS[1]

3

Force, Fraud, and the Founding of the American Constitution

IN OCTOBER 1787, New York wanted nothing to do with the Constitution. So Alexander Hamilton, James Madison, and John Jay began publishing a series of essays in local newspapers to urge New Yorkers to reconsider. As "Publius" they set out, on what would become hundreds of pages, the nature of politics and the future of the United States. What is the first matter at hand? Force versus reason, and force seems to have the upper hand. Against long odds, Publius shoulders the daunting duty of persuasion. Why were the poor authors in such a sorry state and how did they get out of it?

This chapter provides an account of American unification because no good history of it has been written from a realist perspective,[2] and many people, the author included, were unwittingly saddled with lackluster accounts of the period, which may need disabusing. Those comfortable in their competence may skip ahead to the next chapter, while those without a solid grasp may quickly gain one. Those unsure about which category they fall into may scan the brief introduction below and decide for themselves.

The general outline of this chapter is as follows. The first section highlights why the conventional wisdom on the Constitution's birth is not wise. The second section provides a corrective history, starting at independence, passing through the Articles of Confederation, Shays's Rebellion, the Philadelphia Convention, state ratification, and ending with the Bill of Rights. The last section looks at events

after unification, and briefly discusses how we know the United States united and
how the Civil War impacted that.

THE MYSTERY OF AMERICAN UNIFICATION

Many of us learned the civics class version of how the United States acquired its
Constitution.[3] The Articles of Confederation were riddled with problems; so the
great and good met in Philadelphia one steamy summer and crafted the compromises that became the supreme law of the land. Other states were founded on
force and fraud; their laws rammed down the throat of the weak by the fist of the
strong. The United States was triumphantly founded on the powers of persuasion.

Participants cast events in the same terms; Samuel P. Huntington (the Harvard
academic should not be confused with his distinguished ancestor) declared "This is
a new event in the history of mankind.—Heretofore, most governments have
been formed by tyrants, and imposed on mankind by force. Never before did a
people, in time of peace and tranquility, meet together by their representatives,
and with calm deliberation frame for themselves a system of government."[4]

Any political scientist worthy of the name should cock an eyebrow at Huntington's words. External danger is supposed to drive allies closer together and make
cooperation easier. When the threat recedes, cooperation should become harder.
The loosely binding Articles of Confederation were drafted and ratified with an
invading army occupying the United States, while the much more adhesive Constitution was drafted and ratified in a time of tranquility. It took 16 months to draw
up the Articles and three years to ratify them. Contrast that to the Constitution's
four months of drafting and less than a year to ratify. How did the United States
do that?

The conventional view is that the Articles were unworkable—the former colonies faced clear and present dangers. Having their own militias and sovereignty,
states were menaces to each other. States also had to worry about Native Americans and foreign countries, sometimes both in cahoots. Madison fretted "that the
Indians derive their motives as well as their means from their Spanish neigh-
bours."[5] Within their borders, states feared insurrection and slave revolt. Besides
security worries, commercial rights, jurisdiction, and monetary policy were also
points of friction among the states. With toothless executive abilities, the Articles
were no match for the problems states faced.

This view confuses how things look in the rearview mirror for how they looked
through the windshield. The Articles were actually quite impressive and hardly
demanded radical revision. From a security perspective, they had beaten back a

great power and negotiated a favorable peace. Following George Washington's renunciation of command, Congress ordered General Henry Knox to discharge all but 80 soldiers from the Continental Army. From an economic standpoint, the Articles had weathered a postwar depression, the economy was in positive shape, and the population doubled, in spite of seven years of war, from two million to four million. Compared to other states, the young United States were anomalously possessed of free government and free of mass poverty.[6]

American Founders of all stripes realized this. In 1786, Washington wrote, "The people are industrious, œconomy begins to prevail, and our internal governments are, in general, tolerably well administered." Early in 1787, Ben Franklin waxed that prosperity was widespread and obvious. There were those who complained of slack trade and money, but "it is always in the power of small numbers to make a great clamour."[7] Nor did the less illustrious disagree.

The overall impression of historians such as Jack Rakove, Merrill Jensen, and Edmund Morgan is that Americans felt little sense of national crisis and in fact cared more about debates in Parliament than Congress.[8] It is hard for modern Americans to appreciate, but in the 1780s there was little sense of "America" as a single republic with a common interest. Citizens equated "nation" with their particular state and concerned themselves with state and local issues.

The idea of combining all thirteen states into a single government was thought about as likely as the erection of a monarchy. Such a republic "on an average one thousand miles in length, and eight hundred in breadth . . . is in itself an absurdity, and contrary to the whole experience of mankind."[9] Union was thought so distant that one well-intentioned Federalist campaigned for intermarriage between people from different states.

Without polling data it is impossible to get at preferences in Revolutionary America; nonetheless, most agree that if the Constitution had been put to a referendum in December 1787 it would have lost.[10] There is strong evidence to suppose that, objectively, the Articles were not very deleterious and, subjectively, very few contemporaries thought they were. Therefore, general dissatisfaction with the Articles cannot explain the Constitution's origins. Where then did the document come from?

THE MADISONIAN MOMENT

There are two protagonists in this story.[11] Without them the U.S. Constitution would have turned out much differently. The first is George Washington. Lionized general of the Revolutionary War, his dignified manner, imposing presence, and unquestioned courage helped initiate, legitimize, popularize, and consolidate the unification effort.

The second is James Madison.[12] An unlikely hero, he was directionless before the American Revolution, relying on his father for income. Madison cut a drab figure: short, slender, balding, bookish, dressed perpetually in black, and soft spoken to the point that he strained audibility. Yet he outfoxed the Antifederalists,[13] overthrew the Articles, and left the most fingerprints on the world's most successful constitution. Both used their formidable skills, and Virginia as their tool, to shepherd the Constitution into effect. Certainly the two could not have done it alone, but more than anyone else they are the parents of the Constitution.

Independence

On July 4, 1776, the Continental Congress adopted the Declaration of Independence, which transformed the colonies into an alliance of independent states. In Thomas Jefferson's words: "[T]hese united colonies are & of right ought to be free & independent states . . . & that as free and independent states they have full power to levy war, conclude peace, contract alliances, establish commerce & to do all other acts & things which independent states may of right do."[14] The use of "states" in the plural was not a figure of speech; the states were entities with legal supremacy.

Eight days later a draft appeared of the "Articles of Confederation and Perpetual Union" that would draw the thirteen states into "a firm League of Friendship" for their "common Defence, the Security of their Liberties, and their mutual and general Welfare." The Articles spoke on such topics as security, taxes, representation, and slavery, but it vested the federal government with little enforcement ability, and by design—it was crafted not to threaten state supremacy. Article XIII was its amendment clause: "And the Articles of this confederation shall be inviolably observed by every state, and the union shall be perpetual; nor shall any alteration at any time hereafter be made in any of them; unless such alteration be agreed to in a congress of the united states, and be afterwards confirmed by the legislatures of every state."[15] The Articles were a covenant lacking the sword.

Even with such minimal surrendering of sovereignty, the states were reluctant to sign off on the Articles. By November 1778 ten states had signed, but three continued to argue over disputed western lands. By January 1781, only Maryland had not signed. When Maryland requested French naval protection against British raids on the Chesapeake Bay, the French minister advised Maryland to ratify the Articles. Maryland signed the Articles on March 1, 1781, putting them into effect.

From the very beginning, James Madison did not approve of the Articles and tried in vain to reform them through ordinary channels. Two weeks after ratification, Madison and two others proposed amending the Articles to give Congress power to coerce states that did not fulfill their requisitions, by force if necessary. This was not the first such proposal—weeks before the Articles went into effect, Congress had sought a 5 percent impost on imported goods—and it was not the last. Congress considered committee reports to increase its authority over commerce in 1784, 1785, and 1786. For the six years that the Articles were operative, not a single amendment passed. Congress's reputation for inaction spread accordingly.[16]

Procedural motions were not the only efforts to pull states together. From 1781 to 1783, Robert Morris, the virtual financial dictator of the confederation, attempted several wily economic measures to compel states to unify, all of which amounted to nothing. Others tried economic routes to unity until they too ran out of viable schemes by 1786.[17] Ordinary politics was a dead end.

It is worth pausing to note Virginia's size. In population, it was the biggest state in 1790, outnumbering the second-largest state by more than 70 percent, and growing quickly, doubling every generation. Virginia contained one-third of the country's trade and one-fifth of the country's population, though New York, Pennsylvania, and Massachusetts were peers. But as Washington and Madison noticed early, Virginia was penetrated with navigable rivers, possessed feeble naval strength, and confronted the real possibility of slave revolt.[18] Virginia was a prime candidate to coordinate collective action: powerful, central, and vulnerable. At least as important as their personal talents, Madison and Washington were from the right state to spur union.

After the Revolutionary War, Virginia and Maryland had problems with their rivers. Maryland was taxing Virginia's commerce on the Potomac, and Virginia was threatening to tax Maryland's commerce on the Chesapeake. In 1784, Madison was already thinking of a constitutional convention.[19] He happened to be the chairman of the Virginia Assembly's Committee on Commerce, and he persuaded the Assembly to invite Maryland to a conference in March 1785. The conference was not a pressing issue, and Virginia's governor failed to dispatch commissioners to the meeting. When Maryland's delegates arrived in Alexandria, Virginia's delegates were nowhere to be seen. Hearing this, Washington invited the Maryland delegates back to his Mount Vernon estate and personally deputized a Virginia delegation. Once gathered, the group quickly brokered a congenial agreement. While illegal, it was effective.[20]

The conference concluded that the meeting should be held annually. Madison seized upon this opportunity to push for a national convention. So he drafted a resolution calling all the states to a September convention in Annapolis, tamely designated "to examine the relative situations and trade of the United States" and "to consider how far a uniform system in their commercial regulations may be necessary to their common interest and their permanent harmony."[21] But Madison's nationalist motives were suspect, and he found it necessary to mask his proposal's authorship. Someone else introduced the resolution as his own on the last day of the Assembly's session in January 1786.

As September approached, James Monroe reported from New York to Madison that easterners intended to use the convention for more "than the object originally comprehended." Three weeks prior to Annapolis, Madison apprised Jefferson that he and many others, "both within and without Congress, wish to make this Meeting subservient to a plenipotentiary Convention for amending the Confederation."[22] In addition, the convention got a boost from events.

Collective goods problems such as currency and security became more salient. In May, Rhode Island printed massive amounts of money and forced creditors to accept it. In August, John Jay reported on treaty negotiations with the Spanish: navigation of the Mississippi was in jeopardy for 25 to 30 years. This evoked bitter dispute, and elicited thoughts that perhaps the country would split into two to three regional confederacies. In fall and winter, unrest smoldered in Massachusetts and New Hampshire. Jefferson, in France at the time, was unalarmed by the unrest but very alarmed by news of the Mississippi negotiations. In a letter to Madison he predicted:

> the act which abandons the navigation of the Mississippi is an act of separation between the Eastern & Western country. It is a relinquishment of five parts out of eight of the territory of the United States, an abandonment of the fairest subject for the paiment [sic] of our public debts, & the chaining of those debts on our own necks *in perpetuum.* . . . If they declare themselves a separate people, we are incapable of a single effort to retain them.[23]

After waiting a week, only five states' delegates had arrived in Annapolis. This was normal. Travel was hard and costly, and few were in a hurry to attend meetings where nothing much was done. Four more states did not arrive in time and four more did not bother to send delegates. New Jersey was the sole state to authorize its delegates to consider matters beyond commerce. Madison had more patience at the Philadelphia convention, arriving earlier and waiting longer for a quorum to show up. The French representative at Annapolis was wise to why this was so: "There was no expectation and no intention that anything should be done by the convention beyond preparing the way for another meeting, and that the report was hurried through before sufficient states were represented to be embarrassing."[24]

On behalf of the convention, Hamilton issued a report on September 14, calling for another convention in Philadelphia in May 1787. Madison and fellow Virginian Edmund Randolph had to press Hamilton to tone down his nationalist rhetoric and keep the language vague. Otherwise he would scare away states from attending, not least Virginia.

His report decreed that "there are important defects in the system of the Federal Government" which "merit deliberate and candid discussion." It called for a convention that would:

> devise such further provisions as shall appear to them necessary to render the constitution of the Fœderal Government adequate to the exigencies of the Union; and to report such an Act for that purpose to the United States in Congress Assembled, as when agreed to, by them, and afterwards confirmed by the Legislatures of every State will effectually provide for the same.[25]

The proposal looked tame. Honest talk about current problems, drawing up some provisions, suggesting them to Congress, allowing legislatures to ratify them unanimously—very ordinary.

Madison rushed back to Richmond and led the Virginia Assembly to accept the innocuous invitation he helped write. Mighty Virginia's swift action set the tone; Pennsylvania, Delaware, and Georgia modeled their acceptances after Virginia's.[26] As if to illustrate Congress's fecklessness, six states agreed to participate at Philadelphia before Congress convened to consider the idea. Resigned to the unavoidable, Congress called for a convention to be held in Philadelphia on May 14 for "the sole and express purpose of revising the Articles of Confederation" and directed that proposals from Philadelphia be submitted back to Congress for its approval.[27] All states but Rhode Island elected delegates; all state delegations had strict instructions to subordinate Philadelphia to existing rules and institutions. In the end, all state delegations violated their instructions, save one, New York, which abandoned Philadelphia early on.

The Philadelphia delegates were not, of course, selected at random, nor were they picked by unusual methods. The legislatures did not trouble themselves to call special conventions to validate that "the people" were speaking. And there is evidence that those who believed that the Articles were not in need of much revision chose not to go.[28] Seventy-four delegates were elected; of that number, only 55 actually attended the Philadelphia Convention, and most of them hailed from Federalist strongholds, that is, urban, coastal areas.[29] The deck was stacked with Federalists.

Shays's Rebellion

Shays's Rebellion, really a protest in western Massachusetts, is often given extravagant credit for laying the groundwork for the Constitution. Jonathan Smith conveys the common understanding of Shays's Rebellion:

> Probably no other one incident contributed so powerfully to the acceptance of the proposition . . . for a constitutional convention by all the states, or the adoption of the constitution when it was finally formed and submitted to the people as did Shays's Rebellion. The federal government, once organized, under the wise statesmanship of Washington and Hamilton, public confidence was speedily restored and the grievances which lay at the root of Shays's movement [i.e. farmers' debts] quickly disappeared.[30]

As I have argued elsewhere, this view is mostly wrong. Shays's Rebellion was the largest of several small, scattered disturbances in 1786–1787. The rebels spilled no blood, fired no shots, and damaged no property. Remarkable records exist on who participated in the rebellion, and these records show little correlation between participation and debt.[31]

There is no evidence to suppose that Shays's Rebellion added any urgency to nominate Massachusetts delegates for Philadelphia, and no evidence to suppose that it helped Massachusetts ratify the Constitution. Nor is there evidence that the Constitution solved the grievances behind the movement; a 90 percent reduction in taxes did that. If anything, the Constitution would have made matters worse. At the Philadelphia Convention, future vice president and Massachusetts governor Elbridge Gerry complained, "More blood would have been spilt in Massachusetts in the late insurrection, if the general authority had intermeddled."[32]

Shays's Rebellion is important to the narrative for two reasons. First, as we will see in the next chapter, Shays was used for propaganda effect. This media strategy did not work well in Massachusetts, but it may have had a modest effect in more distant, less informed quarters. Shays was the closest current event that elites could wave like a bloody shirt, justifying the urgent need for a Constitution. In essence, they claimed that the country had dodged a bullet with Shays but might not be so lucky next time.

Second, and more importantly, Shays indicates elites' ultimate anxieties. As soon as the rebellion began, Washington and Madison blamed the British. This was characteristic; both had long feared British intrigue. Washington commented, "there surely are men of consequence and abilities behind the Curtain, who move the puppits [*sic*]. . . . They may be instigated by British Councils. . . ." Madison felt sure that Shays had "opened communication with the Viceroy of Canada."[33]

What is more striking is how tenaciously elites feared Shays despite ample evidence to the contrary. Federalist sources contradicted sensationalist accounts of the rebellion. General Shepard, who fired on Shays and his men, stated, "Had I been disposed to destroy them, I . . . could have killed the greater part of his whole army within twenty-five minutes."[34] All to no avail. Madison was stunned when he learned that Massachusetts had electorally punished Shays's opponents and could not conceive of anything but wickedness at the bottom of such conduct. Elites like Washington and Secretary of War Knox never confessed to getting the rebellion wrong. If the British were not behind it, they could have been or might be behind the next one.

The Philadelphia Convention

Heading into Philadelphia, Federalists had quite a bit going for them strategically. They had managed to call a convention with instructions sufficiently ambiguous to exploit. They were clothed with an adequate measure of legitimacy. They had prioritized political problems that few had worried about before. They had assembled a convention of highly influential individuals, biased toward their partisans. They had an unsuspecting opposition. And they had a blueprint for agenda setting: rules and documents that would control the tracks along which the Convention would run.

The Convention began before it started. Madison arrived in Philadelphia on May 5, the first delegate to arrive from anywhere outside Pennsylvania.[35] This allowed time to prepare rules favorable for the Federalist cause and to ready an agenda to steer the course of the Convention. A quorum of seven states did not arrive until May 25, but Madison was busy as the main drafter of the so-called Virginia plan, which was the single negotiating text for what developed into the Constitution. There was still a streak of caution; in the first days not even the most radical delegates suggested scrapping the Articles.[36]

On May 28 and 29, the rules were laid down: Washington was president of the Convention, each state got a vote, straight majority wins, and motions could be reconsidered. Finally, there was to be strict secrecy. Members were "prohibited even from taking copies of resolutions, on which the convention were deliberating, or extracts of any kind from the journals without formally moving for, and obtaining permission, by a vote of the convention for that purpose."[37] Sentries were planted within and without to enforce the rule. On May 29, Madison again obscured authorship of his handiwork and had Randolph introduce the Virginia plan to the Convention. The next day the legitimacy of the Virginia plan was called into question as incompatible with the Articles. This motion was defeated 6–1.

Madison's effort at agenda control was nearly derailed. Despite discussion, attention, and amendments to the Virginia plan, small states were still disenchanted. On June 15 and 18, two other plans were introduced to compete with the Virginia plan. One was the New Jersey plan, which resembled the Articles and treated the smaller states favorably, and it was taken seriously; the other was a plan by Hamilton, which espoused such ideas as a Senate and single executive who served for life, and it was not taken as seriously. On June 19, the Convention had to decide whether to proceed with the Virginia plan or the New Jersey plan.

Madison rose and gave a speech denouncing the New Jersey plan. That plan, he said, is inadequate to remedy the evils of the Articles like treaty violations, encroachments on federal authority, states encroaching on each other, threat of insurrection by armed minorities or the non-voting poor, the impotence and instability of state laws, and the influence of foreign powers in the union. Madison then went on to say that if the Articles were merely amended, then the states would either remain largely independent or form into smaller confederacies. In such a case, small states would either be annexed, or given no better terms than the Virginia plan offered. The Virginia plan prevailed 7–3.[38]

For present purposes, the content of the Constitution is important for a couple of reasons. One is that debate on content aided coalition formation. The famous compromises on issues such as representation and slavery addressed distributional problems, and made the Constitution more palatable. No one was thrilled with the bargain, but everyone got something for their constituency and that made ratification an easier sell. Compromises made the Constitution ideologically more acceptable to the country and strategically bound the document's drafters closer together.[39]

The other reason is that the content of debate exposes what was driving compromise and cooperation. Threats of force bounced back and forth, but the real danger was perceived to be overseas. Larger states hinted at partial union to frighten the smaller states into being more conciliatory, and Gunning Bedford, Jr., responded for the smaller states: if larger states insisted on being overweening, small states could find foreign allies to "take them by the hand." Gouverneur Morris asserted: "This Country must be united. If Persuasion does not unite it, the sword will." Madison, as usual, put the choice most clearly: "Great as the evil [of the international slave trade] is, a dismemberment of the Union would be worse. If those states should disunite from the other states for not indulging them in the temporary continuance of this traffic, they might solicit and obtain aid from foreign powers."[40]

It is not accidental that the language of the Constitution was not novel. The committees of detail and style (which counted Madison among its few members) drew heavily on the Articles. However, soothing familiarity disguised a dramatic shift. Previously, states held legal supremacy, with the new Constitution the federal government held legal supremacy. The framers did not centralize power absolutely, just decisively. And the freighted phrases that fundamentally redirected supremacy required stylistic cover—new wine in old bottles.[41]

Timing plays a key role in the story of how to put the document into effect. By testing the waters gingerly and playing for time, the Founders thinned the ranks to the devoted. Early in the Convention, Madison suggested that an ordinary act of legislature could not ratify the Constitution. Others argued that the Convention might be overstepping its authority, and the ratification subject was dropped. But by July 23, many were arguing that Congress should not have a say on the Constitution because then ratification would never happen: "Whose opposition will be most likely to be excited against the new system? That of the local demagogues who will be degraded by it from the importance they now hold. . . . It is of great importance, therefore, that the consideration of this subject should be transferred from the legislatures where this class of men have their full influence to a field in which their efforts can be less mischievous."[42]

Nonetheless, the real talk on ratification did not come until the very end of the Convention. On August 30 and 31, the delegates debated how many states were needed to ratify. Madison was in favor of seven to nine states to put the document into effect over the whole country, in effect betting that nine could coerce four. James Wilson added that "The House on fire must be extinguished, without a scrupulous regard to ordinary rights."[43] Randolph believed nine was a respectable majority of the whole and was a number familiar in the Articles (nine was a number used in Articles IX and X).[44] But others disagreed and spirited argument ensued. Luther Martin asserted that the people would only ratify if rushed into it. When it was put to a vote, thirteen was voted down, ten was voted down, but nine carried the day.

Some delegates were in favor of a second convention. George Mason and Randolph voiced serious misgivings and worried that "this Constitution had been formed without the knowledge or idea of the people. A second Convention will know more of the sense of the people and be able to provide a system more consonant to it."[45] Gerry concurred. But Charles Pinckney retorted:

The States will never agree in their plans—And the Deputies to a second Convention coming together under the discordant impressions of their Constituents will never agree. Conventions are serious things and ought not to be repeated—He was not without objections. . . . But apprehending the danger of a general confusion, and an ultimate decision by the Sword, he should give the plan his support.[46]

And the rest of the Convention agreed with him. They had come too far, worked too hard, and gotten in too deep to leave their labors at the mercy of further review.

Finally, there was the matter of how to sign the Constitution. Of the 55 delegates who had, at some time or another, attended the Philadelphia Convention, 42 remained and 39 would sign. Of the thirteen states, only eleven states were signatories (Rhode Island and New York were missing.) Two-thirds of the New York delegation had stormed out of the Convention early on, preventing that state from signing (the lone remainder, Hamilton, signed anyway). Less than half of the original delegates from Virginia and Massachusetts signed. The remaining delegates struggled with how to put the best gloss on serious attrition. At Franklin's prompting, they concluded "Done in Convention by the Unanimous consent of the States present. . . ."[47]

State Ratification Debates

At the close of the Convention, the Federalists remained masters of their forces. Although they had not retained all the delegates, they had quietly crafted an acceptable compromise with a claim to legitimacy.[48] And in spite of economic growth before the Convention met, many admitted that there were political problems. Federalists were on the whole united, respected, and influential. Even Antifederalists adored Franklin and especially Washington, and often explained away their Federalist views by blaming it on well-intentioned ignorance or senility.[49]

As the first to the battlefield, the forces in favor of the Constitution could stake first claim on a popular name and divine favor. They dubbed themselves Federalists and their opponents Antifederalists. The labels stuck, though they never really fit. It would have been more accurate, though less politic, to call the Federalists the Nationalist Party and the Antifederalists the Confederalist Party. Naturally, Federalists were quick to conjecture that God caucused with them.[50]

But this propaganda coup should not obscure the virtue of the Antifederalists. Winners write history, and many now view the Antifederalists as reflexive obstructionists or ignorant hayseeds. This is unfair. While the demographics of Antifederalism skewed rural, so did the country. As Merrill Jensen has shown, the quality of their thought and writings was high. Although they had to play catch-up, Antifederalists articulated a tenable vision of America and the modern state—a vision that would become popular within the decade.[51] But Federalists had strategic surprise and could now impose an agenda and procedures for ratification on their uninformed and unprepared opponents.

On September 20, the Constitution was read in Congress and by September 28, Congress sent the Constitution on to the states for deliberation. States were instructed to call special ratifying conventions to debate and accept or reject the Constitution in its totality. No amendments were to be proposed, no second convention called, only union or no. Federalist support tended to come from creditors, merchants, and city-dwellers, while Antifederalist support was drawn from those in agriculture, the countryside, and debt.[52]

The prospects for victory were murky. Hamilton soberly gave the Constitution about even odds; Madison thought ratification on the whole too close to call. Uncertainty persisted into March 1788, when the Comte de Moustier wrote, "The generality of people divide themselves among their Leaders. . . . But every day it becomes more difficult to judge what the outcome of this power struggle will be."[53]

But the playing field was now decidedly different. The Philadelphia Convention had created the crisis necessary for its own acceptance. The Constitution was at least viable, and its advocates created a new incentive structure: the Constitution or disintegration. A different French observer commented:

Indifferent Spectators agree that the new form of Government, well executed will be able to produce good results; but they also think that if the states really had the desire to be united the present Confederation would be adequate for all their needs. Meanwhile they are unable to conceal that after having excited this general ferment there is no longer a means to stop it, that the old edifice is almost destroyed, and that any fabric whatsoever must be substituted for it.[54]

Antifederalists greeted the new Constitution with cries of stunned disbelief. "The Federal Farmer" remarked: "Not a word was said about destroying the old constitution, and making a new one . . . probably, not one man in ten thousand in the United States, till within these ten or twelve days, had an idea that the old ship was to be destroyed, and be put to the alternative of embarking in the new ship presented, or of being left in danger of sinking. . . ."[55] Essay after essay argued that the delegates had overstepped their authority, conspired against the traditional government, and foisted unsolicited innovations on the people.

Even sympathetic parties were surprised by it. "Americanus" proclaimed, "The Convention have certainly acted wisely in throwing the Confederation totally aside. . . . This was a decisive boldness I had not looked for." Overseas, John Quincy Adams was surprised and alarmed by the new document. Jefferson, no enemy of reform, was shocked by a draft of the Constitution when it reached him in France. The document's extensive powers "stagger all my dispositions to subscribe" to it.[56]

Delaware

Delaware was the first state to ratify the Constitution on December 7, 1787. Since the records have not survived, little is known of their convention. We do know that the vote was unanimously for the Constitution and that it only took a few hours to reach that conclusion. Although there were some allegations of electoral irregularities ("sundry persons were insulted and violently assaulted professedly because they were Whigs, Presbyterians, or Irish-men . . ."[57]), they are of dubious origin. Federalist fervor ran high in Delaware—economic and security interests pointed that way. They hoped to get the national capital on their soil, and several members of the state ratifying convention, including its presiding officer, had served under Washington.

Pennsylvania

Pennsylvania was second off the mark, but it is a complicated case. The state was not wed to Federalist principles; its fear of central authority had led it to abolish the position of governor. The state constitution mandated six months between proposing amendments and electing convention delegates.[58] But Federalists called a convention illegally.

Antifederalists in the Pennsylvania Assembly objected, and absented themselves to deny a quorum. The sergeant-at-arms was dispatched to retrieve two of them but repeatedly returned empty-handed. A mob, however, succeeded in forcibly returning assemblymen and the convention was called. The mob was not spontaneous or anonymous; it was led by John Barry, the captain of a ship owned by Robert Morris, and Major William Jackson, who had been a secretary of the Philadelphia Convention.[59]

James Wilson carried the Federalist load in the convention. Keeping to prudent strategy, he phrased the choice succinctly: "The general sentiment in that body [the Philadelphia Convention] . . . is expressed in the motto which some of them have chosen, UNITE OR DIE."[60] The Constitution was ratified by a two to one margin, five days after Delaware.

But an Antifederalist at the ratifying convention indicated why a state that had expressly confined its delegates' powers before the Philadelphia Convention ratified by such a large margin:

> They agreed that the deputies sent by them to convention should have no compensation for their services, which determination was calculated to prevent the election of any member who resided at a distance from the city. . . . public papers teemed with the most violent threats against those who should dare to think for themselves, and *tar and feathers* were liberally promised to all those who would not immediately join in supporting the proposed government. . . . The house was formed by violence, some of the members composing it were detained there by force, which alone would have vitiated any proceedings, to which they were otherwise competent; but had the legislature been legally formed, this business was absolutely without their power. In many of the counties the people did not attend the elections as they had not an opportunity of judging the plan. Others did not consider themselves bound by the call of a set of men who assembled at the state-house in Philadelphia . . . and some were prevented from voting, by the violence of the party who were determined at all events to force down the measure.[61]

Had there been fewer irregularities, it is not hard to imagine rejection.

New Jersey

New Jersey was the third state to ratify. The Revolutionary War was hard on the state; many battles took place there and armies marched through it, requisitioning property and running up debt. The state gave money to Congress after the war and many private citizens lent money as well. Thus, New Jersey felt the financial problems of the Articles acutely and was squarely in the camp that would benefit from the Constitution. There was little uncertainty about the outcome of their state convention. On December 18, the Constitution was unanimously ratified and the delegates retired to a tavern to celebrate "with liquid abandon."[62]

Georgia

The fourth ratifier, Georgia, was something of a non-factor in ratification and the reasons for this are manifest. As Washington aptly noted, "If a weak State, with powerful tribes of Indians in its rear, & the Spaniards on its flank, do not incline to embrace a strong *general* Government, there must, I should think, be either wickedness, or insanity in their conduct."[63] Georgia offered little other than verbal support for the central government, but was more than eager to accept the military support of a central government. Therefore, it unanimously ratified on January 2, 1788.

Connecticut

On paper, Connecticut looks unproblematic. On January 9, it ratified by a healthy margin (128–40), but its ratification is actually more intricate. In the fall of 1786, Connecticut opposed national government; both of her Congressmen voted against the Philadelphia Convention, calling it "a very doubtful measure at best."[64] Yet slightly more than a year later, the vote is lopsidedly in favor. How did that happen?

Unquestionably there was Federalist support in the state. New York taxed many goods bound for Connecticut and kept the revenues, something a national government could redistribute more equitably. There was also a sizable population of merchants and creditors backing ratification. Further, press outlets, like the Connecticut *Courant,* advanced textbook balancing logic.[65] But three ingredients were necessary to produce the lopsided Federalist victory: dishonest delegates, a press that sang in Federalist unison, and political hardball.

First, the ratifying convention turned to their Philadelphia delegates, but their delegates were non-representative and dishonest.[66] While four delegates were elected, one of the Antifederalist-leaning delegates declined to attend, making the delegation more nationalist than the population. Roger Sherman commented that the people "should have as little to do as may be about the Government. They want information and are constantly liable to be misled." To keep the people from being misled, he assiduously propagated the idea that almost nothing would be changed with the new government. Might state and federal government clash over jurisdiction? "The objects of the federal government will be so obvious that there will be no great danger of any interference,"[67] he concluded.

Another active delegate at Philadelphia, Oliver Ellsworth, wrote the influential "Landholder" series of articles campaigning for ratification. He was similarly forthright:

After all, Ellsworth asserted (apparently blind to Article I, Section 10, to the supremacy clause, and to several other parts of the document he helped to write), "No alteration in the state governments is even now proposed, but they are to remain identically the same as they are now." A year later Ellsworth, as author of the Judiciary Act of 1789, wrote the single most nationalizing piece of legislation in all American history. . . .[68]

Second, all the printers in the state were inflexibly firm allies of the Federalists. The characters of Antifederalists were publicly trashed, and the publishers suppressed the fact that town meetings had rejected the Constitution. Moreover, only one Antifederalist article ever saw print and it was never reprinted. As for out-of-state articles, a torrent of Federalist essays appeared in Connecticut papers, but hardly a drop, about five, Antifederalist articles made a local showing.[69]

Third, to these acts must be added the political hardball that ensured ratification. The ratifying convention was moved to a building with a balcony, which was duly packed with Federalists, who drowned out Antifederalist speakers.[70] The vote was 128–40; many of those 40 came from the agrarian area of New Haven County, which rallied behind the unbowed integrity of assemblyman James Wadsworth. He had served ably as congressman, state councilman, and state comptroller before the ratifying convention. After the convention, Wadsworth was removed from office under a law repealed the day after his removal.

The landslide victory in Connecticut masks a host of dishonest and sharp dealings.[71] We will never know how a fairer ratification process would have turned out, but there are ample reasons to believe that the politically mighty would not trust the intrinsic goodness of the Constitution or evils of the Articles to persuade people in the state. At the very least, the people of Connecticut surrendered their sovereignty under false pretenses. It is in this light that we can see Connecticut governor Huntington's comments at this chapter's beginning as either highly qualified or disingenuous.

Massachusetts

Massachusetts, the sixth ratifying state, was another hurdle the Constitution clipped on its sprint to ratification.[72] The state was not eager to revise the Articles, and when the call for the Annapolis convention went out, two sets of delegates were appointed to go, but declined. When the call went out for the Philadelphia Convention, Congressman Rufus King objected on sound legal footing; the Articles invested Congress with the exclusive power to issue such a call. But many states had already elected delegates, momentum had already been built up, and so Massachusetts agreed to attend the Philadelphia Convention.

To understand how narrowly Massachusetts ratified, one must mind the numbers. There were 401 communities in the state; 46 did not send delegates. These 46 were not randomly distributed, and were drawn from communities where the cost of attending was higher. Places that were poor, distant, or inaccessible fall into this category; that is to say Antifederalist towns were more likely to be missing from the convention. Nevertheless, it became clear that Federalists were ominously outnumbered.

And so they played for time to stave off swift defeat. Normally the party in a hurry, the Federalists now insisted on inspecting every cranny of the Constitution. Federalists also faced the task of dampening down Elbridge Gerry's voice. Gerry had been a delegate at Philadelphia and had refused to sign the document. At the state ratifying convention, Federalists did everything in their power to keep him quiet, causing a commotion and calling Gerry out of order when he tried to speak. Humiliated, Gerry left the convention and would only return if he was allowed to defend himself. The Federalists insisted that he had removed himself and refused to allow him reentry. Despite their maneuvers, the Federalists had not won over enough moderates to ensure passage.

Historian Charles Dawson interviewed the son of a prominent New York Federalist who said, "Enough members of the Massachusetts Convention were bought with money *from New York* to secure ratification of the new system by Massachusetts." The Federalist secretary of the Ratifying Convention, George Richards Minot, admitted with repugnance in his diary, "Never was there a political system introduced by less worthy means than the constitution for the United States." He admitted several Federalist designs, "to *pack* a Convention whose sense would be different from that of the people . . .," to use misinformation about candidates, and to spread a rumor that if the Constitution was not ratified that delegates would not be given money to travel home. Federalists also withdrew all advertising from papers that ran Antifederal pieces and tampered with the public mail.[73]

Still, it was not enough to ensure passage. Two factors remained undetermined: potential amendments to the Constitution and the influential allegiance of Governor John Hancock. First, moderates objected to the take-it-or-leave-it nature of the Constitution and wanted to add amendments. Federalists feared that such a precedent would expose the whole document to revision and they doggedly refused. But their options were dwindling, so the Federalists decided to preempt their opponents and offer their own list of amendments that were recommendatory once the Constitution was ratified.

Second, Governor John Hancock was a wild card who had been sitting on the sidelines. He had come down with a conveniently timed case of the gout, and his associates whispered that he was waiting to throw his weight on the winning side. The Federalists opted to try to tie these loose ends together. They approached Hancock, known for his vanity,[74] and allegedly told him that he could introduce their amendments as his own, helping ensure glorious passage for the Constitution, and in return they would support his reelection campaign and back him for vice president (or president should Virginia fail to ratify) of the new country. Catering a banquet to Hancock's ego, the Federalists watched him gluttonously gobble it up. His gout miraculously cleared. On January 30, he appeared at the convention, where shortly thereafter he introduced "his" proposals.

Sam Adams had helped lead the Antifederalists. But with the death of his son, the increasing Federalism of his old friend Paul Revere, and the sudden Federalism of his friend Hancock, Adams's will to resist cracked. He cautiously gave his support of the new Constitution and the new "conciliatory propositions." Such a constellation of stars was barely enough, and Massachusetts ratified with a 52 percent majority—10 changed votes would have reversed the outcome. Had Federalists been slightly slower off the mark, had Gerry not been expelled, or had the alleged bribes not been made, the Constitution would have been rejected.

Maryland

Maryland was the last to sign the Articles and only did so under military duress. Although it was a party to the Mount Vernon conference, Maryland refused to attend the meeting's successor in its own city of Annapolis because the meeting might "produce other meetings, which may have consequences which cannot be foreseen. Innovations in government, when not absolutely necessary, are dangerous . . ."[75] Twelve delegates turned down their appointments to Philadelphia before five were found who would accept. Of those five, two departed the Convention, and three stayed to sign. Despite being one of the closest states to Philadelphia, Maryland had one of the worst attendance records there.

It is hard to reconstruct Maryland's ratifying election. Both sides appear to have manipulated the polls.[76] Less than one-quarter of the electorate turned out, though that quarter was strongly Federalist. Federalists dominated the floor, quickly pushing for its ratification without discussing amendments or answering questions. Federalists successfully challenged the right of Antifederalists to speak. The final vote was 63–11, after which the Antifederalists were outraged.

South Carolina

South Carolina is another example of a deceptively lopsided ratification vote.[77] On May 23, 1788, South Carolina ratified 149–73, yet it is very probable that Antifederalists represented a majority of the population. The reason lay with the segmented nature of South Carolina politics. The state was run by an atypically coherent hereditary aristocracy, thoroughly related by blood and marriage and fearful of slave insurrection, Native American attacks, and bumptious backcountry upstarts. Because of its historical power, a disproportionate amount of representation was allotted to the coastal region, a Federalist bastion. Federalists outnumbered Antifederalists in the convention two to one when it started, and that is how the vote ended up too. Although the vote was not fraudulent or coercive—no government is perfect—it should not be confused with the voice of the majority.

New Hampshire

Before Philadelphia, few in New Hampshire thought the Articles had insufficient power, and, in many places, they thought the Articles had too much. The legislature appointed delegates for the Annapolis convention, but none of them bothered to attend. The legislature authorized delegates for Philadelphia, but— owing to apathy—their two delegates were two months late. Unlike some other states, New Hampshire did not just have a popular Antifederalist majority; it was democratic enough to reflect that majority in its delegates. The Constitution squeaked through more on procedural sleights of hand than debate and deliberation.[78]

The delegates, most of the clergy, and all five of the state's newspapers supported adoption. Debate was lively and the familiar divisions obtained. Antifederalists handily outnumbered Federalists, but Federalists had some compensation for their numeric inferiority. The president of New Hampshire, John Sullivan, was ardently Federalist, and he used his position to maximize ratification's prospects. His leverage brought the Federalists a ratifying convention in the time and place (i.e., Exeter, after many states could already have ratified) that was most to their advantage. Alas, many towns gave their representatives binding instructions not to vote for ratification. To overcome this handicap, the Federalists hatched a plot.

Federalists were told to arrive early for the convention. When a quorum appeared, they would form a committee on the rules, which would check everyone's credentials, lay down ground rules, and pick a temporary chairman. The rules committee would also put in place three safety catches: (1) secret balloting to loosen the hold of binding instructions; (2) motions to adjourn would take priority so quick escapes could be made if a rejection vote looked likely; and (3) no vote could be made without as many members as were initially present. This last rule allowed Federalists the power to sneak out of the convention and stop a rejection vote.

The plan worked without a hitch. Sullivan was presiding over a nearby legislative session, which he did not adjourn until the afternoon, but several Federalist delegates quietly left the session early. Joining their co-conspirators, they formed a quorum, laid down the rules, and installed a temporary chairman. They also assisted Sullivan's election as convention president the next day.

However, all were in agreement that Federalists were in the minority. Try as they might, Federalists could not get a majority, and a vote would mean defeat. Somehow they convinced a small group of moderates to agree to adjournment (bribery has been suspected but there is insufficient evidence.)[79] The Federalists exercised their safety option and postponed a decision until June.

In the interim, the Antifederalists were relatively quiet, but the Federalists stepped up their efforts. The press blanketed the state with glowing accounts of Connecticut's ratification. In addition it launched personal attacks on Antifederalists, accusing them of riots, financial problems, and British service. Federalists also politicked at the local level, picking up a few extra seats at the next convention (one of which is dubious, given that the winner was the fellow in charge of certifying the results).[80] Federalists also applied pressure on individuals from Antifederalist areas not to attend. Of the five delegates absent at the second convention, four were Antifederalist.

The play for time worked. Eight states had ratified and New Hampshire could now be the crucial ninth, the "Keystone of the Federal Arch." Since the Federalists drew up the rules, they were in charge of validating the credentials of delegates. And they decided three disputed delegates unanimously in their favor. The Federalists also availed themselves of recommended amendments to appeal to moderates. Naturally, the pressure continued on individuals caught between Antifederalist instructions and their more nationalist personal sympathies. Four such delegates were marked present but nonvoting in the final tally. With all this, the last vote was 57–47.

Virginia

Virginia was integral to the birthing process of the Constitution, but it was due more to Madison and Washington's virtue than the character of the state. The extraordinary labors of Madison and Washington had created the successes of Mount Vernon, Annapolis, and Philadelphia. Virginia had insisted on separately ratifying the peace treaty that ended the Revolutionary War.[81] Virginia had looked askance on Madison's actions and forced him to mute his nationalism and cloak his handiwork. Virginia elected seven delegates to go to Philadelphia, but four accepted and three ended up signing.

The strongest Antifederalist states were, accidentally or not, the last to consider ratification. The eight states that ratified before Virginia (word of New Hampshire had not yet reached them) did weigh on the minds of the delegates. Washington and Madison kept the debating grounds from the Constitution's problems to union or disunion. Meanwhile, in New York, Hamilton wrote to Madison that the more he understood the Antifederals in New York, the more he feared, should Virginia fail to ratify, "eventual disunion and civil war."[82]

Washington made his allegiances known early and often. To John Armstrong: "I am suprized to find that any person who is acquainted with the critical state of our public affairs . . . can wish to make amendments the ultimatum for adopting the offered system." To Charles Carter: "My *decided* Opinion on the Matter is, that there is *no Alternative* between the *Adoption* of it and *Anarchy*." And to the Marquis de Lafayette: "There is no alternative—no hope of alteration—no intermediate resting place—between the adoption of this and a recurrence of an unqualified state of Anarchy, with all its deplorable consequences."[83]

Patrick Henry led the Antifederalist charge, and he started with a powerful punch: calling the legality of the Philadelphia Convention into question. Had not delegates only been authorized to amend the Articles, not draw up a whole new government? Henry asked to read the act of the Virginia Assembly empowering the Philadelphia delegation. The convention's president reacted with stern severity:

> [Whether the Convention exceeded its powers] ought not to influence our deliberations. . . . Although those gentlemen were only directed to consider the defects of the old system, and not devise a new one, if they found it so thoroughly defective as not to admit of a revising, and submitted a new system to our consideration which the people have deputed us to investigate, [then] I cannot find any degree of propriety in reading those papers. . . .[84]

Henry dropped the matter.

After much resistance, Madison bent and allowed recommendatory amendments, which he later transformed into the Bill of Rights. Edmund Randolph, a non-signer at Philadelphia and an influential independent, also swallowed his misgivings and lent his support to the Constitution. Washington bore some responsibility in kicking the legs out of his resistance. He wrote Randolph in January 1788, "It is the best Constitution that can be obtained at this Epocha, and that this, or a dissolution of the Union awaits our choice, and are the only alternatives before us."[85]

When Randolph relented, he announced his reasoning, "though I do not reverence the Constitution, that its adoption is necessary to avoid the storm which is hanging over America . . ." For if, "in this situation, we reject the Constitution, the Union will be dissolved, the dogs of war will break loose. . . . In case of attack, what defense can we make?" Randolph's conversion correlates with other events. He was "financially embarrassed in 1788 and emerged in 1790 on solid footing and as the holder of more than $10,000 in public securities; that he was politically ambitious and emerged in 1789 as the first attorney general of the United States."[86] It may not be a coincidence that Washington later fired Randolph on suspicion of soliciting bribes.

Even then, Federalists held a slight edge, easily erased by accidents, sickness, and absenteeism. When the vote came: "The Constitution was ratified, 89 to 79. A shift of just five votes would have defeated it, but Madison, for all his concern, had been the master of his forces. Madison, 'Father of the Constitution,' present at its conception in Philadelphia, had also presided as attending physician at its birth."[87]

New York

New York was unquestionably against the Constitution. It profited by the Articles because it collected imposts, which fell largely on residents of other states. New York consistently rejected requests from Congress to help raise money for the central government. At the Convention, two-thirds of the delegation left in July. One delegate remarked that New York "would never have concurred in sending deputies to the convention, if it had supposed the deliberations were to turn on a consolidation of the States, and a National Government."[88] Hence New York is missing from the signatories.

No state debated the Constitution as vociferously as New York, and no state was better informed. Although the New York Federalists were media savvy (even New York newspapers tended to have a Federalist slant) and the deservedly famous *Federalist Papers* were a result of this debate, there is little evidence that persuasion ushered the Constitution past the Antifederalists. Furthermore, the state was exceptionally democratic. Contrary to other states (and the property qualification in the New York Constitution), all free adult male citizens were eligible to vote in the election of delegates to the ratifying convention. And when they did, Antifederalists outnumbered Federalists by a clear margin, 46 to 19.

The Federalists wanted to temporize to let ratification pick up momentum; immediate defeat was certain; future defeat somewhat less so. The Antifederalists wanted to delay so they would not look unfair, so another state might take the onus off them by rejecting first (as they had done with the impost of 1783), and so they could coordinate with Antifederalists in other states to use the New York convention to propose amendments and call for a second convention.

The convention opened with the chancellor railing New York's security position, "Staten Island might be seized by New Jersey, and Long Island by Connecticut. Northern New York would be endangered by Canadians and land-grabbing Vermonters, while western New York would be vulnerable to the British and their Indian allies." Hamilton picked up the thread and continued, "that a rejection of the Constitution may involve the most fatal consequences." All to no avail. Hamilton complained, "Our arguments confound, but do not convince—Some of the leaders however appear to me to be convinced *by circumstances.*"[89]

Circumstances started to go the Federalists' way. Word reached the convention that New Hampshire had ratified and had been the ninth state, putting the document into legal effect. This legality did not dent Antifederalist solidarity.[90] Then Virginia ratified, and cracks became pronounced. New York was alone and surrounded. The only states left were North Carolina and Rhode Island, which would make for a far-flung and inconsiderable confederation. Timing and geography had done New York in.

From this point on, the narrative is no longer about union between equals but rather about absorption of smaller powers. As soon as news of Virginia's ratification reached New York, unification with the remaining states grew much less voluntary. Melancton Smith was the courageous Antifederalist who broke ranks. Previously, he had refuted Jay's argument point by point. Smith's correspondence with his friend Nathan Dane reveals the reasoning behind his change in position. On July 3, Dane was plain:

> Admitting that Rhode Island, New York, and North Carolina all withhold their assent to the Constitution, and propose similar amendments, their situation is such, far removed from each other, and surrounded by ratifying States, that they never can think of confederating themselves. . . . But the ratifying and non ratifying States will immediately have opposite Interests . . . we must conclude, it is at least highly probable that they will have recourse to arms . . . at no very distant period. And what must be the issue of force . . . is not difficult to foresee. . . .

Smith replied on July 15, "I entirely accord with you in opinion."[91]

On July 23, Smith spoke in front of the convention. "He was as thoroughly convinced then as he ever had been, that the Constitution was radically defective— amendments to it had always been the object of his pursuit, and until Virginia came in, he had reason to believe they might have been obtained previous to the operation of the Government. He was now satisfied they could not."[92] Further, there was a threat of civil war within New York; the Federalist Southern part of the state was talking secession. Smith's dissention and the votes he brought with him were just enough to ratify. The final vote on July 26 was 30–27—note the decline in 10 voters from the initial session.

North Carolina

North Carolina played no significant part at Philadelphia and pursued a hiding strategy during ratification. Despite Federalist violence, the result of the ratifying convention was a 184–84 motion to neither accept nor reject the Constitution but instead to offer a series of amendments. Then all the delegates went home. When the United States became a sovereign state in April 1789, North Carolina sent an ambassador to the new government, and struck a conciliatory tone. Public opinion began to change; the new government was the only game in town, and Washington was a respected figure leading a functional state. Further, North Carolina was embarrassed by its association with Rhode Island, the other lingering holdout, that repository of "disgusting, if not dangerous, democracy."[93] On November 21, after three days of debate, the Constitution was ratified 194–77.

Rhode Island

Rhode Island was the pariah state, and its difference was not hard to isolate. Rhode Island had the most liberal charter of any colony; it was possessed of incomparable religious freedom and local self-government. "Home of the otherwise-minded," they called themselves. Others grumbled that the state was "a moral sewer" and a "downright democracy" whose officials were "entirely controlled by the populace."[94]

Rhode Island did attend the Annapolis convention because it was limited to discussing commerce. But the Philadelphia Convention looked excessive, and Rhode Island spurned three attempts to dispatch delegates. When the new Constitution was submitted for ratification, Rhode Island called for a referendum on it. The Constitution called for special legislative assemblies, not the direct opinion of the population. Rhode Island denied a total of eleven motions to call such a ratifying convention. And when the referendum was held in March 1788, the Constitution was rejected 2,711 to 243, though as many as 900 votes were lost by Providence and Newport boycotting the vote.

At the end of 1789, Rhode Island was the sole holdout, a tiny independent state dwarfed by the new republic. On a Sunday in January of 1790, another motion to hold a ratifying convention came to the floor. Because an Antifederalist was attending to his religious duties, there was a four to four tie on the motion. The four-term governor, John Collins, voted his conscience against his party and broke the tie. That vote caused Collins's political downfall but led to Rhode Island's ratification.

When the ratifying convention met in early March, the Antifederalists outnumbered the Federalists 41 to 28. Then things started to change. Congress moved toward an economic punishment strategy. The Antifederalists "must be made to feel before they will ever to consent to call a convention," and they would be made to feel "by subjecting the goods, wares, and manufactures of this state" to the same high duties "as foreign States not in alliance with the United States."[95] Rhode

Island was given a grace period before tariffs were to go into effect, and a convention was called at the moment the grace period expired.

As the ratifying convention continued without issue, Congress grew increasingly impatient. On May 18, Congress passed a two-pronged assault on Rhode Island to go into effect July 1. One measure was a prohibition of all commerce between Rhode Island and the United States; the other was immediate repayment of Rhode Island's share of the Revolutionary War debt. If Rhode Island should fail to pay up, military force could collect. One senator observed the measure "was meant to be used in the same way that a robber does a dagger or a highwayman a pistol."[96]

That news brought more change. The town of Providence issued a statement on May 24, empowering delegates to meet with delegates from Newport to apply to Congress "for the same privileges and protection which are afforded to the towns under their jurisdiction."[97] Under threat of blockade, forceful requisitions, and secession, Rhode Island ratified on May 29, 1790. The vote was close, 34–32, and had all the delegates been in attendance, it might not have passed (three Antifederalists were absent). But the Federalists had calibrated their means to effect their end. The Constitution had, with some bumps and bruises, been unanimously ratified.

The Origins of the Bill of Rights

Nevertheless, the battle was not over. Dissatisfaction lingered in the air, and the Antifederalists still desired a second convention. Making a constitution was hard enough under the generally congenial conditions enjoyed by the first attempt, but a second was a Pandora's box that threatened to ruin all that had been achieved. Madison says as much in *Federalist* no. 49:

> The danger of disturbing the public tranquility by interesting too strongly the public passions is a still more serious objection against a frequent reference of constitutional questions to the decision of the whole society. Notwithstanding the success which has attended the revisions of our established forms of government . . . it must be confessed that the experiments are of too ticklish a nature to be unnecessarily multiplied . . . The future situations in which we must expect to be usually placed do not present any equivalent security against the danger which is apprehended.

Washington expressed the same sentiment: "If another Federal Convention is attempted the sentiments of the members will be more discordant or less conciliatory than the last, in fine, that they will agree to no genl. Plan."[98]

There was a divide among the Antifederalists. Some were staunchly opposed to the whole nationalizing project of the Constitution; others were more open-minded about the effects of the document and were primarily worried about the lack of a bill of rights. Madison muffled his opinions and exploited the Antifederalists' fissure. Formerly the implacable foe of a bill of rights, Madison became its greatest champion, expediently citing the sturdiest of excuses: "Circumstances are now changed."[99]

Madison was elected to the House and soon set about proposing a Bill of Rights. It quickly became clear that his colleagues did not share his sense of urgency and were more interested in implementing the new government. Madison gave a rights speech that was a notable flop. Antifederalists were busy marshaling forces for their own initiatives, and Federalists shrugged the speech off as a dutiful gesture but "innocent, nugatory, premature, and unnecessary."[100] Undaunted, Madison pressed on. Six weeks later, Madison begged the House to reconsider, and they obligingly referred his proposals to an editing committee. When their work was done, Madison sought to have the House consider the matter. Both Federalists and Antifederalists remained reluctant but yielded to Madison.

The debate that followed was inconclusive and acrimonious, issuing in the first ever duel between Congressmen. Madison could not garner two-thirds of the House to propel his proposals. So he sought approval from his friend Washington, who wrote an endorsement of the Bill of Rights: "not foreseeing any evil consequences that can result from their adoption, they have my wishes for a favorable reception in both houses." This was enough to break the jam. In the Senate, Antifederalists started to catch on that "Madison hoped to break the spirit of the Antifederal party by dividing it."[101] Yet after some changes, the reconciled product ended up on Washington's desk, and he forwarded it on to the states for ratification. The Bill of Rights was quietly ratified.

The move was a terrific success. As Jefferson remarked in April 1790, "The opposition to our new constitution has almost totally disappeared."[102] Since 1784, Madison had seized the initiative and pressed his advantage, leveraging success into greater successes. By 1791, when the Bill of Rights was officially ratified, he had attained his goal, and the group that menaced it the most was divided and conquered.

UNIFICATION AND AFTER

At this point, the United States had unified, however imperfectly. How do we know? The Constitution has all the traits of a unified polity where the Articles did not. Under the Articles, nine states had their own navies; many had their own armies. States like Georgia and Virginia retained powers of war and peace, and states like Virginia and Maryland had their own extensive diplomatic activity. England and France asked for thirteen ambassadors. Under the Constitution, state governments were not allowed to keep their own armies or navies, legal supremacy rested at the federal level, and unilateral nullification or secession was not permitted.

Most impressive was the financial turnaround. Federal financial heft went from negligible under the Articles to overwhelming under the Constitution. By 1795, total federal tax revenue was about 10 times what all states raised combined, federal expenditures were more than 7 times what all states spent combined, and federal debt was more than 20 times what all states borrowed combined.[103]

Legal supremacy had moved squarely from the state to federal level. This is how participants viewed matters at the time: "No leading Federalist ever publicly sought to win over states' rights by conceding that a state could unilaterally nullify or secede in the event it later became dissatisfied. The Federalists' silence here was deafening. . . . No state convention, in its ratification instrument, purported to reserve the right of its state populace to unilateral secession."[104]

One could argue that the true founding of the United States was the Civil War. On the contrary, the Civil War is sound evidence that the United States remained on the unified side of the spectrum. A state does not fragment every time a group declares itself independent; states fragment when a group that can uphold legal supremacy declares independence. Theodore Kaczynski, David Koresh's Branch Davidians, and the Confederate States of America did not take the United States from hierarchy into anarchy, and while the historical consensus espouses this view, it is not hindsight bias. Impartial spectators at the time did not bet that any of the above had the wherewithal to uphold legal supremacy, and evidence of this is that none was internationally recognized as a state.[105]

Not only was the South on shaky military ground, it was also on shaky legal ground. Madison, "the father of the Constitution . . . denounced in unmistakable terms the smooth and well-articulated word pattern of Calhoun, condemning secession as utterly without support in the understandings of the men who made, ratified, and launched the Constitution." The accepted view during Reconstruction, advanced by Samuel Shellabarger, was that secession was void, and no state ever left the jurisdiction of the U.S. government. In *Texas v. White*, the United States Supreme Court concurred.[106] Many people believe that the Civil War changed America profoundly and expanded state power and principles; I am among them. But the scope here is narrower, and asks when states cross the midpoint between anarchy and hierarchy. Since 1791, the United States never has.

[F]oreign powers would find means to corrupt our people, to influence our councils, and, in fine, we should be little better than puppets, danced on the wires of the cabinets of Europe. . . .

—JOHN ADAMS, 1775

If general funds were not introduced it was not likely the balances wd. ever be discharged, even if they sd. be liquidated. The consequence wd. be a rupture of the confederacy. The E. States wd. at sea be powerful & rapacious, the S. opulent & weak. This wd. be a temptation. . . . Reprisals wd. be instituted. Foreign aid would be called in by first the weaker, then the stronger side; & finally both be made subservient to the wars & politics of Europe.

—JAMES MADISON, 1783[1]

4

America's Necessity

BEFORE OR AFTER the Revolutionary War, Adams and Madison were essentially staring at the same problem. Dwarfed by the powers of Europe, tenuously tied to each other, security was scarce for the former colonies. Winning the Revolutionary War would not keep Britain at bay, but only some political elites were in a position to know this. The original task of American foreign policy was how to secure independence. It was only after 1850—when continental expanse was assured—that what to do with independence became a live issue. The Constitution solved (and created) many problems, but its first problem and primary cause was insecurity.

This chapter argues that balance of power politics accounts for the creation of the United States better than competing views. To make this case, the first section compares the empirical record to the main argument, and sees how well the background conditions, crisis trigger, and elite persuasion correspond with the evidence. In the second section, I review what alternate explanations get right and wrong about the American case. And in the final section I sum the analysis and tie up loose ends.

ARGUMENT: AN INTERNATIONAL INTERPRETATION OF THE CONSTITUTION

Opportunity: Background Conditions

Like a great politician, the U.S. Constitution has been all things to all people: aristocratic, democratic, radical, conservative, liberating, oppressive, novel, old hat, and so on. It may well be all these things. But the correlates of the document are not equivalent to its causes. In comparative perspective, I argue that the Constitution was a product of the balance of power. Protected by an ocean but threatened on all sides by foreign powers, unable to act in concert and slowly growing apart with time, elites were in a position to solve their security problems by balancing against great powers. The thirteen former colonies faced threats that were optimally intense, abiding, and symmetrical.

Intensity

Trying to unify is not worth the trouble if states confront threats that are either too large or too small. Nothing so drastic as union is necessary when the threat can be met through internal balancing, but unification is pointless if the aggregated power is still not enough to counter the balancing target. Americans found themselves in such a situation in the 1780s. The American Revolution had established that they could fight a great power to a standoff, but just barely, and now their position was eroding. Yet few were in a privileged position to feel these changes.

On the asset side, the threat against the United States was not overwhelming. Wide-open spaces, the Atlantic Ocean, and French assistance certainly helped, but Americans also won their independence by being hard to conquer. One Spanish official took note, "How well it would be for us to avoid the vexations of such a naturally robust people, trained to war and accustomed to the last degree of greatest hardships, as was duly proven when England lost the flower of her troops at the hands of a few naked colonists without military discipline."[2] The United States were fearsome enough when they worked together and balanced against great powers.

On the liability side, victory in the American Revolution was a close call. The Continental Army was constantly plagued by recruitment problems, supply issues, and infighting. Without outside aid, several lucky breaks, and horrible British generalship, the Americans might have lost—and the factors that produced victory could not be relied upon in the future. States were bickering, belatedly repaying debts, and not preparing for future conflict. Their financial position was slipping (on which more in the next section.) Before ratification, American elites felt intense threats, their house was on fire, and they were not shy about expressing these concerns.[3]

If the United States wanted to hold their own against great powers, they had the best chances for success the more they resembled great powers. England, France, and Spain were large, centralized governments; listing federal republics of the period is cataloging weak states: the Swiss cantons, Genoa, Venice, Ragusa, and the United Provinces of the Netherlands. Divided, Americans were weaker, able to be played and preyed upon by great powers, and impartial observers expected the United States to further fragment.[4]

During ratification, security concerns were front and center. Prime evidence of this is *The Federalist Papers*. The early essays zero in on defense; not only were the authors primarily concerned with security, their audience was too. Essays 1–6 and 8–9 were the most reprinted of all of Publius's essays. Essays 4–5 draw on England as a model to emulate, specifically England's unification with Wales and Scotland, which staved off foreign intrigue and kept the Isles free. *Federalist* no. 43 makes an exclamatory appeal to "the absolute necessity of the case; to the great principle of self-preservation. . . ."[5]

These are capital examples of Kenneth Waltz's sameness effect; states copy leaders or fall behind.[6] It was not inevitable that key elites were pro-union, but it was not coincidental that they were. Military elites, like George Washington and Alexander Hamilton, had seen firsthand how precarious American security was; business elites, like Benjamin Franklin and Gouverneur Morris, could hear from their contacts abroad about the former colonies' deteriorating standing; governmental elites, like James Wilson and Madison, were in a good position to watch in horror as the confederation's fissures grew. Unification profoundly improved America's security; that was the Constitution's chief objective and central causal motivation. In brief, the threat that faced the young United States was neither too great nor too small to obviate unification; power politics drove unification.

Duration

The greatest threats the former colonies faced came from foreign states. Great powers had been involved in the New World for hundreds of years and showed little interest in departing. England, and to a lesser extent Spain, had the ability to project force on the northern and southern boundaries of the United States. To varying degrees, they supplied Native Americans in an effort to increase the hostility Americans felt on their flanks, cultivated separatist movements, and left soldiers on or near American soil. Great power involvement in the New World was clearly not going away, and the feeble former colonies did not have the capability to shield themselves from England and Spain's reach.

Again, elites saw matters in similar terms; if balancing was to work it had to be an indefinite union. The objection to the Articles was that it did not have enough enforcement ability; it could not coerce the long-term cooperation necessary to protect the states. Washington complained: "We have probably had too good an opinion of human nature in forming our confederation." Madison echoed Washington; there was "a mistaken confidence that the justice, the good faith, the honor, the sound policy, of the several legislature assemblies would render superfluous any appeal to the ordinary motives by which the laws secure the obedience of individuals." Madison stressed, "The Constitution requires an adoption *in toto* and *for ever*." And Hamilton and Jay chimed in, "A reservation of a right to withdraw . . . was inconsistent with the Constitution and was *no ratification*."[7]

If foreign powers and their proxies chose war to get their way, the United States had dug themselves into a hole: they had bad credit. The early United States could barely finance the war recently passed, and they were in a worse position financing a future war. Ninety-five percent of Congressional expenditures had been on defense during the American Revolution, and defense accounted for 88 percent of debt after the war. Yet states were not repaying their debts diligently, and Washington realized that when war came, the United States could be beaten by a state with deeper pockets and better credit. Worse still, debt was a security liability because it could be forcibly collected. Temporary alliances were unlikely to create competitive pools of resources; solvency took time. One of Washington's earliest stated presidential aims was "to extricate my country from the embarrassments in which it is entangled, through want of credit. . . ."[8]

Whether or not foreign powers were actually intriguing against the former colonies, elites constantly perceived threat. Shays's Rebellion, for example, revealed an acute sensitivity to foreign interference. Elites saw outside threat as a lynchpin to interlocking security problems: foreign garrisons, Native Americans, separatists, and credit. The threat was not expected to change, but balancing could alleviate it.

Symmetry

States that feel their security is interdependent are likely to agree on common policy. There are several indications that elites shared abandonment fears. Although they were a biased population, Madison records unanimity among delegates at the Philadelphia Convention favoring union, a good indication of elite symmetry.[9] In devising the upper house of the legislature, each state received two representatives, regardless of size. More surprising, new states could be admitted into the union on equal terms. Federalist politicians in every state feverishly spent time, money, energy, and political capital to get the Constitution on the agenda and ratified—manhandling representatives in Pennsylvania, politically banishing opponents in Connecticut, alleged bribes in Massachusetts, and so on.

The United States did not have identical interests, of course, but their differences backlight their similarities. One difference is that states were not threatened equally by the same foreign powers. The best illustration of this is Spain's closure of the Mississippi River in 1784, and Jay's failed negotiations to reopen it in 1786. The 1786 incident in particular caused a shudder to run through the elite. Americans were already having a hard time getting the trading terms they desired with Britain, but should the Mississippi stay closed off, the produce of the hinterlands would be bottled up. Then secessionist movements might gain ground, making it easier for both powers to meddle and encroach on American interests. Ominously, areas already contemplating or attempting secession dotted the periphery of the United States and were causing problems that could snowball.[10]

As Shays's Rebellion showcased, malign British interference was seen everywhere. A nonaligned or mal-aligned state could be a base for foreign intervention, an encouraging example to groups contemplating secession, and a resource drain on the Confederation's already meager aggregate power. Moreover, there were good reasons to suspect what would today be called "covert action links" between Native Americans and foreign powers.

"Westerners had an unshakeable conviction that the British aided and abetted every Indian raid." Even small secessionist movements aroused anxieties that European "friends" would annex states and "a spirit of novelty and revolution in the interior part of several of our larger states—which by being refused admittance into the Confederation, may bring a civil dudgeon. . . ." States could resist foreign powers and their local proxies only combined; American defense was a public good that demanded greater participation. Elite writings of the time show how these anxieties fueled thoughts and actions toward union.[11]

Another difference is that states were not equal in size. Central government offered the prospect of improved means to fend off dangers, if only efforts could be concerted. Four states were manifestly larger than the rest and therefore were prime candidates to coordinate collective action: Massachusetts, New York, Pennsylvania, and Virginia. Nevertheless, although those states were strong enough to mount some defense, they did not possess the means to project force very far and secure themselves from future foreign incursions. They were weak and territorially far flung enough to need the aid of many more states to be politically viable. This situation aligned interests because states needed each other a great deal, and some were strong enough to coordinate collective action, but none were strong enough to threaten oppression.

It might appear that multiple outside threats and unequal-sized states make a mockery of symmetry. This is not so. There is often disagreement within alliances and states about who is the primary threat, but security interdependence usually obtains nonetheless. Before and after unification, there was a long-running dispute about whether Britain and Spain—often the South's point of view—or France—frequently the North's point of view—was the bigger threat. Yet that disagreement conceals a deeper abiding agreement. Overall, Britain was considered the preeminent threat.

And if, say, Virginia had gone to war with Spain or Massachusetts with France, both would have been outclassed and likely lost. If either lost, the consequence would be territorial cession, great power aggrandizement, and decreased credit worthiness, which would make all American states more vulnerable. States that stayed out of the fray would be weakened prey to opportunistic outsiders, who could exploit a divided and distracted confederation. As the Swiss showed in 1798 (see chapter 5), leaving one state to its fate can undo everyone.

Aiding unification were three other factors. First, collective action was easier because the number of states was reasonably low. Second, cooperation between the states had been ebbing since the end of the Revolutionary War and this had the perverse effect of underlining how much the states needed each other. Elites were all too frequently reminded of what an inconsiderable confederation they were in; ambassadors were ridiculed, foreign powers did as they pleased, separatist sentiment gathered. Third, the contiguity of the states assisted the symmetry of threat. Facing the same threats from the same geography made it clear to see that states were in the same corner.

Fortune: Crisis Trigger

While I have referred to Shays's protest as a rebellion to keep with conventional usage, it should be clear that convention does damage to meaning. Modern riots do far more damage and kill many more people, and even by antebellum standards Shays wreaked little havoc.[12] For such a minor event, Shays is important for two reasons.

First, he was a useful propaganda tool. Although there was unrest in other states, Shays's Rebellion was the largest such event. Elites needed to point to some visible ill to justify unification and Shays fit the bill. This tactic did not work well in Massachusetts, where people had sound informational networks. But elsewhere the facts were more malleable and media outlets spread histrionic and lurid details.[13]

The Founders could not call for radical change without tying it into (fictionalized) current events. Federalists made hay with Shays, turning him into a bogeyman:

Had Shays, the malecontent [sic] of Massachusetts, been a man of genius, fortune and address, he might have conquered that state, and by the aid of a little sedition in the other states, and an army proud by victory, became the monarch and tyrant of America. Fortunately he was checked, but should jealousy prevent vesting these powers, in the hands of men chosen by yourselves, and who are under every constitutional restraint, accident or design will in all probability raise up some future Shays to be the tyrant of your children.[14]

The Federalist Papers are littered with references to Shays's Rebellion (see nos. 6, 21, 28, and 74), and all of them are caricatures of the conventional view. For instance:

The tempestuous situation from which Massachusetts has scarcely emerged evinces that dangers of this kind are not merely speculative. Who can determine what might have been the issue of her late convulsions if the malcontents had been headed by a Caesar or a Cromwell? Who can predict what effect a despotism established in Massachusetts would have upon the liberties of New Hampshire or Rhode Island, of Connecticut or New York?[15]

Second, and more importantly, Shays displayed elites' ultimate fears. While there is a good case to be made that men like Secretary of War Henry Knox were disingenuous in their reaction to Shays, it seems that Washington and Madison were sincere. Early on, both Founders suspected that Britain was behind Shays, and when time divulged no supporting facts for this perspective they retained their suspicions. There is a strategic logic to this: it makes sense for elites in weak states to be acutely alert to their most pressing threats, even at the risk of false alarms, if the cost of a single error could be catastrophic.[16] But for present purposes, the key point is that critical elites were not most worried about shoring up their social position, getting rich, or going to war with other American states. They were worried about Britain using unrest to subvert governments and take advantage of American weakness. Unless the states united, Britain could gain underhandedly what it could not win on the battlefield.

Virtue: Elite Persuasion

Background conditions, by my argument, tell us how likely it is that unification will be attempted. The crisis trigger reveals other causal forces, but may have some independent effect on when unification is attempted. But it is elite persuasion that explains how unification efforts take place.[17] Elites sought union through three channels: the media, the military, and political procedures.

Media

The best-known reason that the Constitution was ratified is that the Founders won the wars of ideas, but not all good ideas change policy. That Federalists crafted sophisticated arguments does not mean the Constitution was ratified by virtue of rhetorical merit; Antifederalists crafted arguments approximately as intelligent as their opposition. However, there was a stark difference between the two sides: the power of their advocates. Federalists were as a rule more coherent and more elite; they held higher stations in the social, economic, military, and political hierarchies. Federalist words were spoken by people with more authority, and even when not speaking they were better able to manipulate the content and flow of information.

Media conveys particular information to particular people. Newspapers were the primary mode of news, and the printing presses tended to be in wealthy cities, that is, Federalist bastions. For example, when, on flimsy evidence Knox hysterically reported that Shays's insurrection was the size of the Continental army and that it sought to level all property and that there was a Native American uprising too (in an area that had not seen a Native American in a generation), his opinion was carried in papers across the country. He later received no press coverage for calmly confirming that Massachusetts "had proved her ability to put down the rebellion and to defend the arsenal."[18]

America was primarily agricultural—only about 5 percent of the country lived in cities[19]—and since ratification began in October and was more than halfway completed by early February, it was the worst time of the year for political action. Farmers were busy harvesting, and in addition, harsh weather that winter impeded traffic on the poor road system. Consequently, those most likely to oppose the Constitution were ill-informed and unable to act collectively for most of the ratification period.

Furthermore, journalists were beholden to elites. Out of more than 100 newspapers, the Federalists were supported by all but a dozen because editors were "afraid to offend the great men, or Merchants, who could work their ruin." Benjamin Franklin was the influential hub of a colonial printing network, supplying many presses with their newsprint, ink, and start-up capital. Federalists bought up space in newspapers and ran only Federalist speeches.[20]

Beyond this, Federalists were disproportionately perched atop trade and patronage networks. This gave them influence greater than their numbers not only because of their material clout, but also because news often depended on trade networks for dissemination. Federalists therefore sat on critical information nodes, and could use their positions to stifle dissent, amplify their position, and—in at least the case of Massachusetts and New York—open opponents' mail.[21] Federalists ably used market segmentation to mobilize their supporters while minimizing opponent mobilization, and they dominated journalists and the flow of information.

Military

States are loath to give up their sovereignty, and will tend to only when goaded. Goading is more credibly done when one threatens with a big stick, and individuals with access to men and matériel are in the best position to do this. A decisive tool in the Federalists' arsenal was threats of force, and they brandished it dextrously. Although the media and procedural manipulations were stronger causal factors in American unification, and war was not imminent, there is evidence that war in the foreseeable future between former colonies motivated framing and ratification of the Constitution. The centerpiece to credibly threatening destabilizing war and anarchic security competition was George Washington.

It is one thing if someone opines that rejection of the Constitution would bring war, quite another if that person is a heroic former general who could credibly prosecute that war himself.[22] Because elites were disproportionately Federalists, a great deal of the country's wealth and officer corps were squarely on the side of union. All were reluctant to use force on their potential compatriots, but that did not deter many of them from making threats that left something to chance. Threats from Washington, Madison, Hamilton, Wilson, and others all fit into this category, and the more states that ratified, the more credible these threats became.

From the origins of the Constitution, war was always in the background. When the New Jersey plan sought greater freedom for states, Madison successfully defeated the motion, on the grounds that the small states should accept his Virginia plan now or be annexed and accept worse terms later. Wilson also made remarks "meant in terrorem" to the smaller states, and the smaller states threatened to find a foreign ally to "take them by the hand." When the delegates deliberated on the number of states necessary to ratify the Constitution, the "house on fire" and "absolute necessity" were invoked, and nine was thought to be about enough to coerce the rest. When some favored a second convention, the decisive rebuttal was the apprehension of "an ultimate decision by the Sword."[23]

Many states' ratifications witnessed threats of force. Almost every ratifying convention featured discussions on international politics and the perils of disunion.

Pennsylvania was only the first state to frame the issue as unite or die, or alternately to unite or fall into chaos. Yet for three states, ratification hinged on explicit threats of force. The first and most important was Virginia, where Washington's benign belligerence may have swung Edmund Randolph and his followers.

The second was New York, where Melancton Smith painfully admitted that the threat of war led him to defect from the Antifederal bloc and bring over those following him. By this point, the ratifying rule concocted at Philadelphia that nine was about the right number of states to coerce the rest proved to be approximately correct. Once the last of the large states ratified, enough New Yorkers realized that their choices had evaporated. One could build a circumstantial case for similar dynamics in North Carolina, but evidence is wanting. The third use of explicit threats was tiny Rhode Island, which ratified under threat of boycott, secession, and invasion.

Political Procedures

Parties who can set the agenda and frame choices in a manner conducive to their preferred outcome have a distinct advantage, and because Federalists held higher political positions than their opponents did, they were better able to effect their preferred outcomes. Through numerous procedural manipulations,[24] influential Federalists kept opponents on their heels and won victories against superior numbers. They moved fast to minimize Antifederalist mobilization and structured ratification to maximally handicap their opposition.

Because they were a small, coherent, well-connected elite, the Founders could set the rules, time, pace, place, and agenda that favored them most. There is an awkward correlation: where the best arguments, most democracy, and most thorough deliberation occurred, New York and Rhode Island, ratification was staunchly opposed. Although some were disenfranchised, it is still striking that approximately 120,000–160,000 of 640,000 adult white males participated in ratification. Voter turnout for the Constitution compares unfavorably with voter turnout in earlier elections.[25] Through surprise, smart strategy, and wise audacity, the Federalists maximized their political leverage, dividing and conquering opposition.

Getting unification on the agenda in the first place took laborious maneuvering. Others were so suspicious of Madison's nationalist motives that he repeatedly had to obscure his work and its intentions. The Annapolis ploy worked, and Madison quickly set the groundwork and agenda for Philadelphia. In the Convention, the ratification method was not seriously addressed until attrition had drained away many opponents, and then delegates selected a method that defied ordinary politics to maximize ratification's chances. Out of Philadelphia came, unexpectedly, a fully formed Constitution and a host of powerful advocates, organized and prepared to fight on the most favorable terrain. Disorganized groups began to oppose it, but the Federalists moved with speed.

Again, elites were influential by virtue of being elite. They were at the apex of patronage networks; Gouverneur Morris put it: "Loaves and fishes must bribe the demagogues. They must be made to expect higher offices under the general than the state governments."[26] Illegal procedures were also more palatable when done by politicians with sterling credentials. Patrick Henry was technically right that the Consitution was illegal, but he was effectively wrong and knew it. If he had pursued this point during Virginia's ratification, he would have had to accuse Washington of treason under legal standards that were now up for grabs.

In Pennsylvania, ratification was marked by haste and violence; in Connecticut, truncated debate, a balcony packed with hecklers, and expulsion of an opposition leader. In Massachusetts, the governor may have taken a political bribe, an opposition leader was ejected, there were misinformation schemes, the convention was packed with unrepresentative delegates, and there were alleged cash bribes. Maryland's ratification saw electoral violence, and the opposition was not allowed to speak. In New Hampshire, the process included setting the rules under false pretense, certifying delegates unethically, and more allegations of bribery; in Virginia, alleged political and monetary bribes to Randolph.

Most fundamentally, the Founders set the incentive structure. Before Philadelphia, the choice appeared to be between the Articles and some recommended revisions to the Articles. After Philadelphia, the ground shifted to the Constitution or disintegration and conflict. While this blends into the previous remarks on military factors, it is hard to argue that political procedures would have been remotely similar without the glowering shadow of war. For example, Washington stated:

> The legallity [sic] of the Convention I do not mean to discuss—nor how problematical the issue of it be. That powers are wanting none can deny. . . . That which takes the shortest course to obtain them, will . . . be found best. Otherwise, like a house on fire, whilst the most regular mode of extinguishing it is contending for, the building is reduced to ashes.[27]

Some scholars make light of the procedural manipulations in ratification, calling them an "end run" and portraying stepping out of legal bounds in a "boys-will-be-boys" light.[28] To do so is hindsight bias and trivializes how exorbitantly risky the game was. Extraordinary politics is not running outside the tackles, it is

playing a different and dizzyingly more dangerous sport. By such means even talented, well-intentioned leaders have scarred states and wrecked lives. Anyone who
thinks what the Founders did was a mere "end run" should try running such a play
(perhaps by turning NATO or NAFTA into a state) to find out what magnitude of
felony they are committing. There is a time and a place for extraordinary politics,
but there are no easy answers about when and where it is.

To sum up, America unified because crucial elites were sensitive to the precarious security of their states. Without a worthy threat, no elites in the world could
have created a sustainable union. Without able advocates in positions of influence
over the media, military, and political procedures, union attempts would have
been stymied.

ALTERNATE EXPLANATIONS

There are many prior arguments on why the United States united. But if their
explanations on the United States are correct, there should be more unification
happening in places other than the United States. This section focuses on some of
the best analytical work on America's unification—David Hendrickson's constructivist accounts, Charles Beard's economic framing, and Daniel Deudney's binding
explanation—and finds them more provocative than predictive.

Constructivism

David Hendrickson's *Peace Pact* is an analytically eclectic approach to the American
founding. While too ecumenical to fit neatly into a constructivist box, two of his
central arguments fit under that heading:

- that the most potent factors in explaining the trajectory of American politics were the multiplicity of loyalties to and identities with particular colonies and states; the bipolar rivalry that split continental politics on a
  geographic or sectional line; and the exigencies of the union (reflecting the
  impulse to cooperate in a milieu where the first two factors made that quest
  seem eminently problematic.
- that the American reflection on the world of states was "international-
  ist" or "Grotian" in character. It recognized the binding character of the
  "law of nature and of nations" and displayed certain tendencies that set
  it apart from realist (or Machiavellian) and revolutionist (or Kantian)
  perspectives.[29]

Hendrickson uses a lot of neologisms and—like the present author—his prose is not always pellucid. But at the center of his analysis seems to be culture: primary drivers of American conduct are (1) identities and (2) norms.

First, identity is a poor basis for explaining America's union. Constructivism captures some of the ratification process, like the interpretation of facts, and the war of ideas. But the identity of the United States was too nebulous, weak, and ill-formed to cause profound political transformation. Culture cannot account for the alarm and alignment of the period. Canada and Britain were viewed with at least as much suspicion as the Spanish, despite having nearly identical cultures as the former colonies (indeed, zealous patriot John Adams was typical when he referred to Americans as "Britons.")[30] Hendrickson does not posit a process by which sectional and state loyalties grow more (or less) intense and extensive.

Why ideas "take" when they do in the form they do is not specified well. Ideas figure weakly in ratifications that were coerced or procedurally manipulated. The most democratic, best-informed states were the most opposed to ratification. New Yorkers, for example, had no shortage of information and a record turnout, yet the document was widely unpopular.[31] Opinion in New York did not change until Virginia ratified, and Rhode Island was little persuaded until force was on the table. *The Federalist Papers*, one of the finest political works in history, had negligible short-run impact (its long-run impact has been enormous, however)—what hope is there for the impact of lesser articles? Constructivism also has little to contribute to our understanding of the tricky procedural maneuvers that secured ratification in, for instance, Massachusetts and New Hampshire. Even by charitable accounting, a majority of states' ratifications involved forces outside of discourse and ideas.

Second, the Founders were not Grotian in the sense that Hendrickson implies, and international law was a minimal part of even educated political discourse. Jean-Jacques Rousseau rightly observed: "When I hear Grotius praised to the skies and Hobbes covered with execration, I see how few sensible men read or understand these two authors. The truth is that their principles are exactly alike."[32]

When Hendrickson extols Grotius, he is really making an assertion about the causal weight of international norms. Realists think the weight of international law small yet significant, and liberals think it larger and more constraining. But Grotius was not one that thought law should restrain states much. Far from restraining the strong, Grotius approved of slavery, condoned appropriating the land of natives not using it in a civilized manner, and leniently thought it "permissible to acquire for oneself, and to retain, those things which are useful for life."[33] His major work stemmed from a defense of aggressive Dutch piracy. In this sense, I have no objection to calling the early American statesmen Grotian, but calling them realists is just simpler.

Hendrickson, among others, stresses that international legal thinkers are critical in America's founding, but this view is hard to sustain. If it were true, we would be most likely to find evidence at critical junctures in the writings of educated elites. Yet when the chips were down, international lawyers loomed large like pygmies in the discussion. Bernard Bailyn collected the most seminal primary sources during the debate on the Constitution and across 1,862 pages, the founders of international law barely appear: Vattel never, Grotius and Pufendorf two cites apiece.[34]

There is a broader point here: political thinkers were not very important during ratification even in highbrow circles; unification does not have much in common with debating clubs. Montesquieu is the exception that proves the rule. While reverenced and referenced across the political spectrum, his ideas on large republics ran counter to the Constitution and were defeated in debate by people who appealed to common sense and expedience, not Grotius.

Liberalism

Most accounts of the Founding era are kitchen sink explanations; to the extent that causal factors are prioritized, economic factors often receive top billing. Charles Beard's economic interpretation of the Constitution is the most famous of these.[35] Beard's basic idea is that the Founders devised the Constitution to protect their property—it was a way to maximize upper-class wealth. Later work has shown that there is little support for this view, and the correlations that Beard thought were strong are weak. For present purposes, the main point is that the most successful economic interpretation of the Constitution has been badly battered.

One could resurrect a stronger liberal narrative on American union, where initial cooperation over rivers led to greater and greater conventions, culminating in the Constitution. But this too does not fare well. These issues were trade-related but security-inspired issues. Robert Morris tried using financial tools to unite the former colonies but failed, despite being in a good position to succeed (eternal optimists, Americans would later resurrect economic strategies to annex Canada).[36]

Navigation of the Mississippi was an early case in point. Madison was not anxious that Spain would gain more trade or custom duties; he was fearful that river closure would break up the union and make the states vulnerable to foreign countries. Washington minced no words on this score: "The consequences [of river navigation] to the Union, in my judgment, are immense—& more so in a political, than in a Commercial point."[37] He worried that the United States would lose a war to a nation with better credit.

At Mount Vernon and Annapolis, trade did not stir the hearts of the states participating, much less the country. Maryland did not bother attending the Annapolis convention because it did not want any more agreements like the Mount Vernon Compact. Other states attended Annapolis with the expectation that nothing would get done. The demand for the Philadelphia Convention was meager and its mandate was vague to avoid scaring off states that would consider attending. Shays's Rebellion was not about interstate trade and the elites who were agitated by it were on edge about foreign intrusion. While there were economic deals at Philadelphia, the Convention's urgency stemmed from geopolitics. The "house was on fire" not because of economic preferences but because decisions might soon be made by the sword. State economies were growing without the aid of the Constitution.

The Founders were rich, but that has been true of American politicians for some time. Greed is common; constitutional conventions are not. If Philadelphia were a wealth-generating scheme, we would have seen many more events like it. Trade networks had a role to play in ratification, communicating information and perhaps the occasional bribe, and financial issues did help a few minor states ratify. But money was not the sinew of unification.

Binding

Daniel Deudney makes the case that the American system was set up to manage a number of threats: war, revolution, despotism, and empire.[38] On the whole, I concur with him: the United States was founded in auspicious circumstances to protect against revolution, despotism, and war. The point in dispute is whether war avoidance was an independent force for unification. A lot of evidence points in the opposite direction: the epigraphs at the top of this chapter, the secessionist fears in the 1780s, the deepest anxieties during Shays's Rebellion, the threats during the Philadelphia Convention, and the warnings during the ratification debates. Foreigners, not neighbors, were the underlying motivating menaces.

Deudney points to a passage in *Federalist* no. 6, where Hamilton worries about war between the former colonies: "To look for a continuation of harmony between a number of independent, unconnected sovereignties situated in the same neighborhood would be to disregard the uniform course of human events. . . ."[39] From this perspective, a major reason that the United States united was to prevent the evil of war between former colonies.

True, the Founders worried about Americans fighting each other, but I read *The Federalist Papers* differently. It was not war between the former colonies that necessitated union, but war between the former colonies that outside powers could exploit. In *Federalist* no. 4, John Jay speculates:

Leave America divided . . .—what armies could they raise and pay—what fleets could they ever have? . . . Would there be no danger of their being flattered into neutrality by specious promises, or seduced by a too great fondness for peace to decline hazarding the tranquility and present safety for the sake of neighbors. . . . Although such conduct would not be wise, it would be natural. The history of the states of Greece, and of other countries, abounds with such instances. . . ."

In *Federalist* no. 5, Jay returns to a very familiar example: "let us not forget how much more easy it is to receive foreign fleets into our ports, and foreign armies into our country, than it is to persuade them to depart. How many conquests did the Romans and others make in the character of allies. . . ." Hamilton ends *Federalist* no. 7 ominously: "*Divide et impera* [divide and command] must be the motto of every nation that either hates or fears us."[40]

In short, binding did not cause American union. Bad outcomes happen in every cooperative relationship if one of the parties defects or withholds support, but that does not mean that fear of those outcomes is what caused the relationship. American elites feared war between the former colonies, but what decisively caused union was that outsiders could take advantage of any intra-American disputes. Binding logic is analytically unnecessary in unification.

CONCLUSION

The thirteen former colonies were ripe for a unification drive. Elites perceived that they were caught between English and Spanish millstones, poorly organized to handle foreign threats, not to mention domestic unrest and Native American affairs. Union would prevent the states from menacing each other and grant better protection against dark European clouds, which showed no prospect of blowing over. Neither overawed nor underwhelmed, the former colonies felt symmetrically threatened.

Rival views do not address the American case as well as realism does, and that has knock-on effects since the American case is where realism is supposed to do least well. Liberal ideology, shared culture, capitalism, and pacific institutions have all received much credit in the uniting of the United States. Yet ideas and culture do not fit the timing and boundaries of the newborn United States, nor do they capture much of the context of the Constitution's genesis and ratification. Elites tried and failed to use economics to integrate the United States. And though binding theorists make many penetrating observations about early American politics, there is little value added by war avoidance as a cause of union.

Returning to *Federalist* no. 1, now we can see why Publius labored so extensively despite the long odds. Media control was an indispensable tool of the Founders' drive to unify (especially in places like Connecticut), but so were credible military threats in states such as Virginia, New York, and Rhode Island, and procedural irregularities in states such as Pennsylvania, Maryland, Massachusetts, and New Hampshire. Along with the right background conditions and a crisis trigger, the situation was favorable for unification.

Nevertheless, Publius's question is "whether societies of men are really capable or not of establishing good government from reflection and choice, or whether they are forever destined to depend on their political constitutions on accident and force." And the answer to that is mixed. Without propitious circumstances, prudent institutional innovation, a passable security crisis, and strong control over the media, the military, and political procedures, the Founders would have foundered.

As better men have reflected, "Man proposes and God disposes."[41] The Founders' efforts generally met good fortune, and their foresight ushered in an empire greater than Rome's. But Roman corruption troubled the Founders, and they used its history as a cautionary example to build the oldest constitution now in existence—which is why Americans owe the liberty and greatness of their Constitution less to owls than foxes and lions.

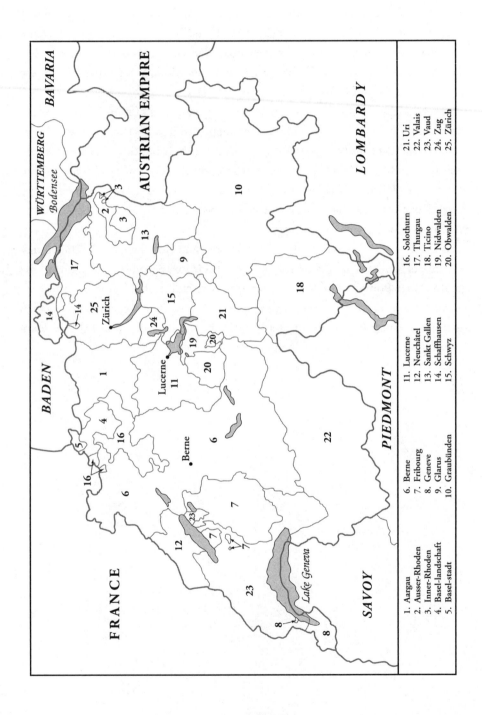

FRANCE

BADEN

WÜRTTEMBERG

BAVARIA

Bodensee

AUSTRIAN EMPIRE

LOMBARDY

PIEDMONT

SAVOY

Lake Geneva

Berne

Lucerne
Zürich

5
16
16
12
6
4
1
14
14
17
25
24
11
19
20
20
21
15
9
13
3
2
3
23
7
7
7
8
8
23
22
18
10

1. Aargau
2. Ausser-Rhoden
3. Inner-Rhoden
4. Basel-landschaft
5. Basel-stadt

6. Berne
7. Fribourg
8. Geneve
9. Glarus
10. Graubünden

11. Lucerne
12. Neuchâtel
13. Sankt Gallen
14. Schaffhausen
15. Schwyz

16. Solothurn
17. Thurgau
18. Ticino
19. Nidwalden
20. Obwalden

21. Uri
22. Valais
23. Vaud
24. Zug
25. Zürich

Good little Switzerland is held up as a shining example to the indocile hoodlums of this world. The peaceful, virtuous, industrious Swiss . . . have avoided the pitfalls into which other nations have been stumbling throughout the centuries and have achieved a state where Latin and Teuton, Papist and Calvinist, worker and banker, cow and milkmaid are all living together in peace and harmony, enjoying the benefits of democracy and watchmaking.

—J. CHRISTOPHER HEROLD[1]

5

Switzerland, *Staatenbund* to *Bundesstaat*

WE TEND TO think of Switzerland as an affluent and decorous land, a place whose crowning cultural attainment is, to pilfer Orson Welles, the cuckoo clock. Switzerland's bland history and pacific union are supposedly models for the world. No less than Karl Deutsch has called Switzerland "a paradigmatic instance of political integration," singling out the charmed course the country took to union: "no unusual foreign military threat played any important role in the adoption of the Swiss federal constitution in 1848."[2] This chapter chronicles the tumultuous history of the Swiss and examines why Deutsch is misled. Like the last case, only mercifully briefer, I adduce the history of unification in the first section, the second section discusses how well the empirics fit my hypotheses, and the third section looks at rival views.

A SHORT HISTORY OF SWISS UNIFICATION EFFORTS

Fortunately for the teller, the basic facts, actors, and periods in Swiss history are uncontroversial. Although unification occurred by all accounts in 1848, Swiss unification was a long time coming. The earliest rumblings began in the thirteenth century, waxed in the fifteenth, waned from about 1500 to 1800, and waxed again into the twentieth century. The main figures in the narrative are the urban and rural states of Switzerland (they go by different names, e.g., town and country,

Protestant and Catholic, liberal and conservative, rich and poor, but they refer to the same states and for narrative simplicity I stick with the urban/rural distinction) and the French, German, and Austrian threats that force them to cooperate to varying degrees.

Switzerland's Infancy

Present-day Switzerland dates directly back to an "everlasting alliance" between three states in 1291. Using anticipatory language, we can say that these three forest cantons and their allies fought against primarily the House of Habsburg for over a century. Because the Habsburgs furnished "sixteen kings to Germany, twenty-two to Austria, three to Portugal, eleven to Bohemia and Hungary, six to Spain, and but for Queen Mary's sterility, might have given England another" many overlook that the family originally hails from Switzerland.[3] The niceties of thirteenth-century imperial politics need not detain us here; Rudolf of Habsburg was plucked from relative obscurity by the German electors to be Holy Roman Emperor in 1273. He quickly set to work increasing his modest empire, conquering swaths of Austria and menacing Switzerland.

Rudolf had been the most powerful and acquisitive ruler in Switzerland before his election, but other polities had enlisted the German crown to balance against him. Now that crown and Habsburg were one, three of the states of central Switzerland, Uri, Schwyz, and Nidwalden, joined together to resist Habsburg encroachments (from this conflict comes the William Tell quasi-myth). What followed was a series of battles over supremacy in Switzerland, only the most noteworthy of which can be chronicled.[4]

The Swiss confederation accumulated amazing victories. In 1315, Leopold, Duke of Austria and grandson of Rudolf, was routed at Morgarten by infantry of Uri and Schwyz. The defeat caused a sensation—peasant footmen trouncing mounted knights and upsetting the social order. In 1386, Leopold's nephew, Leopold III, was routed and killed at Sempach. His brother, Albert III, sought revenge and was routed at Näfels in 1388.

Victory was a lazy disciplinarian. Following this string of successes, there was dissension in the confederation and some civil war. The Toggenburg War began in 1436 when Zürich and its mayor Rudolf Stüssi sought to dominate the confederation. He appealed to Austria for help, and the other Swiss states, fearing foreign penetration and Zürich's ascendancy, joined Schwyz in opposition. Stüssi died in the ensuing fighting and by 1450 Zürich accepted peace, renounced Austria, and rejoined the confederation.[5]

In 1446 tiny Glarus beat the Austrians at Ragaz, almost single-handedly. Yet the biggest victory was in 1476 at Morat. Adrian von Bubenberg led 2,000 Bernese against the Duke of Burgundy and 20,000 of his men. Reinforced by other Swiss states, most notably Hans Waldmann from Zürich, the invaders were slaughtered. This was the last time for centuries that Switzerland was seriously threatened. The country had soundly thrashed great powers repetitively. Reasonable observers found the fearsome Swiss the single greatest force in Europe: "one needs to be exceedingly afraid of them. . . . I fear them alone. . . ."[6]

Coming of Age

After 1476, the Swiss confederation had nullified their chief threats. The "traditional Austrian enemy ventured no more across the Rhine, while the French government was long occupied with greater matters than the intimidation of fierce German-speaking peasants."[7] Although successes continued on the battlefield, the glue for the alliance—more accurately depicted as a bundle of alliances—was losing hold. With security pressures relenting, the confederates indulged the luxury of infighting.

Almost immediately following Morat, the confederates started fighting over the distribution of booty. Squaring off along the familiar urban/rural divide, the states mobilized for civil war and would have commenced hostilities in 1481 were it not for the mediation of the mysterious monk Niklaus von Flüe, also known as Brother Klaus. He brokered a compromise on the spoils of victory, and conflict was delayed for another day.

The confederation lay at a crossroads and had to decide between liberty and greatness. If the confederation were to grow and contend with the likes of France and England—a long shot, to be sure—it would have to become much more unified. Despite the difficulty, some leaders desired a unified state and greatness. Like Stüssi, they all acted from Zürich and sought to make that city preeminent in the confederation. Case in point, Hans Waldmann, mayor of Zürich, started maneuvering to unify Switzerland in 1486. Having risen from lowly birth, Waldmann met with strong opposition, and in 1489 he was illegally arrested, tortured, and killed. The other major city, Berne, refused to see the threats that Waldmann did, and the unification effort lay dormant for another generation.

In 1515 at the Battle of Marignano, the Swiss demonstrated that they were neither united nor invincible. Badly beaten by guns and cavalry, the Swiss phalanx was becoming outmoded, and the states had not the men, money, matériel, or unity to win any other way. Shortly thereafter, the Reformation redundantly layered religious disagreement on top of the urban/rural rift; Luther "gave impetus to a movement which had already started."[8] By this time the confederation had grown to thirteen states, a number that would remain constant until Napoleon.

At this juncture, Ulrich Zwingli, another lowborn high-achiever, entertained notions of unifying the Swiss into a grand Protestant federation. His initial efforts to unify the Swiss met some success. However, the crucial Protestant ally Berne spoke against his efforts, and Zwingli could not assemble a viable coalition. Battles in 1529 and 1531 killed the unification attempt and Zwingli.

The Swiss confederation limped along in this fashion for hundreds of years. Not weak enough to need a stronger alliance, not strong enough to coerce union, urban and rural states circled each other warily. The rural states formed the Borromean league of self-defense in 1585, but little came of it. From this low-intensity acrimony sprung the Swiss policy and principle of neutrality. When the Thirty Years' War broke out, both sides cheered their co-religionists but found common cause in keeping the belligerents out of their lands. Generally, the Swiss decided they were "better off living together as neutrals than dying apart as enemies."[9]

Once the threat of European war had passed and ensuing peasant unrest was suppressed, the confederation continued its squabbles in 1656. The First Villmergen War was a two-month conflict costing about 1,000 lives that went somewhat indecisively to the rural states. The Second Villmergen War of 1712 was also short, but went somewhat indecisively to the urban states. This was the last major battle between Swiss until 1847, and both sides have not tried to upset the religious status quo since. The rural states made a secret defensive pact with the French, called the Trücklibund, in 1715, which, had hostilities recrudesced, may have broken the confederation. But throughout the history of the Confederation, open violence between cantons was relatively rare and minor.

When the French Revolution broke out, the Swiss reacted in the traditional manner: temporizing and vacillating. Through treachery so vile as to disgust the hitherto steel-stomached Talleyrand, the French invaded Berne in 1798, and the rest of the confederation left the city to its fate. Unfortunately, the rest of the confederation had to share Berne's fate, since events revealed no serious defense could be mounted without the town. The French occupation was vile, looting art, jewels, cash, even bears from the bear pit. When Nidwalden ferociously rebelled against foreign rule, the French slaughtered men, women, and children in a horrible struggle to subdue the revolt. Napoleon's wars cost the Swiss dearly. The Continental system choked Swiss industry, forced recruiting depleted manpower, and wholesale theft drained the Swiss people.[10]

Unification: the Most Civil of Wars

Switzerland was ahead of the European curve, not only in being conquered by Napoleon, but also in its conservative reaction after Waterloo, followed by increasing liberalism and the effort to form a centralized state. Conservative forces tried to restore the status quo ante, and they instituted a constitution without an amendment procedure to lock in their restoration. One historian observes, "In 1814, it was internal passions which would tear the confederation apart, while exterior forces would tend to unite and strengthen it."[11]

Yet around 1830, a constellation of internal forces appeared to start aligning for increased Swiss unity. Exacerbating the threats that unification efforts always prompt, radicals committed acts of violence to attain their political ends. Starting in 1831, there were attacks and coups d'état that roiled the divisions between liberal/urban states and conservative/rural states.[12] Nationalist societies sprang up across Switzerland, and they were spurred by foreign affairs. Perhaps the best example is France's 1838 massing of 25,000 soldiers on the border with the threat to invade if Louis Napoleon was not deported out of asylum and into French custody. Fortunately Louis Napoleon defused the crisis by departing to England.

Agitation continued. In 1845, 3,600 disorganized nationalists raided Lucerne, the epicenter of rural Switzerland. The raid was rebuffed, but the rural states were shaken. This led directly to a defensive pact between rural states called the Sonderbund, which approached the Austrian, Sardinian, and French governments for aid. In a revolutionary measure, a narrow majority of the confederation moved to dissolve the Sonderbund as incompatible with the federal pact in 1847 and vowed to enforce their decree. The Swiss Diet's demand was dignified:

> The rights and freedom inherited from your fathers shall continue unaltered, your faith untouched. The Diet desires no oppression of their confederate brothers, no nullifying of cantonal sovereignty, no forced change in the present confederate compact. But the existence of a separate league, endangering the welfare of the whole, can never be allowed. Dissolve it while yet there is time.[13]

The Sonderbund War was short and clean. The confederate commander selected was William Henry Dufour, a conservative whose personal conduct was above reproach. Dufour's orders were extremely respectful:

> Disarm prisoners but do not insult or injure them. On the contrary, treat them as kindly as possible. Allow them to return to their homes if they give their word of honour not to take arms again. At all costs prevent violation of

religious establishments. Carry your respect for these places to the point of
not billeting troops in them, and place guards to protect them.[14]

The balance of forces was 79,000 for the Sonderbund, 99,000 for the confederates,
but the Sonderbund had inadequate plans and lacked unified command. Through
speed and fine strategy, Dufour forced capitulation in less than a month with less
than 130 total deaths. Bismarck, watching from the sidelines, called it a *Hasen-
schiessen* (rabbit-shoot).[15] Foreign powers were displeased and moved to block unification, but before they could intervene, the war was over.

It took two months to write the new constitution and five months to ratify it.
This swiftness had something to do with the kindness of Dufour and the generous
terms granted to the states. Yet the international context also had a hand in matters.[16] Initially, the great powers—Russia, France, Austria, and Prussia—forbade
the new constitution. The European crises of spring 1848 broke out and this freed
the Swiss from foreign interference while motivating them to order their domestic
house well. The new Bund centralized foreign policy, currency, customs, weights
and measures, the military, the post, and secured an independent revenue stream
and an amendment procedure. The shift toward central authority was marginal
but decisive; Switzerland was now a unified state.

Afterword

After unification, Switzerland continued to centralize authority to meet its security problems.[17] In 1852 the canton of Ticino expelled 22 Capuchin monks and in
response Austria imposed a food blockade. The blockade stung Switzerland's vulnerable supply routes and a bargain was reached to pay restitution to the expelled
monks. In 1856 there was armed conflict between republicans and monarchists
in Neuchâtel, which had a title disputed by Prussia. Prussia mobilized in 1857 to
assert its claim, and this action was met with a wave of Swiss patriotism. The Federal Council readied for a fight, reappointing General Dufour and recruiting 30,000
troops. At the behest of the British, Napoleon III mediated a peaceful settlement
to the dispute. Security inadequacy was not evident.

It took German unification to provoke significant constitutional change. After
beating France in 1871, Germany became a much more formidable force in Central
Europe. France's defeat moved the Swiss to further centralize their government.
Given the Neuchâtel crisis, united Germany had the means and the motive to be a
major menace to Switzerland. Since the 1874 constitution, the Swiss have updated
but not fundamentally revised their constitution.[18] And it seems fair to say that
the Swiss have prospered under their constitution.

ARGUMENT

Opportunity: Background Conditions

Switzerland is an ideal case to test theories of unification because there were no less than three separate attempts to unify the country: under Waldmann, under Zwingli, and under Dufour—and at least an attempt at greater unity under Stüssi. Why Dufour alone succeeded has, I contend, a great deal to do with the different threats each faced. Recall that unification threats need three attributes: optimal intensity, long duration, and symmetry.

Intensity

Threats that are too large overwhelm balancing efforts, and threats that are too small render them unnecessary. Initially, the Swiss were graced with a clear and present danger: the House of Habsburg. The Habsburgs pressed the Swiss states into a tight alliance; however, the threat was continually diminished by Swiss victories.[19] Foreign threat was great enough to keep them aligned, but the Swiss states had repeatedly shown that tighter alliance was superfluous for victory.

With this background, we can see why Waldmann and Zwingli had such difficult times convincing other Swiss to unify; it did not seem like a necessity to either keep the other states in the confederation or to keep foreign states out of Swiss affairs. We can also see a critical difference from the American experience: Americans had a different fighting record. They fought only one war against their imperial oppressor before uniting. When American elites appealed to the precariousness of their security situation, there was little body of evidence with which to contradict them. Swiss unifiers had a much stronger headwind.

Over time, the Swiss states maintained their sense of security and saw no need to deepen their loose alliance commitments, until the French invasion. Conquest revealed that internal balancing and loose external balancing were inadequate to protect the Swiss states. Still, the Napoleon anomaly aside, external balancing among the Swiss states had afforded sufficient security for hundreds of years. With more concerted external balancing, there were good reasons to expect that the Swiss could continue to get along better with each other than be absorbed by greater powers or, what was the same thing, by themselves. And time has affirmed this expectation.

Duration

Intense threats need to be abiding to necessitate union, otherwise an ad hoc alliance would suffice. In the Swiss case, the duration of the threat was j-shaped. At first, the Habsburgs and, to a lesser extent, the French frequently troubled the

Swiss confederation. As time wore on, their interference with Swiss affairs, especially after 1476, was minimal. Thus, initially the Habsburg threat was frequent
enough to push Swiss states into an alignment that approached union; nonetheless, Swiss arms deterred incursions, Swiss vital interests were left unmolested,
and their bonds slackened commensurately.

By the nineteenth century, Switzerland's relative power decreased and outside
encroachments grew more durable: Napoleon's invasion, foreign interference in
government following the Napoleonic Wars, France massing troops on the border
in 1838. Swiss interests were frequently, vitally threatened, with no signs of abat-
ing, but few signs of growing overwhelming. By the middle of the nineteenth century, no temporary alliance was up to the task of tolerably meeting the threats that
Austria, France, and Prussia/Germany posed.

Symmetry

Common security interest brought the Swiss states together and kept them
together for centuries. One of the most repetitive facts of Swiss history is the perpetual parity between a small number of neighboring states. Neutrality as policy
grew out of the twin facts that the states wanted to remain a confederation and
they were deadlocked by bipolarity. The Villmergen Wars were essentially stale-
mates that illustrated relative equality between the Swiss states. When the states
mistakenly left Berne alone to deal with the French invasion, the whole confederation was conquered, despoiled, and oppressed. Other themes in Swiss history are
the extreme reluctance to sacrifice sovereignty and the decision to balance with
other cantons rather than bandwagon with strong neighbors.

How leaders spent their political capital is a good sign of symmetry and abandonment fears. As in the American case, when the Swiss states began to drift
apart, it only redoubled the pro-union force's efforts to unify. The losers of the
Sonderbund War could have appealed to foreign powers to renew fighting, but
chose instead to maximize their autonomy inside the Swiss state. Elites spent
their political capital to ensure that the states stayed together; the generous terms
awarded to enter the union, the kind treatment during the war, and the magnanimous forgiveness following the war attest to elites' alignment priorities. The lack
of another civil war is a revealing non-event.

Neighboring states were nearly as threatening as foreigners were. There were
moments, such as the Trücklibund and Toggenburg War, when confederates worried that member states were bigger menaces than were outsiders. However, these
moments were anomalies. By and large, Swiss states cherished their independence, and independence was better secured by balancing in a loose confederation

than bandwagoning with outside powers. Swiss security was, to great extent, indivisible, and defection from the confederation would leave the defector at the mercy of outsiders as well as leaving the confederation with even fewer resources with which to defend itself. Hence, states did not interfere with each other because their survival depended on member states viewing each other as balancing partners, not targets. Swiss states tethered themselves together because they were painted into the same corner: symmetrically threatened more by external powers than each other.

In short, the conditions favoring union were lukewarm for much of Switzerland's history. Originally, the states faced an intense, durable, symmetrical threat that forced them to make great strides toward unification. Yet this approximation of unification was sufficient to allay the Habsburg threat, and the desire to unify abated accordingly. Even with simmering levels of hostility toward other members, the Swiss were generally better off moderately bound to irritating confederates than annexed by unappreciative dominant states. When this arrangement looked unlikely to safeguard their independence, the Swiss states unified.

Fortune: Crisis Trigger

Early attempts at unification never sparked a wide crisis. Despite the best efforts of charismatic individuals in the strongest state in the confederation, union did not get far. Stüssi, Waldmann, and Zwingli attempted integration, but their entrepreneurial zeal was not contagious. Waldmann did not survive long, and Stüssi and Zwingli managed to start wars that quickly killed them and their movements. Without the requisite background conditions, their efforts were seeds on barren soil.

It may be no accident that by the early nineteenth century Switzerland was ahead of the nationalizing and unifying curves. Many states were conquered by Napoleon, but it was Switzerland that pioneered modern European unification. As a weak, vulnerable set of polities, the Swiss states had a clear incentive to learn a systemic innovation like nationalism quickly to defend themselves better, and their small sizes promoted greater organizational agility to respond to their environment.

What took so long to spark the crisis? After all, the Americans were independent allies for about a decade before unifying, as compared to some of the Swiss cantons, which had been independent allies for 556 years. My logic suggests that sometime between 1815 and 1850, the Swiss entered the necessary conditions for unification. However, my argument does not predict the specific timing of Swiss unification. The European distribution of power was casting an increasing shadow over Switzerland and there was increasing agitation, but why unification did not happen another time is hard to explain. My sources offer little help in adjudicating this question, and so I offer speculations.

Some hypotheses are worth discarding: it cannot be because the Swiss were less intelligent than the Americans were; it cannot be because the Swiss had a less onerous occupation; it cannot be because the Swiss faced less dire threats. About a decade after foreign occupation, revolutionary Swiss—like their American counterparts—started rocking the boat to press unification, but conditions checked their advance. These conditions were more moral than material, I suspect. At that world historical moment, revolution had been tainted by France and Napoleon, reactionary statesmen were trying to put the genie back in the bottle. European powers could extend their influence into Switzerland more than into North America, retarding nationalist movements. As the reactionaries lost ground and the idea of revolution lost its taint, the way was cleared for unification in tiny Switzerland.

With the unification of 1848, it is hard to tell when the crisis ends and the bargaining begins. Excluding the French mobilization in 1838, there were attacks, coups, and violence, which culminated in the 1845 raid on Lucerne; "rarely had civil war in Switzerland been preceded by years of such profound disturbance."[20] And naturally, there is the Sonderbund War itself. Because I do not believe the crisis trigger is causally very important, the only reason to include it is for narrative continuity and as possible disconfirmation of my argument. In either case, it is sufficient to note that there was an escalating series of security crises that prioritized unification on the political agenda.

Virtue: Elite Persuasion

Switzerland finally unified because elites managed to persuade all the states that they were better off together than alone or in different company. The most visible tactic was the military, but the media and political institutions played parts as well.

Media

The modern Swiss press was born as an effort to cast off foreign meddling. After the Napoleonic Wars, Metternich and Austria kept Switzerland on a short leash. In 1823, Austria demanded the acceptance of the Press and Aliens Conclusum, which took away Swiss freedom of the press. In an age of Kant, Herder, and Fichte evangelists, shackles on nationalist ideas were bad enough, but foreign censorship of the Swiss press was unacceptable. Zürich and Appenzell led the charge, and by 1829 the Conclusum was repealed. Apart from the nationalist bias in its genesis, urban areas tended to have more media and to reflect the interests of their local audiences, which were pro-union.

When the time came for ratification, the new constitution had another unimpeachable propaganda advantage: foreigners did not write it. As one of the drafters declared, "If the Swiss people accept this federal constitution they may truly claim that it is the first for 50 years which shows no foreign influence. . . ."[21] The Swiss had difficulty agreeing on many things, but they could all agree that they rejected foreign influence. And the new constitution catered to this preeminent collective preference.

Military

Urban areas wished closer union, rural areas thought they would rather not; the military clarified the situation. Dufour's strategy was a model of policy by other means. He had to persuade the rural states that now was the time to unify and that the terms of Swiss unification would be better than what they would get from outside states. In this he did a stellar job. His lightning, clement campaign did not even qualify as a war by the conventional definition. It killed almost no one, injured very few, and did precious little damage. At the moment of greatest emergency and acrimony, cool heads and the common good prevailed. Compared to Napoleon's campaigns and the dallying aid from foreign powers, Dufour's treatment was attractive. He deftly highlighted the abacus of power; the Sonderbund War made plain that the rural states could not survive on their own. Better to pick the domestic devils than the foreign ones with the inferior track record.[22]

Political Procedures

What sparked the Sonderbund crisis in the first place was revolutionary political procedures. Proponents of unification employed violence and novel electoral methods to push their platform. When rural states failed to secure their preferences in the Swiss Diet, they tried force as a last recourse. When force failed, they were given terrific terms and a say in the new constitution. The Sonderbund was billed as the costs of the war, but the debt was forgiven halfway through repayment, and soon all sense of grievance was gone. Political procedures had forced the issue, brought about the necessary crisis, and concluded a mutually beneficial agreement.

It seems manifest, however, that pro-union elites were not procedurally powerful enough to achieve union strictly within the statehouse walls. Compared to the

United States, where elites had a strong grasp on procedures and needed only to intimate force, Swiss representatives had to turn over unification bargaining to the generals. Because Swiss elites had to resort to armed conflict does not necessarily mean that they did not have procedural advantages. It could be that the balance of forces and media domination made procedural manipulation easier. Swiss representatives were agile enough to introduce revolutionary measures, but not so dexterous as to win consent without show of force. It is therefore hard to say whether pro-union elites dominated this domestic political arena.

In conclusion, conditions in the mid-nineteenth century were favorable for unification. Before that time, the Swiss states did not face threats that were optimally intense, indefinite, and symmetrical. When they found themselves suitably threatened, an escalating series of crises brought unification to the fore, forcing a choice between union or no. Through positive media, measured use of military force, and generous use of political procedures, elites structured incentives to effect union.

ALTERNATE EXPLANATIONS
Constructivism

Deutsch lists five background conditions for political integration: (1) values and expectations; (2) capabilities and communication processes; (3) mobility of people; (4) multiplicity and balance of transactions; and (5) mutual predictability of behavior.[23] At base, Deutsch sees causes where I see consequences.

Deutsch realizes that cultures are heterogeneous and tries to clarify his point:

> Briefly, we may consider a *people* a community of social communication habits. Its members usually have common habits of speech, such as language, or common cultural memories permitting them to understand one another's ideas, even if they are expressed in two different languages, as among the German-speaking and French-speaking Swiss.

He goes on to explain how social scientists should test his argument:

> The survey, or measurement, of communication habits must be supplemented by a survey or measurement of actual communication experiences. What are the concentrations of populations, the patterns of settlement, the volumes of traffic and migration, the distribution of radio audiences and newspaper readership, the frequency and range of face-to face contacts? . . . Surveys of communication experiences, and of the cultural and social status assigned to them, indicate the essential material with which

any political integration process has to work, as well as some major sources of its potential strength.[24]

At some level, everyone agrees that values are important in deciding who is inside or outside a political group, and people prefer to pattern their behavior in such a way that they tend to cooperate with others who share their values. But then we are not agreeing on much. Conceptually, Deutsch is making distinctions that are hard to understand and harder to test. What is an "actual communication experience" and with what is it to be contrasted? How do we know what the relevant political values are for integration? In some countries, religion is a deadly dividing line, sometimes between different religions, sometimes within the same religion. In other countries, it is differences in ethnicity, language, history, and/or culture. Deutsch seems to be asking us to take on faith that particular values matter because people value them, and not ask where these values came from or how they attained such salience in one place but not another.

In the intervening 40 years, Deutsch's claims have received little empirical confirmation, and surely not for want of time. In the case of Switzerland, it is a motley crew of states who do not share a language, a religion, or an ethnicity. Before unification, Swiss states were well behind other European states in their economic integration. The only value the states shared was their desire to avoid being consumed by Austria or France; apart from that, they could not even agree on standard weights and measures. What uniform culture they now possess is due mostly to unification and mandatory military service.[25] If Deutsch could have measured communication flows across Europe in the 1840s, it is highly unlikely that his results would have predicted much. Some areas, I conjecture, had minimal communication yet were considered as part of states, for example provinces of France, while others had more communication and were not considered unified, for example Portugal and Spain.

My main criticism is that Deutsch does not seriously consider security threats as a driving force aligning interests and facilitating the transaction of goods, services, people, and ideas. Deutsch misses that anticipatory effects are still effects; they signal real causes. It is as if patterns of trade, migration, traffic, settlement, and norms are uninfluenced by power politics. Certainly states do not entirely dominate these phenomena, but if for reasons of state a government chose to alter the above patterns, it is not controversial that the outcome would be dramatically different. Deutsch seems to believe there is some baseline communication level, which exists apart from what states do. That may be, but I am unsure how he has access to that information. The Swiss were savvy observers of the balance of power; they had to be, their livelihoods as mercenaries depended on it. Yet Deutsch implies that political considerations did not suffuse the economic and social lives of the confederacy's citizens.

Swiss patterns of communication were also becoming more strained as unification approached. Again, as in the American case, it is growing apart, not growing together, that fueled union. Urban and rural cantons disputed each other for years, growing more hostile with time. This does not resemble the social learning dynamic that constructivists postulate. If Deutsch is right, social patterns should converge as political integration proceeds, but this is not what we see. After unification, the Swiss increasingly integrate until after World War II. But why does integration level off when the German threat dissipates? Today technology has made communication and transportation easier than ever, making the price of interactions historically low. Nevertheless, contrary to Deutsch's logic, political integration has not continued in Switzerland.

In a sense, Deutsch is right to point out that foreign powers were not up to any unusual activities in 1847; there were no menacing treaties signed, no verbal threats, no foreign mobilizations. Yet Switzerland was facing a shifting balance of power and increasing military threats. Warfare was growing more intensive and expensive. As a small state, Switzerland needed all the power it can muster to keep its borders safe from giant neighbors. If a number of cantons defected or did not assist the confederation with alacrity, everyone would be at the mercy of foreign states. It is no wonder that Dufour was so lenient and the peace terms so magnanimous; external threats required that the Swiss be on very good terms with each other. When Switzerland's military capability was sufficient to keep foreigners out, unification drives never got off the ground. But when its neighbors grew too strong, Swiss union was approved and expanded. Communication patterns cannot explain Swiss unification and consolidation, but the distribution of power can.

The pre-unified Swiss were already *in* a security community. Yet for some reason, a preponderance of the legendarily rational Swiss people sought to upset this charmed arrangement through the application of force. The whole civil war makes no sense from a constructivist standpoint; for this reason, among many others, constructivism is not a useful account of Swiss union.

Liberalism

The problem with liberal theory in the Swiss case is that there was little talk of trade in the buildup or course of the Sonderbund conflict. There was some talk of inefficient tolls, but such grumbles had been around for centuries.[26] But if elites were worried about trade, they could have pushed for a customs union, and they did not. Businessmen were not the leading edge of unity; it was politicians and nationalists. Elites wanted union to defend their nations as best they could, and that was becoming less feasible as foreign states grew increasingly powerful. Security, not trade, was the prime driver of Swiss union.

Binding

Although they have shed the reputation today, for most of their history the Swiss were anything but afraid of war. Exporting soldiers was a major industry, and Swiss citizens were almost constantly at war, just not with each other. It is hard to extricate binding arguments from balancing arguments because the cases in this work are never between great powers. This fact in itself weighs against binding because if states were more worried about fighting each other than they were about harming their balancing prospects, then at least some of the cases would be less peripheral states. But even in the Swiss case, the history is an imperfect fit with a binding narrative. If violence interdependence drives integration, then the cantons should have federated with France in 1815. The Napoleonic Wars were incredibly destructive, and afterward the biggest threats facing the cantons did not come from each other but from outside great powers.

CONCLUSION

Deutsch is right that Switzerland is a paradigmatic instance of political integration—it looks very similar to other unification efforts.[27] But he is wrong to think that the case militates against the dictates of power politics. Switzerland is a country because foreign threats forged it into one. Most of what Deutsch and others like him applaud as causes of Swiss integration was in fact consequences of external threats. His ideal of political integration uncaused by outside threat remains just that.

Nevertheless, history reflects well on the Swiss. I have argued that they have balanced autonomy and security adroitly over centuries. They have seized opportunities that have come their way over time and, when forced to make a virtue of necessity, unified with stunningly little violence. It was not until the middle of the nineteenth century that conditions were ripe for unification. That the attempt was successful was due to the relative power of elites favoring union, particularly their skillful handling of the media, the military, and political procedures.

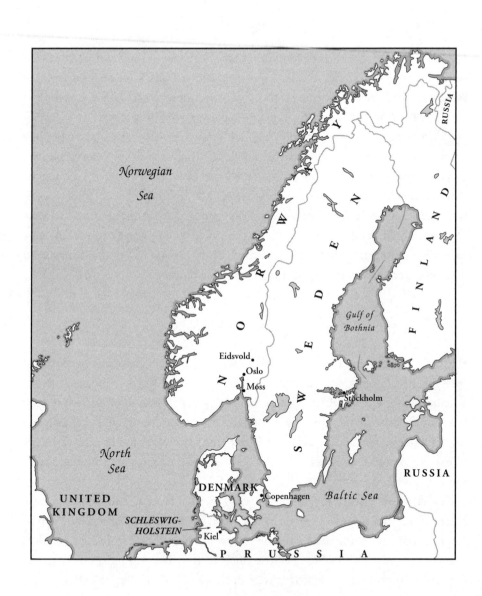

Now that the most powerful princes in Europe together make it a point of honour by their superior physical resources to compel fulfillment of the treaty for the withdrawal of Norway—you, my gracious lord, must also from your side weigh up Norway's strength in relation to that colossal power. That it is irresistible, especially when England gives way, is incontestable. . . . Try therefore to negotiate for this loyal people the best conditions that can now (perhaps never again) be secured as a federated state with Sweden. Then nobody will ever have benefited Norway so much as you.

—CHRISTIAN COLBJÖRNSEN[1]

6

The Liminal Union of Sweden and Norway

WHAT SORT OF union might be formed if countries came together after a cataclysmic great power war, stayed together during a period of long peace, and shared similar language, cultures, laws, and religion? Many Europeans would like to know. The union between Norway and Sweden is an excellent example. Following an increasingly familiar pattern, I first elaborate a brief history of this unification, then analyze how my argument relates to it, and finally discuss how rival perspectives fare comparatively.

A SHORT HISTORY OF SWEDEN AND NORWAY'S INTEGRATION AND DISINTEGRATION

Ninety years is a long time to maintain an experiment. The experiment with union between Sweden and Norway lasted longer than Soviet communism and German fascism combined, but all led to failure and fragmentation. This section traces the development of a union whose beginnings in 1814 aspired to Pan-Scandinavianism and whose end in 1905 reaffirmed traditional nation-states.

Post-Vikings to Pre-Napoleon

Let us start by leaving aside the marauding and pillaging of Viking and medieval Scandinavia.[2] We begin in Denmark, at the end of the fourteenth century. Through the Kalmar union and subsequent advances, Denmark established supremacy over

Norway, turning it into a Danish province. The interests of the two polities were, while not diametrically opposed, far from identical. When Danish rule grew oppressive, Norwegians would protest and occasionally form ill-starred rebellions.[3] It would be historically inaccurate to say that the Norwegian nation existed in this period, but the tension between Danish interests and Norwegian interests laid the groundwork for later growth in Norwegian nationalism.

For four hundred years, Norway suffered famines, expropriation of its wealth into Copenhagen's coffers, and armies traversing its territory. Many of those armies were Swedish, attacking Norway at irregular intervals during centuries of border warfare. The 1644 Hannibal War, hostilities following the 1658 Treaty of Roskilde, the 1676 Gyldenløve War, the 1709–1720 Great Northern War, skirmishing in 1788, and the 1792 conflict that almost escalated to war are all illustrations of routine threats and incursions.[4]

Indeed, while prohibitions against Catholic and Jewish immigration are partly responsible, modern Norway's anomalously high homogeneity is probably due to this history of political conflict. With prohibitions keeping outsiders out, and external threats keeping insiders in, Norway likely saw less migration than other areas of Europe. Union with Denmark was a mixed bag, but there were enough negative experiences to sour Norway on cooperating intensively with Sweden or Denmark.

The Napoleonic Wars and the Unification of Norway with Sweden

As Napoleon battled his way through Europe, the Scandinavian countries did their best to stay clear, but their policy of armed neutrality did not fare well. Denmark-Norway signed a treaty with France and Russia in 1807, and consequently English ships ravaged Denmark and defeated nearly the entirety of its naval fleet and merchant vessels.[5] It was bad enough that Denmark had dragged Norway into a hopeless war, brought starvation and blockade, and deprived Norway of its commerce, yet it was insanity for Denmark to declare war on Sweden in 1808, on the principle that Sweden opposed Russia and France.

Once Denmark cavalierly initiated war, Norway was left alone to face the Swedish onslaught. One Norwegian recorded in his memoirs: "This war prepared the way for the separation of Denmark and Norway, and some Norwegians began, though vaguely, to think of the advisability of a union [with Sweden], the very possibility of which had hitherto wounded their innermost feelings."[6] Seventeen thousand poorly equipped and trained Norwegians repulsed 15,400 Swedes (three-fourths of Sweden's fighting force was on its eastern front), inflicting heavy defeats in the battles of Toverud, Trangen, and Prestebakke.

The Russian threat prompted talk of Pan-Scandinavianism and a union of the three kingdoms: Denmark, Norway, and Sweden. Bickering and infighting pushed the proposal into dormancy, as well as Danish impotence. The English controlled the sea-lanes, and effectively severed the Danes from the other two kingdoms. Norway had demonstrated the ability to defend itself against Sweden, and Denmark had to delegate authority to a power it could little govern. Denmark and Norway drifted apart, while Norway and Sweden began drifting toward England.[7]

Meanwhile, Russia pressed its advantage on Sweden's eastern front. In 1809, Sweden lost one-third of its territory to Russia, including the painful loss of Finland. Panic ensued in Sweden; a German statesman noted, "Sweden lies in her death-throes and she should be permitted to die in peace."[8] Radical circumstances demanded radical actions; Sweden deposed its king through a coup and installed a royal relative, the king's uncle Charles XIII. The Swedish parliament elected a Danish prince in the place of the childless Charles, but the prince died shortly thereafter.

With Napoleon on the ascendant, the parliament thought it judicious to elect a French field marshal (Bernadotte, who later changed his name to King Karl Johan, or Charles John) to assume the throne and lead the Swedes. He wrote a constitution that endured into the 1970s, and joined the alliance of England and Russia to defeat France in 1812. In return for this allegiance, Russia and England agreed that Sweden would compensate for its loss of Finland by linking with Norway, thereby securing its western border, raising the odds of future English support, and ensuring that no single state would control the entry to the Baltic Sea. Along the way to defeating Napoleon, a Swedish army menaced Denmark and requested the right to rule Norway. In a weakened state, Denmark turned Norway over to Sweden in the Treaty of Kiel, January 14, 1814.

On January 15, the king of Sweden wrote his son, "Norway is united with Sweden, and forms a separate and independent kingdom." To another he wrote, "Norway is to be taken possession of, not as a province, but only to be united with Sweden in such a way as to form with it a single kingdom."[9] From the very beginning, there were incompatible intentions for union and independence.

Back in Norway, there was uniform, albeit ambivalent, rejection of the Treaty of Kiel. No one solicited Norway's opinion on unifying with Sweden, and if they had, the answer would have inclined toward the negative.[10] Finns and Swedes had a long-standing common enemy, while Sweden and Norway had engaged in long-standing border warfare. Although elites realized that Norway was defensively no heavyweight, they wanted more autonomy than they had possessed under Denmark, and the people were even more eager for independence.

The great and good met at Eidsvold, a city north of Christiania (modern Oslo), to write a constitution. They drafted eleven propositions and approved ten—the eleventh was a proposal for uniform military compulsory service—and on May 17, the document officially became the Norwegian constitution. Claims were made concerning the originality of this constitution, echoing its American uncle; British politician Samuel Laing remarked, "There is not probably in the history of mankind another instance of a free constitution, not erected amidst ruins and revolutions, not cemented with blood, but taken from the closet of the philosopher, and quietly reared and set to work, and found to be suitable without alteration to all ends of good government."[11]

Predictably, Sweden, and to a lesser extent the great powers, gave Norwegian nationalism a chilly reception. Sweden and Norway negotiated to a standoff, and Norway braced for an assault, which arrived shortly. The Swedish king warned the Norwegians that their resistance was "contrary to their own interests as well as to the true and unchangeable principles of political science."[12] Inexplicably, this failed to mollify the Norwegians.

While the balance of forces was not lopsided (20,000 Norwegians vs. 16,000 battle-hardened Swedes), Sweden had twice the population of Norway, Russia promised 30,000 reinforcements, England pledged military stores, and the naval balance was grossly unequal. On the other side of the ledger, Norway had the defender's advantages, low population density, rugged, tenable terrain, and faced a fragile coalition. Early fighting favored the Swedes, but the Swedes did not want to harm the reservoir of goodwill they might have with their potential partners.[13] Austria, Prussia, and England all made evident that Sweden would merge with Norway and would receive material aid to effect that end, provided Sweden respected Norway's domestic politics. But the Swedish did not put much stock in their great power backers; it was not clear that the great powers would incur significant costs over the matter. With a strong but not unbeatable hand to play, Sweden pressed for a compromise.

Seeing the writing on the wall, Norway agreed to integrate with Sweden but stubbornly stuck to its guns that Sweden recognize the constitution of Eidsvold. Sweden was under duress to do this anyway, and the constitution was duly recognized on the condition that all matters relating to union would be done jointly. The head of the union, the king of Sweden, calmed unifying fears by stating on August 30, 1814, "The kingdom of Norway, without being regarded as a conquered country, in the future shall be in an independent state united with Sweden; and its present constitution shall be properly protected, after the changes necessitated by the union of the two countries shall have been made."[14] Terms of the Treaty of Moss were brought into effect on November 4.

Thanks to hard bargaining by Norway, the crucial component of the Treaty of Moss was its incompatible commitments to Norwegian independence and union.

The ambiguity between independence and union was never resolved and ultimately brought down what little union there was. The Norwegian parliament believed that it retained supreme authority—which the historical record later validated—but even at the time, it was clear that troops could not be summoned from Norway without the Norwegian parliament's approval. Following the Treaty of Moss, Norway foreshadowed that real union was not in the cards; its first actions were preparations for continued military conflict with Sweden.

State of the Union: Rotting, 1815–1886

From the outset, the terms of the agreement were strenuously contested, though the Swedish parliament agreed on complete formal equality between the kingdoms in 1815. Legal authorities were repeatedly consulted and reached no consensus. Sweden believed that in time it would achieve the prerogatives and supremacy not clearly attained initially. Norway was equally determined to deny those prerogatives and supremacy, believing its trump was inscribed in the constitution.[15] In the background, nationalist doctrines had been contagiously contracted from Germany and were gathering momentum in Norway. The first and most constant avenue along which Norway struggled with Sweden was over veto power. The king could veto measures passed by the Norwegian parliament (Norway's legislative body is called the Storting and Sweden's the Riksdag—or archaically Storthing and Rigsdag—but both are parliaments by another name, so for simplicity's sake I call them that), but the king's veto could be overridden if the measure was passed three times.

The first such test of supreme power occurred in 1821. In 1815, 1818, and 1821, the Norwegian parliament passed a bill noxious to the king, and on the third time declared it law. The king was manifestly irritated and upset. He issued a circular, vehemently denouncing the ingratitude and perfidy of Norway.[16] That summer Sweden's armed forces held maneuvers near Christiania and there were indications that a coup was brewing. The coup failed to materialize and the maneuvers ended in parades and balls. The king shortly thereafter sought wider powers, such as the right to dissolve the Norwegian parliament, remove government officials (except judges), order new elections, and create a new hereditary nobility. In 1827–1830, the king challenged the Norwegian parliament over their celebration of May 17 as a national holiday, as opposed to the more union-centric November 4. In both efforts, the king lost.

During this period, Sweden-Norway experienced very little international conflict. The chief cause of concern, Russia, made little waves. There were some muffled anxieties bruited about concerning the rights of migratory reindeer hunters, and the king made noises about the Russian threat, but he named his grandson after the Russian czar, and the Norwegian parliament called his bluff about external threats necessitating integration. There was the "Ships Crisis" of 1824–1825, an incident involving the sale of ships to South American liberators, but it was minor and quickly passed.[17] Another minor event was the alignment with France and England prior to the Crimean War. But the largest foreign policy events centered on Schleswig-Holstein.[18] In 1848, Sweden committed some troops to deter Prussia from attacking Denmark, but in 1864 Sweden left Denmark to fend for itself. Denmark's defeat revealed Pan-Scandinavianism as a farce and eviscerated it as a political force. General weakness, along with public opinion in Sweden and Norway solidly supporting neutrality, curtailed the capacity for foreign adventures. From 1864 to 1914, Sweden and Norway were not involved in any notable international incident; the union hardly had a foreign policy.

All the while Sweden lost legal ground against Norway. In 1842 the Norwegian parliament passed its own free trade legislation; in 1844 Sweden failed to gain passage of more unifying legislation; in 1859 Sweden lost a fight over political appointments; in 1866 Norway defeated a reorganization of its armed forces.[19] And still the legislative challenges kept coming: 1867–1871, 1877–1880, and 1882–1886—all defeats for Sweden. Norway had hollowed out the ambiguous and creaky agreement that was the Treaty of Moss, and union had persistently been crowded out by independence.

The most decisive political victory to date was 1886. Tensions grew after Sweden vetoed appropriations for shooting clubs in Norway in 1882, fearing that they could be used for national defense; money was later appropriated. There was also friction with regard to the Norwegian parliament voting in 1884 to decrease its military contribution available to the union to one-third of its total army. In these, among other issues, Norway had asserted its supremacy with impunity; parliament successfully upheld its rights "as an independent kingdom placed on equal footing with Sweden in the union." As one observer noted in 1886, "All attempts to amalgamate the two nations have failed, and have, long since, been abandoned."[20] This string of successes came with a cost, however. Victory, that bane of focus, splintered Norwegian liberals for a brief period, delaying the drive for formal independence.

Crises and Dissolution, 1887–1905

The final issue that crushed the Sweden-Norway union was foreign policy. Although both sides had extensive control over their armed forces, they did have a unified foreign service that was predominantly Swedish.[21] Norway had a much larger merchant marine and believed that its interest would be better regarded if it had its own consular service. Yet a unified diplomatic corps was the last remaining vestige of union, and Sweden was loath to give it up.

The debate over foreign policy began in 1891 and escalated until 1894, at which time the conflict began to escalate militarily. Swedish leaders sympathetic to Norway warned, "The new act of union is to be adopted by the Rigsdag, and will then be submitted to the Storthing. If . . . no agreement can be reached with the majority in the Storthing, the Swedish army is to march against Norway." Norway's defenses had fallen into desuetude and were in no shape to repel invasion, though in fairness, Sweden's defenses were not in top form either. German General von Moltke was said to have laughed twice in his life: once after beating the French at Sedan, once on being told that a forlorn structure outside Stockholm was a Swedish fortress. Further, emigration was a rival pursuit to military service, prompting the quip that if Sweden increased its military service, "we shall, indeed, have our officers here at home but our soldiers will be in the United States."[22] Whatever the sorry state of the Swedish forces, the Norwegians were yet worse, and Norway, for a change, was forced to back down.

Norway quickly set about improving its defenses. After 1895, it paid more attention and budgeted more money for its army, updated its navy, built fortresses on its coasts and along the border with Sweden, and stockpiled munitions. In 1902, a joint commission on consular service was appointed—by some accounts because a growing Russian threat encouraged Norway to press for such a commission and Sweden to accept it—and by 1903 the commission reported that Norway could indeed have its own consular service. By 1904 the matter had become a crisis, bargaining grew intense, and Norwegian towns sent petitions to the capitol stating their willingness to fight. Shortly after, the Norwegian government floated an immense loan to be ready for war.[23]

Still, conquest was highly unlikely. The crisis caught Sweden in the middle of a military revamping, and even had its military been up to date, tactical victory was far from assured and strategic victory was out of reach by all accounts. England sympathized with Norway; the two were long-standing trading partners, though of timber, a commodity of declining strategic importance. To this must be added the king's mild reputation and popular demonstrations in Sweden protesting for peace. It is a great testament to Sweden that in a time of upheaval it acted with such grace and prudence, making a virtue of necessity.

In 1905, the issue was put to a plebiscite, at the suggestion of the Swedes. In a revolutionary vote, the Norwegian parliament declared that the king no longer ruled. The plebiscite results were ugly: on August 13, 1905, with 85 percent turnout,

367,149 voted for dissolution and 184 against.[24] Soldiers remained on both sides of the border and fleets remained on alert during August and September, but by October all the relevant authorities approved dissolution. And in November, Norwegian citizens voted to install their own constitutional monarch. So ends the Swedish-Norwegian union.

The Union Ledger

As the chapter title suggests, Sweden and Norway's union was neither here nor there. Their alliance had elements of union and elements of independence, with the latter predominating over the former. To make my accounting and analysis transparent, I here lay out the balance as I see it.

On the union side, the two states shared a foreign policy, however limited it was in practice and consequence. Against this must be weighed that legal supremacy de facto and de jure rested with the state governments, that the power of the purse rested with state governments, that militaries were independent, and that trade policy was set at the state, not the federal, level. According to my definition of union, states: (1) must centralize the means to pursue a single foreign policy and (2) cannot legitimately resort to force to resolve disputes between each other. If one wanted to place a phone call to Sweden-Norway, there would not have been anyone on the other end (in fairness, there might not have been anyone on the other end of the Norway line either). Overall, the Treaty of Moss was in practice a covenant without a sword, and so union was largely, though not totally, false.

A related concern is that the Sweden-Norway union was not voluntary. How does Sweden-Norway fit in the scope of this work? Awkwardly. Recall that the cases in this work are relatively equal (i.e., the ratio of the unifying states' population and GDP does not exceed three to one) and not forced by outsiders. Sweden-Norway is at the outer bounds in both regards. In 1815, Sweden was about two times larger than Norway, and great powers pledged support of Sweden's overtures. As the epigraph shows, Norwegian elites were under acute pressure.

It is hard to say in retrospect how events would have played out if Norway had held out. During the Napoleonic Wars, Norwegians had defeated Swedish forces repeatedly, and in 1815 Swedish forces needed to do more than win battles; they had to take and hold Norway. Further, Sweden and Norway had deep doubts about how serious great power commitment was to the issue. In brief, there were good reasons to suspect that if push came to shove, Sweden would not get its way. If Norway and Sweden really thought that 30,000 Russians and the military stores of England—in addition to the full might of the Swedish army—would potentially invade, the terms at Moss would have been drastically different.

In addition, some Norwegian elites were also concerned about Russia's future ambitions. If Norway had escalated the conflict, it would have alienated an attractive alliance partner, which might be costly later. The case is complex; great power arm-twisting bleeds into small power self-help. Since there are fine arguments on both sides of the issue, I err on the side of inclusiveness.

ARGUMENT

Opportunity: Background Conditions

Hence Sweden-Norway is an example of a quasi-union forming and dissolving. Sometime in the Napoleonic Wars, Norway transferred out of hierarchy with Denmark and into anarchy on its own. But after 1814, Norway did not transfer back into hierarchy with Sweden; there was alignment without full unification; and thereafter the two states drifted apart. In this section, I detail how and why.

Intensity

Moderate threats pressed Sweden and Norway into a lethargic approximation of union, and as those threats dwindled the two states grew apart. True to traditional realism, Norway grew more restive the less international pressure it was under. So too Sweden pressed for union following the devastating loss of one-third of Swedish territory to a very large neighboring state, but when the union did not yield the hoped-for security benefits, Sweden allowed Norway greater and greater autonomy. England, France, Germany, and Denmark did not menace the territorial integrity of Sweden or Norway, and Russia's ambitions lay elsewhere.

From the deliberations of Norwegian elites, we know that security was the main cause for concessions to Sweden. Many worried that Norway was too small to be a viable state on its own (by population it is smaller than Scotland).[25] Nevertheless, Norwegian elites were not frightened enough by foreign threats to give up their constitution, and Swedish elites were not so terrified of foreign threats to ignite the issue. At Eidsvold, Norway did not feel an exigent enough threat to include the eleventh proposal in its constitution, which related to compulsory military service. As time went on, external threats were minimal, making it much easier for Norway to chip away at its bonds to Sweden. Sweden and Norway generally stayed out of world politics, and world politics generally returned the favor. Absent the sense of threat, though, union was a dead engine.

Duration

The Russian threat was clearly the one viewed as most pressing and abiding. Witness the loss of Finland and Norway's balancing behavior during that episode. Outside this event, however, relations with great powers were strikingly tranquil. Great power interference in Scandinavia was occasional and limited, and elites were wary but unsure that foreign powers threatened them indefinitely. Unsurprisingly, an alliance masquerading as a union was the result.

Symmetry

Sweden and Norway felt similar security threats throughout the period under study. The relatively equal terms at Moss, Pan-Scandinavian ideology, and many period alignments attest to moderate symmetry. Yet, there are important exceptions: Denmark's alliances during the Napoleonic Wars and Schleswig-Holstein in 1864 demonstrate that at times of high danger, Scandinavian states were not painted into the same corner. Separation by water caused a separation of interests that stranded Denmark. Denmark aside, the differences in trade and security desires attest to the asymmetry of interests between Sweden and Norway. The Norwegian king and parliament spent a great deal of political capital—risking invasion more than once—in high-stakes brinkmanship to lessen intimacy with Sweden.

Because Sweden and Norway were so peripheral to European power politics and had mildly divergent foreign policy goals, common foreign policy was not necessary. Norway had a significantly smaller fear of abandonment than Sweden, and evidence of this can be found in the plebiscite results of 1905. One commentator remarked that the two countries were "like two twins grown together in the back, and therefore continually turning away from one another, the one looking eastward and the other westward."[26]

Fortune: Crisis Trigger

Sweden faced a clear and present danger that forced it to rethink its security in different directions. The Napoleonic Wars and their fallout triggered Swedish thoughts of union; the loss of Finland to Russia was especially harsh. Sweden deposed its king, anointed a foreign general, and immediately sought compensatory territory. To deal with a threat on its eastern flank, Sweden shored up its western flank by uniting with Norway.

As for dissolution, there were two serious efforts to dissolve the union: one that ended in 1895 and the other in 1905. As disunion became a greater possibility, both sides readied for an armed confrontation. Norway was unready to offer stiff resistance in 1895 and so relented. But in 1905, Norway moved at a time when Sweden could no longer win at low cost. Nonetheless, there is an important difference between unification and de-unification. When states unify, a security crisis is needed to justify new thinking and policies as radical as unification. When states dissolve, three kinds of security crises, on my logic, may arise. A security crisis may be so intense it reveals that balancing is futile; a crisis may underscore asymmetries in vulnerability; or elites may manufacture a crisis to loosen ties against an insufficiently durable threat.

Sweden-Norway's dissolution was all of the above. The security crisis that ensued was created to aid dissolution, but because the two states were not fully unified, the response was not what one would expect as an ideal-type de-unification response. When states centralize their coercive authority, they have to overcome commitment problems. These commitment problems are even graver if the parties decide to break apart because there are severe incentives to prevent one of the new states from becoming a threat to the other. Although they engaged in joint exercises and were committed to integrated defense, Sweden and Norway retained supreme control over their militaries. Their relationship was distant, not intimate, and this encouraged a safer, more amicable divorce.

Virtue: Elite Persuasion

Elites in Sweden and Norway were busy advocating their agendas for and against union for decades. They set up leagues, started newspapers, and lobbied legislators. At the end of the struggle, conditions favored Norwegian elites and they ultimately carried the day. Yet there was a lack of perceived threat for some time; structural conditions were biased toward dissolution of union well before dissolution took place. How and when Norwegian elites won was a noisy, drawn-out process, and deserves greater detail.

Media

Both sides armed themselves with formidable propaganda arsenals.[27] On the Swedish side there were pro-union societies, Pan-Scandinavian ideology, and (ineffective) attempts to influence the Norwegian press. On the Norwegian side, there were nationalist shooting clubs, nationalist political movements, and the propagation of Norwegian folklore and culture, which boasted lights such as Henrik Wergeland, Bjørnstjerne Bjørnson, and Henrik Ibsen. At the time of unification, coercion necessitated Norwegian concession, but over time unthreatening conditions supported appeals to Norwegian nationalism over Swedish Scandinavianism.

Sweden never controlled the Norwegian press, and the popular sentiment in Norway was against union. Norwegian elites and the king went through many exertions to get the public to accept the Treaty of Moss. From this I infer that the media had little to do with helping unification. However, a better case could be made for the media aiding the deterioration of relations between the two countries. Although the media was probably a reflection of public opinion, the marketplace of ideas in Norway was dominated by anti-union feeling. Swedes received the message and were genuinely puzzled by the clamor, but could not prevent it.

Military

Military bargaining explains a great deal of when and how Sweden and Norway came together and split apart. Early on in the Napoleonic Wars, Norwegians invested in a reputation for toughness. Despite being half as powerful as Sweden, Norway's determined resistance made up for some of its material weakness, and this tenacity yielded political dividends when Sweden sought union. With Norway's impressive record fighting Sweden, docile acquiescence was not to be relied upon. When the king of Sweden needed a quick victory in 1814, he was compelled to seek it more at the negotiating table than on the battlefield. Had Norway been bested in 1808 or had the king of Sweden tried to unify by conquest rather than diplomacy, Norway may have received a more decisive settlement. And it was the shrewd indecisiveness of the settlement that Norway used to lever itself out of its Swedish commitments.

The military balance also played a part in explaining dissolution. Sweden was manifestly reluctant from the beginning to use force on Norway (e.g., the potential coup of 1821); not only would that offer dicey prospects for success, it would also contaminate relations with a state whose cooperation might be helpful for common endeavors. Norway took advantage of this reluctance by strengthening its defenses prior to deunification such that invasion was all but certain not to pay. On this view, Norwegian forces deployed on the border could not miss. If they were successful on the battlefield, they repelled the invasion. If they were unsuccessful on the battlefield, their deaths would be a trip wire that would trigger revulsion with the Swedes and make Norway ungovernable.

Political Procedures

Regular conflict took place in the political procedures of Sweden and Norway. The Norwegian parliament eroded Sweden's power steadily for decades until what passed for union toppled. Veto after veto was voted down, exasperating the Swedish king and preparing both sides for independence. By the time dissolution was impending, Sweden and Norway had essentially been dealing with each other little differently from any other two foreign nations for some time.[28] Yet it took a revolutionary vote in Norway to end the union, and there were measures undertaken to suggest that the split might not take place pacifically.

To sum, Sweden and Norway were probably closer to an alliance than a union. Even in theory it was not clear where supreme authority lay, but when push came to shove, Norway asserted its sovereignty with nearly unanimously success. As it became clear that the two states did not face an intense, durable, symmetrical threat, they drifted apart until Norway punctured the legal fiction of union. Both the attempt at union and attempts at dissolution ran along tracks determined by elites, though in this case more than the others, popular sentiment played an important role.

ALTERNATE EXPLANATIONS
Constructivism

Sweden, Norway, and Denmark are difficult cases for constructivism because their identities are so similar and connections so extensive. For Sweden and Norway, poor communication was not an obstacle to union—they could hear each other just fine. Better communication was not a cause of increasing integration—they grew further apart as modern media expanded its reach. Improving communication correlates with Sweden and Norway becoming unbound.

This addresses constructivist talk of we-ness and identity. Despite many efforts, Pan-Scandinavianism never got off the ground, and this in the face of massive cultural, religious, legal, and linguistic congruence. Of course, Swedes and Norwegians do not see matters in this light. Where outsiders see vast cultural congruence, insiders immediately see differences between the two peoples, and this is instructive. Emmanuel Adler and Michael Barnett assert that union is a factor of shared values, yet on nearly every formulation of values the Scandinavian countries have more in common across them than most states have within them. "Shared values" and "a distinct way of life" either predict unification poorly or are hopelessly amorphous and in dire need of reforming. Compared to previous cases of unification like the United States and Switzerland, Sweden and Norway should have unified long ago if culture drove union. But the tyranny of small differences triumphed for reasons that a lack of overriding security concern could explain but constructivist variables cannot.

No doubt the tide of nineteenth-century nationalist discourse played a role in the efforts to unify and deunify the two states; there is much to Miroslav Hroch's account of nationalism.[29] Elites did champion folk culture and traditions; they did lead the nationalist mobilization movement through communication and a nationally relevant conflict of interest; propaganda was a key component of these efforts. However, these actions happened within an international political context. Folk traditions were incubated within Norway because political forces contained them there; long-standing strategic factors helped create Norwegian culture, and those same factors encouraged elites to spout nationalist ideas and publics to listen to them.

By Adler and Barnett's logic, Sweden and Norway have successfully formed a security community. The Napoleonic Wars threw Sweden and Norway together, far-sighted elites fomented a common identity around a core of strength (i.e., Sweden), and through discourse and social learning the states forged expectations of peaceful change. But why the backsliding? Union has worked well for Switzerland, a much more heterogeneous place, which also had negative experiences during the Napoleonic Wars. Why were the forces of political integration so much weaker in Scandinavia, when Pan-Scandinavianism was a more developed ideology than whatever the Swiss could muster?

Swedish and some Norwegian elites were busy disseminating Pan-Scandinavian ideas, but their ideas resonated less because external threats did not nurture or make such ideas profitable. Conservative Norwegian elites longed for "the organic beginning of an articulation of civilized human society which we regard as the task of the new age,"[30] but such integration grew little under the cold indifference of distracted threats. Factors like mobility and communication do not explain radical changes in government policy well in the case considered here, and the nationally relevant conflict of interest (here depicted as a crisis trigger) was often epiphenomenal and constructed by elites. Ideas play a role in threats, but threats explain more about ideas than vice versa.

Liberalism

Trade is a weak explanatory variable in the Sweden-Norway case.[31] In 1814, the king of Sweden couched unification predominantly but not exclusively in terms of protection. There were few gains from trade before, during, or after union. Norway and Sweden had different trade orientations and policies. Although both were a source of timber, Norway espoused free trade much more than Sweden did, and their economies never realized returns from scale.

Likewise with dissolution, trade was an issue of contention but not the decisive one. It was the dispute over united foreign policy and consular service that led to the breakup of the union. It is possible that foreign policy was a subterfuge issue and that trade was really the ulterior motive for dissolution. Yet then we should see changes in trade policy after the split, and we do not—Sweden continued its economic nationalist course, and Norway continued its free trading.

Binding

War weariness was an element bringing Sweden and Norway together, but not a dominant one. Again and again, the two sides prepared to fight and fought. Some elites were tired of war after 1815, but the Norwegian public was ready for battle. Immediately following unification, Norwegian elites passed legislation that brazenly provoked Sweden. In 1821, Norwegians refused to be intimidated by fiery rhetoric and Swedish military maneuvers. The long string of provocations continued until the two states came apart. Despite explicit threats of war, Norway went ahead and overtly worked for disunion and readied for war. While Sweden and Norway were adept at staying off the international agenda and managed their internal conflict short of violence, it would be hard to describe either state's behavior as war avoidant and harder to explain their union with that motive.

CONCLUSION

The union of Sweden and Norway is not a prototypical case of unification because it was more alliance than union. Tellingly, the states did not centralize the authority to control armed forces, they did not espouse comparable trading policies, and no federal body overruled a state parliament with much success. The lack of an intense, abiding, symmetrical threat predicts the loose association that elites negotiated. Along the way, this chapter made a case for running the logic of the argument in reverse to explain de-unification. With a decline in union-worthy threats, elites championed de-unification through the media, the military, and political procedures.

One remaining issue is why Norway did not continue to fragment after distancing itself from Sweden. I conjecture that Norway fragmented into the smallest possible defensible state, and the record with Norwegian autonomy since formal independence has tended to bear out the belief that Norwegian elites gambled rationally in separating from Sweden[32]—and something similar can be said of Sweden's endurance. However, one should not lose sight of the small number of possible outcomes in the fragmentation process. There were not several likely successor territories; the bargaining range was lumpy. Path dependence probably explains part of this lumpiness; historical happenstance, domestic institutions, and nationalism likely had a seminal impact on what later became the Norwegian nation.

Yet like decisive battles or game-winning plays, some historical moments reflect abiding, underlying, geopolitical realities. While the forces that forge nations appear and often are arbitrary in fine detail, in broad strokes they may not be as capricious as thought. Over the sweep of history, randomness is likely to be canceled by later randomness. And though an event can always be found that indicated an outcome in hindsight, deeper causes may cause both the event and the outcome. In short, despite many historical accidents, Norway's stable borders may not be accidental.

There are many analogies between Bolívar and me. We both owe our rise to our swords and our merits; we are both beloved by our people; we are faithful to the cause of liberty, distinguishing ourselves from Napoleon in this matter.

—KARL JOHAN[1]

7

Bolívar's Dreams of Gran Colombia

THE KING OF Sweden could have added another similarity: both he and Simón Bolívar were unifiers manqués. But Bolívar was the more ambitious of the two, pursuing his dreams with exceeding ferocity and flair. He pressed for closer, greater union and achieved fast, painful fragmentation. Bolívar's dazzling successes and dismal defeats illustrate the fate of redoubtable elites who lose touch with reality. To chronicle the details of a fascinating case, the first section outlines the history, the second presents my argument, and the third addresses counterarguments.

A HISTORY OF GRAN COLOMBIA

The rise and fall of Gran Colombia is inseparable from the biography of Simón Bolívar.[2] Since the plot of his life is quintessential tragedy, the information will be delivered in three acts, with a short denouement. The first segment introduces the scene and conflict, the second charts Bolívar's rise, the third chronicles his abysmal fall, and the fourth assesses the extent to which Gran Colombia was unified. Before beginning, it should be noted that the name "Gran Colombia" was not used during the period considered here. The state Bolívar tried to establish was called "Colombia" by contemporaries and it was only later called Gran Colombia to avoid confusion with present-day Colombia, which was then called the Department of New Grenada.

In the Beginning

In the beginning, there was calm. To be sure, there was dissatisfaction with Spanish colonial rule, but a central fact of South American liberation is the anomalous lack of protest before it begins. North Americans were agitating for years, fighting the Tea and Stamp Acts, but no equivalent period exists in South America. There were isolated revolts in the eighteenth century, most prominently under Tupac Amaru II in 1781, but these were not nationalist movements.[3] There were liberation stalwarts prior to 1808 (e.g., Bernardo O'Higgins of Chile and Francisco de Miranda of Venezuela), but they were voices in the wilderness. There were some elite complaints, but little clamor—popular or elite—for independence.

War in Europe sparked the chain reaction that led to South American liberation. Napoleon's rise led directly to South American independence movements, and it is fitting that Bolívar was in Paris, living the dissolute life of an overprivileged Venezuelan aristocrat, at the time of Napoleon's coronation (Bolívar was attracted to Napoleon's power but repulsed by his anti-republican actions.) In 1805, much of the Spanish navy was lost in the Battle of Trafalgar and with it a great deal of power projection capability. The British attacked Buenos Aires in 1806 and 1807, and while the Argentines repelled these assaults, the Spanish were powerless to help. By 1808, Napoleonic France installed Joseph Bonaparte to rule over Spain, triggering a legitimacy crisis. Authority to rule descended from the Spanish king, and South American elites debated whether to follow King Ferdinand VII, the usurper Bonaparte, or to strike out on their own. At first they rallied around the fallen king and set up their own ruling councils to manage business in his absence. But self-government proved addicting, and elites soon pushed to make their de facto autonomy official.[4]

Liberation and Unification

Action in two theaters combined to liberate South American from Spanish colonialism. To trace this sequence in the most congenial way, we will begin in the South, switch to the North, then proceed until the armies of Bolívar unite with those of San Martín in 1822, and the narratives become one.

In the South, on July 4, 1811, Chile convened a congress, still professing loyalty to King Ferdinand VII. By the following year the government took on a decidedly anti-royalist cast, civil war broke out, and the Viceroyalty of Peru attacked Chile. The liberal factions failed to reinforce each other and in October 1814 they lost, their leader, O'Higgins, escaping into Argentina. From 1814 to 1817, royalist rule returned to Chile. During this period, Argentina declared independence and invaded Peru multiple times, losing each time and winning no hearts and minds in the process.

José de San Martín turned the tide, though it helped that the end of the Napoleonic Wars brought more manpower and matériel to the side of the liberators. The opposite of Bolívar, San Martín was simple, reserved, constant, continent, and efficient. He sought to secure the independence of Argentina by expelling the Spanish from their Peruvian strongholds. In 1817, San Martín, practically on his own, assembled an army in Argentina and charged across the mountains, winning the key Battle of Chacabuco. In 1818, at the decisive Battle of Maipo, San Martín liberated Chile. O'Higgins had joined the Argentine after the 1814 liberal loss, and when the government offered the dictatorship to San Martín, he declined rule and turned the country over to O'Higgins. San Martín's army then continued on, dislodging Spanish forces as it headed north.

Chilean independence was secured with Argentine arms, but shortly after independence, the Chilean senate sought to control San Martín, procure its own army, and attack Peru. Although his rule was upright, O'Higgins was thought too powerful, and was deposed and exiled to Peru, which was a better fate than other Chilean revolutionary leaders met, like José Miguel Carrera and Manuel Rodríguez, who were assassinated. O'Higgins's replacement, Ramón Freire, governed on and off until 1829, when he too was exiled to Peru. Later, Freire attempted an invasion to regain power and was mercilessly punished with exile to Australia.[5]

In the North, on July 5, 1811, Venezuela declared independence when 38 of 44 deputies signed the act proclaiming Venezuela a confederation of free, independent, sovereign states (from the beginning there was an aversion to unitary states.) There, Bolívar was initially subordinate to Miranda in the fight against the royalists. The rebels fared well until an earthquake struck in March 1812, ravaging liberal towns and sparing royalist towns. Apparently divine right monarchy had something to it: God was evidently a royalist. Support for the revolution bent and Miranda buckled. Bolívar, incensed, sought to shoot Miranda for wanting to quickly gather supplies and retreat. Instead, Bolívar and others turned their leader over to the Spanish before fleeing Venezuela. Miranda died in a Spanish prison four years later.[6]

Soon Bolívar was back battling in Venezuela, against both the Spanish and domestic strife. Santiago Mariño declared his own state in the eastern portion of Venezuela. By 1814, history had repeated itself, minus the earthquake—Bolívar sought to gather supplies and retreat just as Miranda had two years prior—but this time junior officers stayed in line. Exiled in Jamaica, Bolívar collected himself, autopsied his mistakes, and prepared for another invasion. During 1815 he wrote his celebrated "Jamaican Letter" outlining the future of South America and the need for union. In 1816, he resumed his campaigns, and through the loss of Mariño's army and the execution of Piar, an insubordinate protégé, Bolívar became the undisputed leader of liberation.[7]

With Haitian aid, Bolívar continued to hurl his army against the Spanish, to limited effect. But then things started to change, and this was likely due to Spain's deteriorating finances. There was general consensus among Spaniards that the colonies ought to be retained; only the means were debated. But during the Napoleonic Wars, the Spanish economy fell on hard times, and British support for Spanish forces was contingent on fighting Napoleon, not rebellious colonies. Money was so short for colonial counterinsurgency that forces had to be raised with private funds. After the war, sufficient credit was available to send forces to the New World, but not in the desired numbers over a number of years. While Britain did not interdict Spanish reinforcements, it did not financially support Spain's effort, and that had an equally arresting effect.[8]

The 1819 Congress of Angostura brought to life many of Bolívar's ideas, including creating a nation of three departments: New Grenada, Venezuela, and Ecuador. Union was the stated goal, in spite of the facts that vast distances separated the people and much of this territory remained in Spanish hands. Simultaneously, Bolívar integrated post-Napoleonic recruits, trained his army, and joined forces with José Antonio Páez, the hearty, illiterate leader of a hinterland army.

The two men defeated the Spanish in Venezuela and continued on, perilously crossing the Andes, into New Grenada (the current Colombia proper) where they routed the Spanish at Boyacá. As soon as he entered Bogotá in triumph, Bolívar had to return to Venezuela to put down a revolt. While there, he prompted the Venezuelan Congress to approve the union of Venezuela and New Grenada on December 17, 1819.[9] His grand hope in union was geopolitical and similar to that of the U.S. Founders: to ward off great powers and avoid Europe's bloody balance of power fate. The following year was spent mopping up Spanish resistance in New Grenada. A liberal revolt in Spain stopped the flow of Spanish troops for good and opened negotiations. Europe and the United States believed that Spain's departure was inevitable.

The negotiated truce disintegrated and hostilities renewed. In 1821, at the second Battle of Carabobo, Spanish power in Venezuela was broken, though pockets of resistance remained until 1823. Bolívar became the Liberator. Also in 1821, the Congress of Cúcuta gave legal form to Gran Colombia. Bolívar was named president, but he accepted on the condition that he be allowed to liberate Ecuador and Peru, and delegate his responsibilities to a vice president. At Bolívar's suggestion, Francisco de Paula Santander became vice president. Subordinate to Santander, in charge of Venezuela, was General Carlos Soublette, and below Soublette were Páez (later to surpass Soublette), Mariño, and Francisco Bermúdez.

Domestic unrest smoldered, Caracas and Valencia protested the union, and Páez, the military commander of Venezuela, acquired an immediate deafness to Santander's requests for soldiers.[10] But Bolívar was absent to witness this; he and his superlative lieutenant Antonio José de Sucre marched down to liberate Ecuador, Peru, and Upper Peru (the later Bolivia). The victories, accolades, and laurels rolled in, boosting Bolívar's blossoming reputation and blinding him to his coming destruction.

In a famous 1822 meeting, San Martín and Bolívar met for the first and last time to plan final strategy. The contents of the discussion are unknown, but the meeting resulted in San Martín turning his army over to Bolívar, getting on a ship, and leaving politics for good. With characteristic flamboyance, Bolívar sent San Martín, as a parting gift, a portrait of the Liberator. San Martín silently returned to Argentina. Unwilling to watch the liberated states devour themselves, he wisely went into exile with his daughter in Europe, where he stayed out of public affairs and died in 1850.[11] A sad fate, until one compares it to his peers: O'Higgins and Freire involuntarily exiled, Carrera and Sucre murdered, and Bolívar, lowest of all, stripped of everything dear to him and forced to watch his life's work implode ignominiously.

After 1822, Bolívar and Sucre destroyed the remaining Spanish resistance. The Monroe Doctrine the following year did not preclude great power intervention, but it did make an unlikely event even less likely—South American liberation garnered little European attention or assistance, especially compared to the American Revolutionary War. At the Battles of Junín and Ayacucho in 1824, Spain's back in South America was broken, though it was not until 1826 that the last Spanish flag was lowered in South America.[12]

Decline and Fall

As soon as Spain left South America, Gran Colombia started to fall apart. Politically, the South American map divided along administrative lines.[13] For hundreds of years, South Americans had been ruled by kingdoms linked only by their subordination to the Spanish crown. Capital cities—Caracas, Lima, Quito, Buenos Aires—had promulgated laws to their territories for so long that it was straightforward expedience for the liberators to use these political nerve centers for their own ends. The principle of *uti possidetis*, the status quo of 1810, was held up to maintain the territorial integrity of liberated states and avoid boundary disputes.

The first serious instance of fracture was Upper Peru, the first territory to try to throw off the yoke of Spain and the last to successfully do so. Upper Peru had been a province of Peru until 1768, when it became a vice kingdom. Too removed from Lima, too far from Bueno Aires, too mistreated by Peru and Argentina to cooperate with either, Upper Peru was a buffer state waiting to happen. When Sucre set about ordering the territory in 1825, he found that *uti possidetis* was in conflict with popular sovereignty. By a vote of 45 to two, Upper Peru chose to be independent for the first time. Knowing that Bolívar would not be pleased with a step away from union, they sought to assuage him by naming the country after him and inviting him to write their constitution. The ploy worked. Bolívar presented them their constitution in 1826, announcing with typical panache, "This constitution is the work of centuries, because in it I was successful in combining the theories of experience and the advice and opinion of wise men."[14]

Bolívar consoled himself that in time, Peru and Bolivia would grow ever closer. In the meantime, he sent his Bolivian constitution to Argentina, Chile, and Bogotá, hoping to displace the Constitution of Cúcuta several years before its ten-year expiration date. Part fame addict, part gambler unable to quit while ahead, part maniac seducer, Bolívar planned greater conquests: liberating Paraguay, Havana, Puerto Rico, the Philippines, and unifying the South American continent. He laid plans for a great convention at Panama, to extend and consolidate his union. He shrugged off two conspiracies against him, one of which implicated high-ranking Peruvians and Argentines, as isolated incidents unrelated to his public standing. And he basked in the fickle adulation of crowds while his resented army consumed the countryside, Venezuela scrapped republican government, and Santander and Páez grew ever more estranged.[15]

Border disputes flared up between Bolivia and Argentina, and between Peru and Colombia. Bolívar's Congress of Panama was received coolly. Only Peru, Colombia, Guatemala, and Mexico sent delegates, and they made meager provisions, adjourning after three weeks. This emerging chaos unnerved Bolívar. During this time he bandied about the idea of putting the newly liberated states under British protection. He realized a protectorate was risky, but thought the risks worth the security that a foreign pacifier could provide. Great Britain did not consider Bolívar's request.[16]

Páez, concurring with the prevailing sentiment, led Venezuela to revolt against Gran Colombia in 1826. Santander summoned Bolívar to deal with the rebellion, though Bolívar sparred with Santander over legal supremacy. Turning to Páez, Bolívar prophesized: "My enemies are sent to their ruin according to the will of Providence, but my friends, such as Sucre, ascend. . . . There is no legal authority in Venezuela but mine."[17] Páez did not escalate or deescalate. Neither man wished to tangle with the other, and by 1827 the result was indecisive: the revolt went dormant and no one was punished.

Santander was furious; Bolívar would not allow the union to break up, but he would not keep it together. Bad news came regularly: Peru abrogated the constitution Bolívar had bestowed on it the prior year. Peru menaced Ecuador. There was an unsuccessful coup against Sucre, who was blamelessly governing Bolivia. The Gran Colombia army mutinied; refusing to take orders from Venezuelan officers, it sailed home.

In 1828 matters continued to unravel. The Ocaña Convention produced nothing but frustration and faction. It revealed that Bolívar's party was extremely obstinate and distinctly in the minority—Bolívar's party would have to accept the terms they rejected at Ocaña two years later, after creating much ill will. There was a revolt in southern New Grenada, Peru invaded Bolivia, and Bolívar turned reactionary, gaining dictatorial powers. Citizens feared that he was becoming a power-hungry tyrant, and attempted a coup that nearly killed him. Soublette beseeched the head of Bolívar's party, "Better to separate in peace and harmony than at the point of the sword, and not to waste our time and energy defending ourselves against our brothers when we should use it in organizing ourselves."[18]

By 1829 and 1830, Bolívar reached the bottom of the wheel of fortune. Not that he believed it. He was still convinced that union could happen, and he tried the same tired remedies, expecting better outcomes. Four years before, he was the adored liberator of South America—now Bolívar's charisma was spent; everything he touched turned hostile or futile. Another of his former officers, José María Córdova, took up arms against him; Bolívar earned not a single vote in the presidential election, was thrown out of New Grenada, and outlawed in his homeland. Nonetheless, upon leaving power, he implored his countrymen to keep his sham state united.[19]

Venezuela, already a state within a state, inaugurated the final dismemberment of Gran Colombia. Making official the obvious, Páez sensibly declared Venezuela's independence from Gran Colombia, threatening war to any challenger. In the Caracas Act of Separation on November 26, 1829, 400 notables signed on to independence, among them Bolívar's cousin, his brother-in-law, and Soublette. The Bogotá Convention met in January 1830 to announce the death of Gran Colombia; New Grenada and Ecuador went their separate ways. Venezuela did not bother to attend. Sucre was assassinated not long after.[20] Bolívar's degradation was complete.

Beaten, betrayed, prostrate, powerless, expelled, and outlawed, his handpicked successor murdered, his states fallen into anarchy, his reputation ridiculed, and his health ruined, Bolívar died of tuberculosis on December 17, 1830.[21] He clutched his dreams to the end. In his last will and testament marked December 10, 1830, Bolívar stated, "I, Simón Bolívar, Liberator of the Republic of Colombia, born in the city of Caracas in the department of Venezuela. . . ." On his deathbed, Bolívar issued a proclamation declaring, "I aspire to no other glory than the consolidation of Colombia. You must all work for the supreme good of a united nation. . . . If my death will help to end party strife and to promote national unity, I shall go to my grave in peace." His last words were: "Let's go. These people don't want us in their country." News of his death in Venezuela elicited a proclamation announcing: "Bolívar, the evil genius, the anarchist, the enemy of the country, has ceased to exist."[22] Only years after his death was his reputation resurrected into the cult of the Liberator.

The Union Ledger

Was Gran Colombia a union? The answer is a heavily qualified yes. There are two practical criteria by which to judge whether states have unified: (1) Have they formally centralized the means to pursue a single foreign policy? (2) Can members legitimately use force to resolve disputes with other members? On the pro-union side of the ledger, the Congress of Angostura and Constitution of Cúcuta did formally centralize the means of foreign policy and delegitimize the use of force among members. There was a governmental hierarchy set up, it did have its own army, and it appears that all sides considered Páez's 1826 and 1829 revolts to be rebellions against established authority.

Against this must be weighed a bevy of other facts. First, the members did not have much of a foreign policy, so it is hard to tell to what extent it was unified. Second, while details are sketchy, it appears as though there was little policy convergence among members. Third, from the outset Caracas protested the union and viewed it as illegitimate, and when Venezuela refused to supply troops or comply with central government, no punishments were forthcoming. Fourth, although Gran Colombia did have an army, it was more attached to Bolívar than Gran Colombia, mutinied without reprisal in 1828, and could not keep domestic peace. A state is hardly a unified state if it cannot control policy and its own army. Thus, for a brief period after the Constitution of Cúcuta, Gran Colombia was a unified state, but shortly after the Spanish departed it started dissolving. The process was complete by the beginning of 1830, but it was probably de facto dissolved sometime around 1828.

ARGUMENT
Opportunity: Background Conditions

In plainest form, Gran Colombia amalgamated around 1820 to face the Spanish threat and came apart sometime between 1826 and 1830 when that threat receded. Although the states were young and Bolívar had inertia, circumstances swiftly turned the tables and nourished the power of states at the expense of Bolívar's union. Absent an intense, abiding, symmetrical threat, elites militating for disunion gained the upper hand in the competition for power.

Intensity

Intensity of threat caused most of the observed alliance behavior in South America. During the Napoleonic Wars, the decline in Spanish power in its colonies created an opportunity for a balancing coalition to fend off Spain. As per usual, the coalition was slow to form, but it was ultimately effective. One would have thought that, with the loss of Spanish ships at Trafalgar, Spain could no longer menace the New World. But it took time for colonial structures built up over centuries to deplete their resource reservoirs. When uncoordinated liberation movements attempted to cast Spain out of the New World in 1811, they fared poorly. Internal balancing was insufficient and alliances slowly blossomed (e.g., the 1819 Congress of Angostura).

Spain was at first a formidable foe, and South American liberation was an incredibly destructive process. Scholars estimate that between one-quarter and one-third of Venezuela's population was lost during the war against the Spanish. Such an intense threat is the impetus of unification, and indeed we see the beginning of union. Then power began to shift. This was partly for non-realist reasons: revolutionary ideas sapped Spain's recruiting, drew people from all over the world to fight against Spain, and led to domestic faction in Spain, which undermined the war effort. Yet a realist lens captures some of the foundations of this; Spain's power was evaporating, its finances were in ruins, its power projection capability was weak, it was ripe for robbery, revolution, and retrenchment. After initial setbacks, liberation movements improved and by 1819 were holding their own. By 1822 they fully united and were turning the tide, and by 1824 Gran Colombia won the decisive victories for liberation. External balancing was manifestly effective.

But Spain was a declining power. The North American colonies had the fortune to face Great Britain, the preeminent naval power, one of the most powerful states in the world, and growing stronger with time. In contrast, the South American colonies faced a sinking Spain, less powerful, more distant, and of dwindling ability. The next most likely threats, the United States and the United Kingdom, displayed no interest in territorial aggrandizement in South America. Threat had dried up.

One should not overlook the correlation: in 1826 the last Spanish flag goes down and Páez's flag of rebellion goes up. It took concerted effort to wrest loose the heavy hand of Spain, but once the Spaniards departed they had not the wherewithal to return, and almost everybody knew it. The desultory and quickly destroyed Spanish expedition to Mexico in 1829 is the exception that proves the rule. Even Bolívar, seemingly the last person to realize, came to see it. In an 1829 letter to his trusted confidant, General Daniel O'Leary, he wrote: "Men and conditions cry out for separation, because the dissatisfaction of each region makes for a general unrest. Spain herself has now ceased to threaten us. This is the final proof that the union is no longer necessary, for it served only to concentrate our forces against our former rulers."[23]

Had another foreign threat stepped into the breach, unification would have been bolstered. For better or worse, no such threat was forthcoming. The United States made several friendly overtures to South American liberation, and far from being the next threat, Britain tried to outbid the United States to be the champion of South American independence. Bolívar noticed that Britain was the friend of South America in 1814: "Nobody doubts, that the powerful Nation which has defended . . . the Independence of Europe, would not equally defend that of America, were it attacked." And in 1823: "Do not fear the Allies, for the ditch is large and the English fleet still larger."[24]

Bolívar proffered the idea of making the newly liberated states protectorates of Great Britain. Despite the fact that British and South American citizens expressed little interest in such a league, Bolívar was hyperbolic. Before the Congress of Panama, he wildly speculated, "This Congress seems destined to form a league more extensive, more remarkable, and more powerful than any that has ever existed on the face of the earth."[25] Bolívar was crassly out of touch.

Institutional inertia prevented immediate dissolution. The states of Gran Colombia were new and weak. The armies of San Martín and Bolívar were largely recruited along personal and charismatic lines—formal states hardly existed, much less controlled organized armed forces. So when San Martín stepped aside, Bolívar headed the largest army, and he was a focal solution to liberation legitimacy problems. He had a centralized multistate army, a reservoir of goodwill, and a mind for unification. Although no one matched Bolívar's zeal for union, for a time he was the only game in town.[26]

That reversed as Bolívar's stayed the same while reality changed. His army grew fractious and mutinied, conspirators plotted to take his life, Páez and Santander quarreled over supremacy, elites in different capitals were not interested in cooperating with each other, and revolts broke out in the countryside. With no foreign threat to speak of, Bolívar's actions and state alike grew incoherent. Concentrating power in some faraway capital was unlikely to quiet domestic unrest, which was often caused by reaction to excessive concentrations of power. States could be secure through internal balancing; external balancing was no longer necessary.

Duration

Initially, there were good reasons to think that Spain might be an enduring threat. South America had been oppressed by Spain for hundreds of years, and ridding the continent of Spanish influence would not happen overnight. Nevertheless, the Spanish threat declined swiftly. Separated by an ocean, the British navy, and a consistent inability to raise funds, Spain vanished as an abiding threat. As mentioned, no other state stepped in to fill Spain's former shoes; the United States and Great Britain's attentions were elsewhere, they did not seek territorial changes in South America, and South American elites, including Bolívar, did not perceive them as threats. Without an enduring threat, an enduring alliance was useless, and Gran Colombia fell apart.

Symmetry

At first, the Spanish threat bearing down on the colonies did so relatively equally. No third parties intervened to provide aid; the former colonies were on their own to purchase liberty. Bolívar observed: "America stands together because it is abandoned by all other nations. It is isolated in the center of the world. It has no diplomatic relations, nor does it receive any military assistance; instead, America is attacked by Spain, which has more military supplies than any we can possibly acquire through furtive means."[27]

The more distant colonies—Argentina and Chile—were liberated earlier and struggled with fewer Spanish forces than their northern cousins. Yet Venezuela, New Grenada, and Ecuador were painted into the same corner, and reacted with predictable solidarity. Politicians spent their political capital assisting Bolívar until their cooperation paid off in the form of independence and a dearth of external threat, which made symmetry no longer of any value. Fissures were quick to form and spread. Elites then fought nasty fights and burned bridges to exit Gran Colombia, ruining reservoirs of goodwill.

Fortune: Crisis Trigger

A cataclysmic struggle for independence qualifies as an exigent security crisis. It was in the context of widespread warfare and atrocities—a "War to the Death"[28]— that Venezuela and New Grenada coordinated their union, and it is transparent that a security shortage motivated parties to talk of union. Bolívar pointed to Spanish atrocities and oppression to justify the sacrifices necessary for liberation, and union was conceived as a way to keep Spanish power out of South America.

There was ample evidence for any spectators that security was scarce in South America, and union appeared a reasonable remedy.

As for dissolution, recall that unions break apart through three types of crises: an overwhelmingly or underwhelmingly intense threat makes balancing useless; a crisis reveals asymmetric vulnerability; or elites manufacture a crisis to loosen ties when they face an insufficiently durable threat. Like Sweden-Norway, Gran Colombia faced threats that underwhelmed in multiple respects. Intensity and duration were lacking, making symmetry irrelevant. The member states of Gran Colombia could barely keep domestic order and, as the quote from Soublette above indicates, they sought to stabilize government by decentralizing power. Páez created crises by making manifest Venezuela's disobedience to Bogotá, and in 1826 and 1829 he gutted Gran Colombia until it was a husk. Páez did not work alone; Santander, Soublette, and many other elites worked to hollow out a union that provided no additional security at a cost of too much sovereignty. Elites presided over conferences showcasing that Gran Colombia was designed for a situation that no longer existed.

Virtue: Elite Persuasion

With most of the population politically atrophied from Spanish rule, elites were the dominant players in unification and de-unification. The main means of bringing about each was military, but the media and political procedures also contributed. As a prior section has argued, circumstances initially tipped the playing field toward Bolívar and then against him, conditioning thought and action to create then dismember Gran Colombia.

Media

Bolívar was a consummate propagandist, and his powers of persuasion are legendary. But most of the population—and some of the leaders—could not read, and so any media effects were weak, top-down, and unlikely to be as widespread as in cases with higher literacy rates. Through voluminous writings, Bolívar made the case early and often for South American union, winning many elites over to his cause. Nevertheless, once the war against Spain was won, the media unmade Bolívar. The press in Venezuela and New Grenada deprecated his motives and his policies, and Bolívar, to his credit, largely chose not to silence these voices.[29] If anything, the structure of the marketplace of ideas favored continued union, since Bolívar had the power to control the media. With the Spanish threat gone, his former allies were no longer convinced of the Liberator's logic, and elites like Santander, Páez, and Soublette put their booming voices, and their influence on the media, in the anti-union chorus.

Military

The main means to effect union and dissolution was the military. Gran Colombia came to be because the Spanish threat compelled concerted action. Once the army was unified under Bolívar, he had the most influence over postwar settlement, and he had long resolved to establish a massive South American political entity. But absent an external threat, the elites whom Bolívar entrusted in the capitals were soon working for greater independence for their states. They had not fought the Spanish to give up sovereignty to some ungainly union, nor did they fight to become a protectorate of Great Britain. The distribution of power had always been in the capitals, and while Bolívar temporarily surpassed these centers to defeat the Spanish, their departure reverted power back to the capitals; military power congregated there, and drove separation.

In the case of Venezuela, Bolívar was gone only a short time before Páez was in visible revolt. Neither Bolívar nor Páez wanted to fight the other—both were well acquainted with the fearsome competence of the other—but that revealed, in part, that both could be expected to command respectably balanced forces. Three years later, when Páez was more brazen about Venezuela's independence, he made clear that an invading army could not hope to win at an acceptable cost.[30]

Venezuela was representative. With no foreign threat to discipline behavior, faction broke out across Gran Colombia between and among subnational groups and states. Bolívar could not field a big enough, fast enough, coherent enough army to keep order. His constitution was abrogated shortly after he wrote it; his troops mutinied not long after he left them; his subordinates challenged his authority overtly. Bolívar bemoaned, "If I go north, the south will disintegrate; if I go south, the north will revolt."[31]

Union would not solve the rebellions and invasions that plagued South America, and only Bolívar thought otherwise. Conditions favored independent states, and states swiftly found themselves in possession of their own militaries, which facilitated extrication from Gran Colombia. Bolívar and his policies quickly found themselves outside the parameters of competitive politics. Left alone, most cooperation and loyalty stayed local. It was as if an invisible hand prevented international cooperation where there was no danger of external threat to corral defection. South American states could hardly conquer each other, and Spain caused little further anxiety. Why should soldiers take orders from foreign nationals?

It was in fact very hard to project force in South America, and controlling territory from the traditional capital cities was hard enough without making soldiers fight for a novel political entity. Beating foreigners was one thing, taking and holding land against natives was another. Bolívar's army was united because everyone hated Spanish rule more than each other, but that same army mutinied because without the Spanish threat they saw no need to be under the thumb of Venezuelans.

Political Procedures

Procedural measures had only a marginal effect on Gran Colombia because domestic institutions were so weak. With regard to union, Bolívar did receive aid from the New Grenada government, on which he had more rhetorical than procedural influence. The Cúcuta and Bolivian Constitutions were imposed essentially by an occupational force, albeit one of benevolent intent. My explanation poorly covers the participation of Páez, who could be described as elite only by stretching the term.

Bolívar was no respecter of legal formality—he sought to replace the Cúcuta Constitution with his Bolivian Constitution well before the former was legally supposed to be revised. One biographer states:

> In fact, Bolívar never governed constitutionally. Whenever Congress elevated him to the presidency, in Augostura [sic], in Cúcuta, in Bogotá, he hastened to turn over the civil command to the vice-presidents and, under the pretext of conducting war, always maintained his character of supreme chief, in accordance with his autocratic tendencies and the necessities of the situation.[32]

He said cavalierly of his Bolivian Constitution: "Throw it in the fire if you don't want it—I don't have an author's vanity," which was true if only because his vanity more nearly resembled a brittle beauty queen's. Opposition infuriated him, and he admitted that he could not play any complicated game because, "I would break it."[33]

Political procedures also played a marginal role in disunion. From 1826 on, Santander was actively opposing Bolívar in the legislative process of Gran Colombia, and Páez was leading anti-union measures in Venezuela, culminating in the Caracas Act of Separation. Procedures did signal intent, but we are speaking of states run by strongmen; political institutions were simply too nascent to have great effect.

ALTERNATE EXPLANATIONS
Constructivism

Gran Colombia is another tough case for constructivism. Bolívar agitated for union expressly on constructivist lines; many South Americans shared an identity, a religion, a history, and a language.[34] If anyone had generous endowments to be a political entrepreneur, it was he; Bolívar united an international army that successfully liberated a continent. And yet for all the convergence of identity and values, for all the cooperation and previous positive experiences, for all the pull of charisma and cores of strength, as soon as the Spanish threat fell into obscurity there was a sudden resurgence in local identity over Gran Colombian identity.

Certainly there were not extensive interactions between the Spanish South American colonies, but that was equally true about the British North American colonies. Increased contact did not lead to unification, and unification did not lead to increased cooperation. This all runs counter to constructivism but fits well with the shifting balance of power.

The social learning of Deutsch, Adler, and Barnett is not in evidence. The struggle for independence was long and hard; in the fight against Spain, many states and individuals had ample opportunity to work together and learn to trust each other. And the historical record indicates that during hostilities, they did. In a historical rarity, San Martín trusted Bolívar enough to turn his army over to him. Despite the common struggle, despite the shared past, despite the prominent ideas of Bolívar, common consciousness never flourished. South American states were arrested in the second tier of Adler and Barnett's process. Why such favorable conditions did not evolve into a common identity is something constructivism misses.

Liberalism

There was no prewar economic protest, no prewar recession (actually, prewar growth was robust), and no major prewar class struggle. There is also no discussion of trade during or after unification. With the possible exception of Chile, most countries' economies fared more poorly on their own than under Spanish domination—some union was evidently more economically beneficial. One indication of this is that traditional trade links with Spanish markets collapsed. After independence, Spanish overseas trade fell 75 percent.[35] As Gran Colombia divided, the main concerns were domestic security and the power of neighboring states, not tariff policies.

Were Dani Rodrik defending his explanation, there is a standby fallback position. A liberal defense could be that the pull of economic forces was too weak in 1820s South America for sustainable integration; the world economy was underdeveloped, and South America was not tightly enmeshed in it. Very well, but the same could be said for 1780s North America and, to a lesser extent, 1840s Switzerland, and they managed to unite. If liberal explanations abandon this part of history, realists will happily claim it. But as the next chapter tries to show, liberal explanations of the Rodrik variety do not do work even in the optimal conditions of contemporary Europe. Regardless, the balance of threats, not trade, combined and dissolved Gran Colombia.

Binding

There is some circumstantial evidence for binding. Although we do not know what Bolívar and San Martín said to each other in their sole meeting, there is suggestive evidence that they sought to dampen the possibility for war between the former colonies. Period sources contain regular appeals to avoid shedding fraternal blood. But talk is cheap and binding language had a limited shelf life. Once the Spanish had departed, the newly independent states fell to quarreling, coups were common, and border disputes cropped up. If South American states were truly serious about stopping war between each other, they would have federated as the United States had, or at least kept Gran Colombia together longer. They did not because their love of autonomy outweighed their hatred of war.

CONCLUSION

In the sixteenth century, Cortés supplanted the Aztec empire with the Spanish empire, and almost exactly three hundred years later, Bolívar tried to supplant the Spanish empire with a South American empire. At first he met partial success, forming Gran Colombia around 1820 in the expectation that it would help fight an intense, durable, symmetrical Spanish threat. But when entrenched Spanish power was dislodged, no foreign threat materialized. Inertia kept Gran Colombia together briefly, but without an external threat, conditions were ripe for fragmentation. By 1826 cracks started to widen, and no later than 1830 Gran Colombia was broken apart. A security crisis facilitated the union, and a security crisis destroyed it. Primarily through military means but also marginally through the media and political procedures, the distribution of power effected a reversal of fortune. The leader who rose to supremacy against the Spanish threat sunk below his subordinates when the times changed and he did not.

At the risk of dullness and worse, pedantry, I hazard some final points. First, I would like to refute those who see the failure of Gran Colombia as no fault of Bolívar's. To list just a few authors: "He had liberated the greater part of South America by the sheer force of his own personality, and when it was done, could not save it from itself!" "By his own strength he freed them from Spain. More he could not do, for his people lacked the genius for self-government. . . ."[36] On this view, if only the people were smarter, if only other elites were not so self-aggrandizing, then South America would be living in mirth and plenty.

Spain infantilized and oppressed many under its rule, and poor economic conditions, bad infrastructure, and too few trained officials were also inhospitable to self-rule. But it is incorrect to portray the South American masses as bovine and elites as preternaturally petty, while Saint Simón escapes without stain. It was Bolívar who pressed for utopian schemes, Bolívar who widened the gap between rhetoric and reality, Bolívar who solipsistically clung to delusions of grandeur. The masses and elites have their imperfections as well, but they were sensible enough to know bad policy when they saw it, and with admirable rationality they dethroned Bolívar when his compulsiveness was obvious.[37]

Second, could Bolívar have sustained union? With the personality of Attila and at the cost of oceans of blood, union was possible for a time. Yet with vast distances, no foreign threat, maladapted economies, widespread opposition, and the demand for constant oppression, it is more likely that the ultimate result would have been similar, only at a higher price. Stubborn systemic pressures penalized, deterred, and selected out elites who advocated union from leadership positions—indeed Bolívar was almost alone when he died. Faulting Bolívar for thinking on a grand scale is fastidious; faulting him for dismissing mountains of negative feedback is only responsible.

Third, people are not always rational, and systemic imperatives do not mean that they will be; it only means that non-competitive actions will be punished. Bolívar is an epic example of martyrdom on the system's cross.[38] Unlike other tragic figures, it is not ignorance that lays him low—he knows full well why he failed. Intelligence he had plenty of, it was weakness of will that kept Bolívar from correcting his course.

Thankfully, Bolívar was determined not to be another Napoleon, and he caused less bloodshed than he could have. Longing to see Gran Colombia free and great, he pursued both ends and consequently secured neither.[39] He is an intriguing man and a great liberator, but his romantic visions of union gratuitously lacerated half a continent. Had Bolívar never been born, one could make a good argument that San Martín or Miranda would have founded South American independence on less violent foundations, and ultimately would have made a lasting improvement in the development of the region.

One last point: tragedy in drama aside, tragedy in politics happens, I argue, when leaders fail to make a virtue of necessity. Although this chapter is not meant to be a morality lesson, Bolívar's peripety can be read as a cautionary tale to those whose waking dreams are several sizes too big.

The European Union itself [must] become a major pole of international equilibrium, endowing itself with the instruments of a true power.

—JACQUES CHIRAC

We're not here just to make a single market, that doesn't interest me, but to make a political union.

—JACQUES DELORS[1]

8

Europe's American Idol

THE JACQUES OCCUPY a popular position. A parade of elites and a majority of citizens want a United States of Europe to be a peer competitor of the United States of America.[2] Europeans wish for American unity and power, but is it wishful thinking? Will Europe unify?

The conventional wisdom is that it will, through "ever closer union." Europe has learned the folly of balance-of-power politics and now practices postmodern politics. Not through balancing but through communication, trade, and institutional ties will Europe gradually grow together to avoid another major war. Yet communication, trade, and democratic institutions have burgeoned in Europe while integration seems stalled.

One of the most important issues in world politics is what it would take to make a union out of Europe. How integrated it grows in the coming years affects the bedrock of great power politics for generations. Even skeptics of the European Union (EU) concede that, unified, the continent would be a juggernaut. If unifiers are looking for models for Europe, the cases in this book are the most excellent examples.

Although it smuggles "union" into its name, the EU is not a union by my definition. The EU has an impressive array of powers, but monopolizing the ends and means of foreign policy has never been among them. Moreover, no legislation to do so has been viable. However, Europe's potential unification has profound implications, shares key traits with the other cases in this study (i.e., it would be a self-help, relatively equal union), and therefore merits inclusion and comparison with the other cases.

However, no parallel is perfect and no guide inerrant. Much time has passed since the examples in this book united, and today's EU is an entity with regulatory and redistribution powers that states of old hardly possessed. Unquestionably all cases have different histories, geographies, linguistic and ethnic compositions, and so on.[3] In addition, the present sometimes parts company drastically from the past—all of which adds a healthy dose of caution to our findings, but does not remove the imperative for using the best materials for purchase on pressing problems.

This chapter objects to the prevailing notions of how Europe will unify, and spells out why the odds are long for Europe to truly unify. The following section provides some brief background on recent attempts at European unity, and the next section discusses how the main argument explains European integration to the present. In the third section, I analyze rival views and criticize the logics behind ever closer union, and the fourth compares predictions about Europe's future.

A HISTORY OF MODERN EUROPEAN UNITY

The protagonists of this story are the relatively equal states at Europe's core: Germany and France. Secondary characters stand in the background—the United Kingdom, Spain, and Italy—but they are simply valuable supporting cast. Europe has integrated as much as it has due primarily to the labors of its lead states, and if Europe unifies it will likely be because these states are in the vanguard.

If one were to map European integration over time, the topography would show a ridge during the Concert of Europe and some minor hills in the late nineteenth century. World War I would be a valley surpassed only by World War II, with the interwar years registering trivial integration. It is only in the late 1940s and early 1950s that integration in Europe peaks; this is when unifying policies are most appealing. By the mid-1950s, unifying proposals become markedly less ambitious, and that mediocre level of integration persists until the end of the Cold War. The 1992 Maastricht Treaty is an echo of the earlier bid for European integration, and progress has flagged since then.[4] This is not to take anything away from pro-integration elites; as I will explain shortly, Western Europe has done well for itself.

Europeans Talk about Union, 1815–1945

Modern Europe, like ancient Europe, has seen many attempts at unity.[5] The Habsburgs, Napoleon, and Hitler are the most famous and need no elaboration here, but the more voluntary attempts do. After the Napoleonic Wars, European great powers met regularly in the Concert of Europe to manage their relations and diminish tensions, by most accounts quite successfully. Over time the Concert withered, but a residue of cooperation remained. With the birth of a new great power in the middle of Europe, Germany in 1871, that residue started to disappear.

Without question, there were efforts to voluntarily integrate European states. William II of Germany talked of a European union to balance the United States, but he had an economic union in mind. In the Boxer Rebellion, European armies united briefly under a German general. In A. J. P. Taylor's words: "It is often said that the world will only unite against another planet; in 1900 the Chinese served much the same purpose."[6] Economic interdependence, though separate from political integration, was at historic highs in Europe before World War I. During World War I, the Supreme War Council was a flickering flirtation with unification that went poorly. Between the world wars, there was some idle talk of making war illegal and heading toward a United States of Europe. And during the fall of France, Winston Churchill made an overture for an Anglo-French union, but the offer was probably neither made nor taken seriously. Churchill would make the next overture for integration, reiterating the call for a United States of Europe in 1946.

Europeans Consider Union, 1946–1954

After World War II, the United States was reluctant to continue its formal military presence in Europe. American policymakers increasingly sought to improve the counterweight to the Soviet threat, and planners mulled over creating a "third force" in Europe, independent of the United States and the USSR, capable of tying down the West Germans as well as rebuffing Soviet pressure. The American presence in Western Europe would remain to soothe fears of West Germany and lubricate the integration process until the Europeans could stand on their own.

The original American plan for postwar occupied Germany was the Morgenthau Plan, named after Treasury Secretary Henry Morgenthau, Jr. The Morgenthau Plan aimed to deprive Germany of its war-making ability by partitioning it and dismantling its industry. American policymakers foresaw that this policy would lead to widespread suffering, but clemency was a low priority. Morgenthau was explicit: "I don't care what happens to the population," and Franklin Roosevelt refused "to say that we do not intend to destroy the German nation."[7] With some softening, Morgenthau's tough logic was implemented as JCS 1067 (privately in early 1945 but publicly in October of that year). The deleterious consequences of the policy were fast to arrive, but stirred little sympathy in Washington. American policy remained unmoved, even when it became plain that it was economically inefficient to make the most productive country in Europe unproductive when the continent was short of necessities.

Roosevelt, and decreasingly Truman, stuck to Morgenthau's course from 1944 until mid-1947. Then policy changed abruptly, but not for humanitarian or economic reasons. Citing national security grounds, Truman issued JCS 1779, which stated that an "orderly, prosperous Europe requires the economic contributions of a stable and productive Germany."[8] The death of the Morgenthau Plan went hand in hand with the birth of the Marshall Plan, announced in June 1947, which invested tremendous sums of American capital to rebuild war-torn Europe.

Why such an enormous volte-face? German suffering clearly did not bother American elites much, nor the prospect of offending the German people, nor negative economic externalities among America's allies. What inspired the proponents of the Marshall plan—George Marshall, George Kennan, Chip Bohlen, and Lucius Clay—was communist influence. The first burst of Marshall Fund aid went to Greece and Turkey, the states most in jeopardy of communist subversion. NATO followed not long after. The Soviet threat propelled European integration.

Over the same time period, Britain was undergoing its own policy reversal. When William T. R. Fox coined the term "superpower" in 1943, he had three states in mind: the United States, the Soviet Union, and the United Kingdom. Although Britain was not on a par with the other two, it was initially considered to be in the same league. British postwar planning optimistically sought to lead a power bloc independent of the other two superpowers to maintain maximal autonomy. Before the Potsdam Conference in July 1945, the British Foreign Office analyzed their postwar prospects. According to Anthony Adamthwaite:

> Sir Orme Sargent . . . drew up *Stocktaking after VE Day*. Sargent did not sugar the pill. Britain, he said, was "numerically the weakest and geographically the smallest of the three Great Powers." [the report goes on] ". . . in the minds of our big partners, especially that of the United States, there is a feeling that Great Britain is now a secondary power and can be treated as such." . . . [I]t was "essential to increase our strength." This was to be achieved in two ways: by encouraging "cooperation between the three Great Powers," and by British leadership in the Dominions, France and smaller West European powers—"only so shall we be able in the long run to compel our two big partners to treat us as an equal". . . . Attack was the best form of defence. Britain should take the offensive in "challenging Communist penetration . . . in eastern Europe and in opposing any bid for control of Germany, Italy, Greece and Turkey". . . . Early in 1947 the Foreign Office updated Sargent's 1945 *Stocktaking* paper . . ."the balance of military strength, particularly in Europe, had

altered to the advantage of the Soviet Union". In 1945, Sargent had envis-
aged Britain's economic recovery; by 1947, economic ills seemed incurable:
"we have seldom been able to give sufficient economic backing to our policy. . . . Too great independence of the United States would be a dangerous
luxury. . . . We do not seem to have any economic resources available for
political purposes."[9]

By 1947, the British were quickly becoming disabused of their illusions. They
gave up hopes of leading an independent Europe. Unable to control areas they
formerly grasped firmly, like India, Palestine, Greece, and Turkey, they turned to
the United States to help manage their security. They began channeling their influence through the "special relationship" with America.

Meanwhile, West German and French ministers were working to overcome their
recent hostilities by using a combination of functionalist and realist theory. If they
could cooperate in industry, it would make it harder to go to war and may even
spill over into a greater range of cooperative endeavors. At the same time, the clear
and present danger of the USSR focused minds. As Sebastian Rosato and Michael
Sutton nicely demonstrate, balance of power thinking shadowed European policymakers, particularly in France and Germany, and fueled the success of the European Coal and Steel Community (ECSC) in 1950.[10]

The United States was concerned that it could not underwrite the defense of
Europe indefinitely and pressed Europeans to integrate more. Neill Nugent succinctly covers the key series of events:

In the early 1950s, against the backdrop of the Cold War and the outbreak of
the Korean War [June 1950], many Western politicians and military strate-
gists saw the need for greater Western European cooperation in defence matters. This would involve the integration of West Germany—which was not a
member of NATO—into the Western Alliance. The problem was that some
European countries, especially France, were not yet ready for German rear-
mament, whilst Germany itself, though willing to re-arm, was not willing to
do so on the basis of the tightly controlled and restricted conditions that
other countries appeared to have in mind for it. In these circumstances the
French Prime Minister, René Pleven, launched proposals in October 1950
which offered a possible way forward. In announcing his plan to the National
Assembly he stated that the French government "proposes the creation, for
our common defence, of a European Army under the political institutions of
a united Europe". . . . In May 1952 a draft EDC [European Defence Commu-
nity] Treaty was signed, but in the event the EDC, and the European Political

Community which increasingly came to be associated with it, were not established. Ratification problems arose in France and Italy, and in August 1954 the French National Assembly rejected the EDC. . . . [There was] a feeling that, with the end of the Korean War and the death of Stalin, the EDC was not as necessary as it had seemed when it was first proposed.[11]

The Americans were looking for West Germany to join NATO, but France was not eager for its erstwhile enemy to rearm under such terms. So, as an alternative, France put forward the Pleven Plan, which, merging with the logic of the ECSC, evolved into a call for a European Defense Community (EDC). The EDC was not a strictly European entity; it would be an adjunct to NATO and serve under the NATO commander. Armies still answered to their national governments (except West Germany's, naturally) and states still preserved ultimate authority, but the EDC would have created something like a European army with central budgeting and procurement.

Nonetheless, even with compromises, France quickly backed away from the supranationalism it had introduced. The United Kingdom's interest in the proposal was lukewarm at best; the UK always feared that too much European cooperation might provide an excuse for America to abscond. West Germany could never spearhead such a plan. By 1952, the French were asking for American guarantees to militarily intervene if West Germany tried to withdraw from the EDC. France feared that it could not control West Germany; Britain feared that Europe could not manage the Soviet threat; everyone agreed that American involvement was tolerable in order to keep, as the saying goes, "the Germans down and the Soviets out." With no champion, the EDC died.[12]

What ensued were several rounds of European states pressing the United States to help Europe, while the Americans were wary of sacrificing their autonomy and infantilizing their allies. American policymakers would have preferred that Europeans centralize the tools of statecraft and did all they could to encourage the project, but efforts repeatedly fizzled. Ideas for unification were tossed about, but, like the EDC, the ideas were non-starters and by the mid-1950s all were dead. The next best solution was for the United States to underwrite the system of European defense.

The United States commitment to Europe, made partly as a desire to facilitate union, hampered unification. With the American security guarantee, Europeans had less incentive to integrate militarily and less incentive to unify. John Foster Dulles suspected the United States had made this error: "It is possible that the historian may judge that the Economic Recovery Act [Marshall Plan] and the Atlantic Pact [NATO] were the two things which prevented a unity in Europe which in the long run may be more valuable than either of them."[13] With an American pacifier firmly in place, Europe was protected against the Germans and the Soviets, and European politicians could safely speak bromides about "union."

Originally, American policymakers had feared that they could not sustain the public support and financial drain of provisioning European defense. Over time, they realized that those assumptions were false, but they still felt that the Europeans were behaving poorly. Dean Acheson was irritated by what he saw as ingratitude and idiocy: "What was so hard for me to understand was how the Germans and French, who had seen us go to great lengths to respond to statesmanlike efforts on their part, could risk their own defense and future, as they were now doing, in petty political squabbling."[14]

Europeans Talk about Union, 1955–1990

With the failure of the EDC, pro-union advocates cast about for a way to pick up the pieces. In 1955, the Western European Union (WEU) was formed. Basically a watered down consultative body for defense matters, the WEU was designed to mask the failure of the EDC and get integration back on track. The WEU was found wanting, so in 1957 the Rome Treaties called for a European Economic Community (EEC) and European Atomic Energy Community (EURATOM), organizations that would eventually transform into the EU.[15]

Progress in the 1960s was mostly economic. Several states agreed to a loose European free trade association as an alternative to the EEC, and the EEC approved its Common Agricultural Policy (CAP). The big news in the 1960s was France under Charles DeGaulle championing a more assertive role for states' rights. DeGaulle denied Britain's request to join the EEC and pushed for greater Franco-German cooperation, at the expense of American leadership. Incredulous and annoyed, President Kennedy implied that if the Germans wanted the French instead of the Americans they could have them. The West Germans were not about to swap their American benefactor for a French one, effectively isolating the French and undercutting their leadership bid. From the mid-1960s on, Europeans would dicker over the details of their reliance on the United States, but the reliance remained sturdy.

The 1970s and 1980s were not a notably productive period for integration, though several new members joined the EEC and pro-union advocates could point to some institutional attainments, such as parliamentary elections, advances toward monetary union, and diminished border controls. An exception to this generalization is the Single European Act of 1987, which laid the groundwork for the Maastricht Treaty five years later.

Europeans Consider Union, 1991–1995

December 1991 was an extraordinary time in Europe. Germany had reunified, the USSR was in its death throes, the Maastricht Treaty had been approved by the European Council, turning the EEC into the EU, and many Eastern European states were gravitating toward the EU. In the unpredictable days of the Cold War's demise, the EU strung together a swift, surprising series of successes. In spite of the odd setback, the Maastricht Treaty gained assent from key states, a raft of legislation was completed, and steps were made to bring numerous new states into the agreement—by 1995 there were fifteen members, up from the original six in 1957. Large strides were made in European integration at a time when America became peerless and geopolitical uncertainty was high. Certainly Maastricht was a product of many forces and negotiations had gone on for years, but as Robert Art shows, geopolitics was uppermost in leaders' minds.[16]

Europeans Talk about Union, 1996–Present

European politicians have been busy over the last 15 years, but their accomplishments have largely solidified integration rather than advanced it. A sequence of treaties were drafted at Amsterdam (1997), Nice (2001), Rome (2004), and Lisbon (2009), conservatively tinkering and streamlining the rules of the EU. In a 1996 meeting in Berlin, NATO members agreed to the European Security and Defense Policy (ESDP, now called the Common Security and Defense Policy, CSDP), which permitted European states to act in concert where NATO chose not to. And France and Britain met in Saint Malo in 1998 to develop joint force projection capability to give credible support to the ESDP. These developments deserve emphasis: Europe has institutionalized the ability to act militarily without the United States or NATO.

In 2003 the EU issued a European Security Strategy, laying out a common, if vague and non-binding, foreign policy perspective from Brussels. As part of the Lisbon Treaty, the European External Action Service (EEAS) is in the process of setting up a foreign ministry and diplomatic headquarters for the EU. These are all good indications of an intention to set up the forms, if not always the functions, of a confederal foreign policy. And the recent world financial crisis has rocked the EU, but in spite of some loose talk and minor friction, no policies indicate that the Franco-German relationship is in anything other than rude health.

For all this activity though, the overall impact has been stasis and the effects specifically on foreign policy cooperation have been modest. European states have moved slightly closer to each other, but in terms of foreign policy cooperation they remain far from unifying. The rapid reaction force (RRF) is not an independent army at the disposal of the EU but a group of national units, whose participation is conditional on the consent of member states. The EU develops security strategy, though to date that has been largely aspirational. Authority continues to rest in state capitals and, most germane for this study, there is little institutionalization with teeth. States receive the lion's share of the tax revenues, states have ultimate authority over foreign policy, and national militaries weakly integrate their planning, training, and doctrine.

Today it appears that integration has hit a glass ceiling, and unification in the sense used in this work has not been a viable policy in over 50 years. Yet it is worth pointing out that Western Europe has done quite well for itself. With their own Herculean labors and a hefty dollop of outside help, Western European states have consistently defied pessimists' conclusions, achieving an economic miracle, economic stability (albeit with sluggish growth of late), monetary union, entrenched democratic institutions, a favorable diplomatic reputation, and security on the cheap. Not all of these attainments will last and some are likely to look less attractive with the passage of time, but relative to the rest of European history, the last several decades are marvelous.

ARGUMENT

Opportunity: Background Conditions

Intensity

European political integration has varied with external threat, and Europe has not been in the security environments that successful unions have.[17] Early in the Cold War, there was some hope that a unified Europe could balance against the USSR on its own, but as the Soviet threat cast a longer shadow, more and more people came to the conclusion that Europe could not balance independently. The threat became too intense and unification would have been a treacherous, exhausting exercise to arrive at the same fate. Only in the infancy of the Cold War did the USSR approach what might have been an optimally intense threat to Western Europe.[18]

But Dulles's concern at the time turned out to be spot on; the American security blanket obviated the need for greater integration. Acheson was arrogant to view his European counterparts as foolish ingrates; Europeans were simply maximizing their security through external balancing. Unifying would have been more expensive and dicey—colossal Soviet forces were massed on the Inner German border; mounting a timely and credible deterrent with only Western European forces looked unlikely. Nonetheless, the pressures of geopolitics and American policy left institutions and indentations. Their legacy can be seen in the uneven steps taken toward integration and several generations of Europeans socialized to new values.

When great geopolitical uncertainty returned to the continent at the end of the Cold War, integration efforts reignited. Yet Russia was not the Soviet Union; when the latter collapsed, the former had more in common with the Third World than the First. Such a basket case could not motivate unification. Today, Europe's vital interests are secure, and one can see this in European defense debates and public opinion data.[19] The same security that makes it easier for places like Scotland and Catalonia to move away from the British and Spanish governments also makes it harder for France and Germany to move toward each other.

Duration

The United States transforms Europe's security environment and makes it much harder for the forces of self-help unification to work. The United States is irritating, and current alignments reflect this.[20] But the United States has yet to disturb Europe's vital interests and, perhaps redundantly, makes sure that continental conquest would not pay, effectively rendering incredible the nudges needed for unification. Russia, imploded or resurgent, has to date provided only passing nettles to Europe (e.g., interrupting energy supplies). China remains too weak and aloof. In short, no state or combination of states on the horizon appears close to constituting a threat necessary for union.

Symmetry

On the face of things, European integration has much going for it. History does not support Europeans' excuses for their lack of union. For instance, some blame Europeans' lack of interest in integration on EU institutions not demonstrating functional competence.[21] In the most excellent examples—the United States, Switzerland, Sweden-Norway, and Gran Colombia—nowhere were federal institutions revered for their great efficacy.

Others ascribed failure to a host of intractable issues: concerns about accountability, transparency, and relative gains. In historical perspective, these excuses look lame. The United States faced these problems too—plus the monstrosity of slavery—and still managed to craft a country. Sweden and Norway were deeply distrustful of each when they attempted union, and Switzerland could have wrangled over linguistic, ethnic, or religious differences—instead, it unified. Gran Colombia is a poor parallel in this regard, having few rancorous issues at the time of unification, but in all cases what helped quell internal issues was external danger.[22]

All of the closest comparisons overcame mammoth obstacles. The United States balanced against offshore powers and overcame ill-defined identity, a democratic deficit, and thorny bargaining issues to build their state. Americans may believe their presence spares Europe from itself, but that may be an irony of history. In the 1770s, the British justified their dominance of North America by contending that the British pacifier spared Americans from falling victim to each other or French depredations. The period following American independence gave the lie to that claim, though barely.[23] Switzerland came together after centuries of bickering and several civil wars. Gran Colombia surmounted inchoate nationalism, paltry foreign aid, fierce foreign resistance, and incredible logistical problems. Sweden-Norway was born in the ashes of major European war and in spite of long-standing mutual antipathy and occasional wars. The EU's present problems pale in comparison.

On the bright side, Germany and France now have a long history of cooperation under their belts. They form a powerful, compact core that would not suffer from collective action problems and they share borders, which aids security interdependence. They possess an institutional foundation and strong democratic traditions on which to build a union and, ostensibly, popular support from the great and the many. These are all good reasons for sustained integration, but not union.

Yet more importantly, Europe is at the core of world politics; all of the cases in this book were on the periphery. Peripheral states are probably not worth much bother, but a new superpower would frustrate the foreign policies of other powers. Great powers would be tempted to prevent such a union or break it up once unification got under way by playing off some Europeans against others. This touches directly on EU enlargement. As the number of EU member states grows, it will be harder to solve collective action problems.

If EU proponents aim to expand the economic pie and promote democracy, then enlargement is all for the better. But if proponents are serious about creating a pole of international power or a political union, contraction is wiser. Of course, one need not choose. Due to the multiplicity of institutions in Europe, large and small groupings are possible at the same time.

According to Christopher Layne and others, the United States has a long track record of employing divide-and-rule strategies in Europe when European cooperation could aggravate American foreign policy. There are plenty of cleavages to take advantage of. British interests have historically been quite separable from those of its continental cousins, and more recently Secretary of Defense Donald Rumsfeld distinguished between "old Europe" and "new Europe."[24] The situation is more intricate, though; the more actively the United States intervenes in European affairs, the more likely unification becomes. So long as American interference stops shy of threats to vital interests, European unification will stall.

Fortune: Crisis Trigger

Crises come and crises go, but without adequate background conditions, no crisis is likely to bestir Europe to unify. Keep in mind the crises Europe has experienced without unification efforts getting off the ground: hundreds of Soviet divisions on the Inner German border, the Berlin Crises, the Cuban Missile Crisis, German reunification, economic booms and busts, and the list sprawls on. Yet should a crisis or crises reveal conducive background conditions, unification could suddenly become a live option. Union has come as something of a surprise in many of the cases in this work.

Virtue: Elite Persuasion

Pro-union Europeans are scattering seeds on inhospitable soil. The most dynamic, persuasive sages would have an impossible time unifying contemporary Europe. The media landscape is more treacherous than it used to be, and there is a limit to what can be attained through political procedures. Perhaps critically, military cajoling is off the table in Europe as it was not in prior examples.

Media

The previous cases in this study all unified prior to 1850, and changes in the media since then have been massive. On the one hand, dog whistle politics may be easier. With the diversity of media forms, segmented audiences, and significant government presence in European media, it would be possible for pro-union forces to mobilize backers without mobilizing opposition. Countervailing this is that the reach of modern media is much greater, the speed at which news travels much faster, and the coverage of modern media is more expansive. Elites in advanced democracies cannot control the media like they used to, and this makes unification a battle at an even steeper incline. Surely manipulating the press is still possible, but doing so has grown more demanding.

Military

Conditions are poor for European elites to use the military instrument to facilitate union. The American security umbrella is a formidable barrier to threatening force in Western Europe. Even without American guarantees, taking and holding territory by force does not have the allure it once held. Professional militaries are more tied down than they used to be, and the core European states either possess nuclear weapons or are spitting distance away from possessing them. A George Washington or William Henry Dufour born in modern Europe would live out his days in obscurity.

Political Procedures

Given the byzantine bureaucracies of the EU and the elaborate machinery of advanced states, one can imagine political procedures cutting both ways. One logic is that the complexity of the EU and its component states allows small, dedicated groups to move faster than cumbersome institutions in effecting union. Another logic is that the cumbersome institutions have many veto points that can block change. I believe the historical record supports the first view more than the second. All of the cases under consideration circumvented obstructionist institutions, some of which were entrenched.

This raises the matter of Europe's "democratic deficit." This excuse for Europe's failure to integrate further is largely a myth; European institutions and legitimacy actually compare favorably to national institutions. But if Europe follows the best cases of integration, constitutional ratification will not be a triumph of pristine democracy. Europe is already practicing this page of its predecessors' playbook. As Eric Hobsbawm notes, "The EU was explicitly constructed on a nondemocratic (i.e., non-electoral) basis, and few would seriously argue that it would have got where it is otherwise."[25] I would add that it is unlikely to get where it is ostensibly going otherwise. Institutions are important, but, in spite of years of wrangling with verbiage and rules, no institutional fix would make European unification palatable. A legal cast of mind cannot solve these problems.

ALTERNATE EXPLANATIONS

How will Europe unify? The received wisdom is ever closer union, a gradual process of trial-and-error economic and administrative cooperation, where success is neither continuous nor automatic yet is nevertheless occurring —and at a respectable clip too. Analysts at the CIA predict that Europe will unite by 2015, and Charles Kupchan makes the case that European integration is faring well, relatively speaking, and that Europe faces problems the United States faced at the end of the nineteenth century.[26] Three logics underpin the ever closer union notion: constructivist, liberal, and binding.

Constructivism

Craig Parsons advances the most persuasive constructivist argument on European integration.[27] He contends that adverse events in the first half of the twentieth century shook up how elites thought about Western European politics. After World War II, a small group of elites, who had radical ideas, came to positions of prominence. They had "a certain idea of Europe," and this perspective informed their choices to build supranational institutions in the 1950s.

At base, Parsons makes an idea entrepreneur argument, which ties directly to Adler and Barnett's claims. In every case in this work, peoples were thrown together, and farsighted elites labored to stitch them together. These elites all had "certain ideas" in their heads, and doubtless material conditions did not foreordain detailed political outcomes. But this is beside the point; no one is making a structural determinist argument. The issue is one of causal priority, and the evidence suggests that the international environment was the most important factor. Elites met bad ends when their ideas did not match a favorable distribution of power, but within those parameters they had freedom of maneuver.

Parsons's argument is provocative, but has an ad hoc element to it. He does not say why leaders with visions of a European community came to power in the right places at the right times, nor why they were more or less ambitious. The "certain idea of Europe" is posited exogenously, and it is not clear where it came from, when it will return, or why other people who did not share it went along with it for years. Rigorous empirical scrutiny reveals that the role of EU entrepreneurs has been greatly exaggerated.[28]

Moreover, the causal logic on war and memory is double-edged. Parsons argues that memories of war were an inducement to integration. One may equally argue that negative memories of war were a barrier to integration—the French and Germans could not trust each other after the World Wars. And one may also argue that both of these pressures were active simultaneously. But without a causal mechanism about when one tide will overwhelm the other, wartime memories may explain everything and nothing.

Parsons's model is underspecified and does not say how memory works and over what sort of time spans. Furthermore, empirical support in the present universe of cases is weak. The North American states fought a successful war together and then unified. The Swiss cantons fought a series of wars against each other over centuries, the last and least bloody of which led to unification. Sweden and Norway showed few signs of war fatigue and were readying to fight each other before they formed a quasi-union. South American states fought a destructive war for independence, but this led only to a temporary union. None of these instances fit Parsons's narrative. Constructivist causes are too frail to explain or predict unification.

Liberalism

There is no case where economic preferences and coalitions caused unification, not in Europe, not anywhere. The best liberal work on integration in Europe does not make this point, and so this section switches to discussing Andrew Moravcsik's sophisticated liberal intergovernmental arguments. The core of his argument is: "EU integration can best be understood as a series of rational choices made by national leaders. These choices responded to constraints and opportunities stemming from the economic interests of powerful domestic constituents, the relative power of states . . . and the role of institutions in bolstering the credibility of interstate commitments."[29]

He and I agree that security considerations are the primary cause of unification and that institutions help stabilize political integration moves. Where we come out differently is on the source of state preferences and the importance of economic factors. His study is more geographically (i.e., European) focused than mine but more conceptually broad (i.e. he examines more than foreign policy unification), and this may account for some of our differences.

Moravcsik pays special attention to domestic interest groups as a source of policy preferences. This is empirically true some of the time, but if security considerations are the primary cause of foreign policy integration, then it is theoretically superfluous. Domestic interest groups will generally have the same preferences as governmental elites; thus we arrive in the same place with an extra step. If security considerations are primary and economic interests secondary, then we are only quibbling over details.

The overriding point is that the original liberal plank for ever closer union has rotted out. Where Ernst Haas once extolled economic interests as more important than security factors for uniting Europe, now the most distinguished liberal scholar on Europe has reversed Haas's causal priority. Realists and liberals will never run out of things to debate, but on the issue of European unification they are more alike than not.

Binding

The basic logic of binding is that states try to tie down or defuse the threat of war by intertwining themselves with their potential enemy. Seth Jones makes a convincing case that politicians weave a mesh of institutions over Europe because they fear that an independent Germany might spark war.[30] Pushed to its logical conclusion, binding could unify Europe.

Surely at lower levels of integration, binding explanations have much merit. Post-Cold War European politics featured marked concern, inside Germany and out, about an untethered Germany generating war. Art sums the evidence well: "Therefore with the French trying to 'Gulliverize' Germany, with the British balancing against it, with the other states of Europe warily watching it, and with its citizens having their own concerns about their future, [German Chancellor Helmut] Kohl strongly supported the creation of a meaningful European Defense Identity and the preservation of a strong NATO."[31]

Still, binding appears to be a feeble foundation for union. Several horrible European wars and anxious decades have passed without leading to a binding union. Britain and France are nuclear powers; Germany could become one in record speed if it decided to; there is at least the technical possibility of destructive war. But union in the sense of this work is not necessary to keep the peace tolerably; Europeans seem to be doing just fine without it. States speak with their deeds that they are keen on autonomy. A range of American officials have repeatedly solicited European troops for NATO missions, and their pleas have generally fallen on deaf ears. A range of European initiatives to boost the CSDP have been modest and fanned few passions.

There is an interesting counterfactual that binding theorists should answer: What would Europe have looked liked without the Soviet threat? If one believes binding arguments, the "German problem" would have led to approximately the same levels of integration. American elites would have feared Germany lighting another war so much that they would have spurred the institutional tethering that led to the EU. The logic of binding suggests accommodation would have been a priority with postwar American planners, at least on a par with balance of power considerations.

But this view receives little support from the historical record. Alliances frequently feature worries about what would happen if one of the partners slipped its leash, but that is different from establishing that this caused observed behavior. Fear of an independent Germany was real, but the evidence suggests that, were it not for the gathering Soviet threat, the United States would have implemented something closer to the Morgenthau Plan. Absent the red menace, Germany would now look like a cross between Poland and France.

There is more than one way to defang a potential adversary, and a binding story is not confirmed by the early choices of postwar U.S. policy. When external threat was lower, between 1944 and 1947, American policymakers were worried about future recrudescence of war within their bloc, but that was an insufficient cause of significant integration. Only increasing external threat did that. And this is no crude correlation. American policymakers were clear and consistent: it was the Soviet threat—not the desire to accommodate Germany, France, or Britain and avoid war—that quickly swung policy from the Morgenthau to the Marshall Plan.

Individually or collectively, the three planks that bolster hopes for Europe's ever closer union are too rickety to support union. Europeans have had ample contact and been exposed to extraordinarily talented idea entrepreneurs, yet integration seems to be plateauing. There are outstanding economic reasons to increasingly integrate Europe, yet even the foremost liberal theorist on Europe rates economic factors as a secondary cause of unification. And binding has had modest success in politically integrating European states but no success in unifying them. That does not mean that the three arguments are a flimsy basis for other forms of integration or that efforts to unify Western Europe are futile. But if the desire for unification is more than a velleity, plans for ever closer union should key on external threat.

PREDICTIONS

So much for the past, what about the future? Rosato is of the opinion that, with the Russian threat gone, the EU will wither away until it is at best a free trade area. On the other side, Moravcsik believes that the EU will emerge from the current world financial crisis stronger than ever because European states would rather swim together than sink apart.[32] My crystal ball is cloudy, but paradoxically my pessimism predicts a guardedly optimistic middle course between these two views. This section lays out what I think I know, what I think I do not, and how I see these factors unfolding.[33]

How Europe balances in the future has much to do with what quarter the threat comes from and how much. The most likely source of danger is Russia, but one cannot rule out competition with the United States or China in the distant future. Table 8.1 is a rough estimate of Europe's relative power. One should keep in mind that geography, proximity, technology, and synergy complicate the picture, and that different states track defense expenditures differently. Nevertheless, it is an adequate first cut at how states might countervail each other. What the table underscores is that Western Europe need not balance strenuously against Russia; if anything, Russia needs to balance to catch up.[34]

In the short run, with a conventional definition of vital interests, the outlook is favorable that no state will endanger Europe. It seems probable that the prolonged period of great power peace will continue; land is harder and less valuable

TABLE 8.1

Europe's Balance of Power, 2007

Country	Population	GDP	Defense Expenditures
Germany	82	3.0	38
France	61	2.3	53
United Kingdom	61	2.4	52
Italy	58	1.5	31
Spain	40	1.3	13
Ger+Fr	143	5.3	91
Ger+Fr+U.K.+It+Sp	302	10.5	187
Russia	142	1.7	59
United States	298	13.2	583

Source: International Institute for Strategic Studies 2007. Population is in millions for the year 2007; GDP is in trillions of U.S. dollars and in official exchange rate terms for the year 2006. Defense Expenditures are from 2005 and given in billions of dollars in market exchange rate terms, except the United States, which indicates 2007 authorized total national defense expenditures.

to take and hold; security is not scarce; hostility spirals are unlikely to get off the ground.[35] This may be good for the world but not for European unification. So too, it is striking that the focus of this chapter, Germany and France, do not really need additional states to form a world power. Their growth and birth rates are slow, but unified they would create a technologically adept state significantly larger than China or Japan (at market exchange rates) and about as relatively capable economically as the Soviet Union in its prime—that is, a bipolar world— in short order. Without conditions demanding unification, however, no union will be supplied.

In the longer run, hegemonic states are particularly prone to lapses of judgment and overbearing behavior. Without a Soviet-scale threat, American accommodation and German deference cannot be taken for granted. If unipolarity endures, America's growing footprints in Eastern Europe and the Middle East have the potential to snowball into the kind of anxiety and acrimony that galvanize integration efforts. Nonetheless, unipolarity is unlikely to endure, America's attention will be directed primarily at China, and nuclear weapons and the changing calculus of conquest make threats to Europe less exigent.[36] But this is no sure bet, and threats, like icebergs, can come from unexpected places. American policy gaffes, a rebounding Russia, and great power resource competition are not negligible risks, and prudent elites will act accordingly.

Laying my cards on the table, here is what I think I know: the most important factors in Europe's future will be growth rates and defense spending among the world powers. Balance of power theory suggests that coalitions form to check each other, but it says little about which of the numerous potential coalitions will turn into actual coalitions. My working assumptions have been that, because of proximity and relative power, Germany and France are the most likely coalition partners, and could ultimately form a union. But these assumptions may prove false.

As for what I do not know, only economists can predict growth rates and they intercept the future intermittently, no one can predict revolutions, and anyone can predict that over long periods of time surprises and accidents will jostle the best models. States may adopt risky or reckless foreign policies despite contrary incentives, new ideas may constrain how the game of politics is played, and unforeseen technologies may contort the direction of international relations.

My best guess of how this will play out is guardedly optimistic for pessimistic reasons. Since I believe unification too distant a prospect, my remarks relate to the lesser goal of sustaining present integration. American policy in Europe has been so successful it has made itself redundant. This is an accomplishment for which we ought to honor George Marshall, George Kennan, Chip Bohlen, and Lucius Clay.[37] Germans and French have no plans to fight each other and are strong enough to fend for themselves. States love autonomy; when 1940s Britain and 1960s France thought they were strong enough to lead a more independent Europe, they tried to. Contemporary Paris and Berlin are in a stronger position to lead Europe and show little compunction about doing so. That looks like the future.

Rosato and I view the causes of European integration, the course of European history, and the present threats to Europe in essentially the same way. And yet our predictions diverge, I suspect, because my pessimism is greater: he sees threats to Europe as benign and likely to stay that way; I do not. Obviously, politicians obsess about the next election, and much political thinking is myopic. But my interpretation of history is that states think long-term in foreign policy far more than is appreciated. Alliances are insurance policies, and Germany and France could use expensive insurance.

America's continental commitment is waning and shows every sign of continuing to wane. Europe cannot count on conditions staying as congenial as they are currently, and no one knows Europe's best interests better than European powers. Cooperation is the best preparation for the inevitable storms over the horizon. In sum, the changing distribution of power is a powerful incentive for the hedged status quo to continue, with or without secondary states. But for now, no outside power has much incentive to tamper with Europe's vital interests, and so union will have to wait.

CONCLUSION

Europe is not the only potential candidate for a modern voluntary union, but it has gotten the closest.[38] My central finding is that the abiding arguments behind ever closer union are false idols. However, a realist explanation is more promising: states unify to balance against threats to their vital interests. This could be good news for the EU's present malaise, but likely it is not. The blessing of the Atlantic security community has been a curse for European unification, sapping the need for unification. Only when America's continental commitment grows intrusive or inadequate can Europe unify.

Unification between equals is hard, messy work. There are terrific templates for would-be unifiers, but they should be aware of what a daunting, dangerous task unification is. When it comes to union, all good things do not go together, and grave trade-offs must be made with respect to democracy and threats of force. Union proponents should be aware that the prospects are inauspicious for uniting non-peripheral states in response to non-state threats.

As I said, voluntary unions—the United States, Switzerland, and Gran Colombia— are the most excellent examples for Europe to follow. But different examples are more relevant at different times, and for contemporary Europe one example stands above the others. Discussing attitudes after World War I, A. J. P. Taylor observed that Europeans dreamed "of a painless revolution, in which men would surrender their independence and sovereignty without noticing that they had done so."[39] No nation has come closer to living that dream than the United States, and the politicians who founded it were guided by an extensive knowledge of history.

In *Federalist* no. 18, James Madison pondered the example of the Achaean League, a confederation of Greek city-states that squabbled among themselves rather than unite.[40] Rome befriended the Achaeans and defeated their nearest enemy, becoming the sole superpower in the Mediterranean basin. With a foothold established, Rome kept the peninsula divided, relegating it to a political afterthought. America avoided repeating the Achaeans's pitiable experience, and in so doing left an instructive example for succeeding generations. Those who desire similar ends may have need of similar means.

Unity is always effected by means of brutality . . .

—ERNEST RENAN[1]

9

Conclusion

THIS WORK HAS investigated how and why states unify, not revising realism so much as returning to its origins. I argued that unification occurs when states face an optimally intense, indefinite, and symmetrically shared threat; a security crisis opens a window of opportunity; and elites persuade relevant audiences of union's necessity through the media, the military, and political procedures. This logic, run backwards, helps explain state disintegration.

The competing explanations were tested against the complete universe of cases, and a main finding is that my argument did not depict the best way to voluntary union; it depicted the only way. What remains is threefold. The first section summarizes the cases, the second discusses theoretical implications, and the third is devoted to policy implications.

CASE PROFILES

We have examined the universe of cases: two successes and two failures. What they have in common is that they are attempts at voluntary political union—that is, unifications where conquest was not a viable option and where great power patrons were not compelling union. They are efforts at egalitarian, self-help unification.

The first case of successful union is the United States, a hard case for my argument. Following the Revolutionary War, Great Britain still posed an intense threat to its former colonies, through its perceived hostility to them, through its presence in Canada, through its reputed use of Native Americans against the former colonists, through its maritime supremacy, and through its failure to fully withdraw. Spain posed similar if lesser threats in the South; its bottling up of the Mississippi River endangered states with secessionism and sectional rivalries. Key American elites felt these threats acutely and began agitating for unification. Seizing upon Shays's Rebellion, elites were in prime positions to control the flow of information, make credible military threats, and manipulate political procedures. Luckily, like other major steps in 1803 and 1848, America's unification around 1790 benefited from distractions in Europe.

The second instance of successful union is the Swiss. Switzerland unified after the French conquered the country and demonstrated that the previous system of Swiss alliances was untenable. Attempts to push back the clock were unsuccessful and, ahead of the European curve, several cantons saw that they would be safer unified with their longtime allies than by themselves or as tiny provinces of larger states. Elites pressed the issue in print, in procedures, and by arms, forcing the other cantons to choose between the devil they knew and the devil they did not. Through an almost bloodless war, the Swiss cantons decisively banded together indefinitely to balance against shared symmetrical threats, and tightened their bonds as those threats grew.

The first example of liminal union is Sweden and Norway. The two states came together after the Napoleonic Wars to brace against future great power threats. But Norway had acquitted itself well during the war and did not share the same level of threat as Sweden. Lacking intensity and symmetry, Norway resisted unification, and the ambiguous terms of union were made a shell by subsequent Norwegian actions. Finally, when the fear of foreign interference had ebbed and the two states had divergent foreign policy interests, Norwegian elites stepped up propaganda measures, started procedural initiatives, and militarized their border. Sweden and Norway were brought together by moderate pressures, and as the pressures faded, their quasi-union faded too.

The second case of union undone is Gran Colombia. It came together to face Spain and became incoherent because the Spanish threat vanished. Initially, Spain was a ferocious threat, symmetrically afflicting the northernmost states of South America, and was expected to remain a danger for some time. Following Spain's removal, no foreign power posed a threat to the members of Gran Colombia, making unity unpalatable. Despite brandishing legendary powers of persuasion, possessing a mighty army, and installing his candidates in critical positions, Simón Bolívar fell from power because he refused to adjust to a power distribution antithetical to union. South American states threatened each other more than foreign powers threatened them; elites who acted in line with this reality were rewarded, while those who did not were pummeled. For this reason Bolívar's quixotic mission failed.

Europe, the area with highest hopes for unity, has poor prospects. All the conventional wisdoms behind ever closer union are deeply flawed, and advocates of a united Europe should rethink the path to union. Without a threat like those the Americans or Swiss faced at their births, the core European states will fail to merge. Even should a unifying threat emerge, elites must be aware of what difficulties and compromises lie between the current EU and true union.

In sum, the evidence strongly supports the argument. I am aware of no case where voluntary union happened without the conditions described in the argument. It is a promising finding that the causes of union appear not to be distinct from the causes of disunion.

IMPLICATIONS FOR THEORY

Alternative explanations may fare well with less intimate forms of integration, but only geopolitics causes unification. With globalization transforming interactions, constructivist causes should be leading states around the world to unify. While highways, airplanes, telephony, and the Internet may bring people closer together socially, there are sharp limits to what they can do politically. The only successful unification efforts occurred in societies before the communication and transportation revolutions transformed them.

Liberal theories also performed poorly. If integration happens to increase market penetration, then the United States would be just another district in the United Kingdom, and Switzerland would have been absorbed into its neighbors. Instead, both countries have stoutly guarded their independence. Marxists famously thought their revolutions would happen on the cutting edge of capitalism; instead, backward Russia and China led the charge. Like Marxists, liberal theorists believe their unifications should happen on the cutting edge of capitalism; instead, they happen only in the occasional backwater, like postcolonial America and 1840s Switzerland.

Many liberals assert that the distinction between high (security) and low politics (everything else) is bunk; there is little hierarchy of issues in politics.[2] It is this thinking that has led liberals to overoptimistism, overpredicting political integration victories. This book has looked at cases where the liberal view is most likely to work, and has found five cases where high politics was essential to explaining the outcome and no cases where it was inessential. The gauntlet is down; has there ever been a unification through low politics?

Binding theorists are right to stress the security sources of union and the dangers of unifying too much. Yet there is little empirical support for the view that binding can work on the scale that its advocates hope. The fear of war between states has been an impetus behind some alliances, but no unions. Nevertheless, my criticisms should not be pushed too far. There is no sense in letting the best be the enemy of the good; if voluntary unifications are improbable ventures, other paths to peace look comparatively attractive. Realist prescriptions for lasting peace short of union have demonstrated little advantage over the competition and display at best a checkered record.

All unifications are shotgun weddings. Duress and deceit are indispensable elements in even the gentlest unifications. These are hardly hallmarks of voluntarism, and an impartial reader could inquire if the contents of this study have been improperly labeled. To this charge there are several defenses. The claim was only that the focus would be on the more voluntary end of the spectrum, and while all unifications require force and fraud, that does not mean it is force and fraud all the way down. How could it be? It is inordinately difficult for relative equals to coerce each other to stay in a union, especially during the youth of a new state. Dissatisfied partners can choose to exit and summon foreign support as needed.

As for deceit, it is at best a temporary expedient. At some point the moment of extraordinary politics must end. When it does, the new institutions will channel political dissent into less potent alleys, but regimes—and new regimes especially—are not immune to subsequent protest and revolution. If people feel that they have been hoodwinked and their institutions are not serving their needs, extraordinary politics is always an option. Citizens are not sheep; they have rightly shucked off odious unions—for example, Gran Colombia and Sweden-Norway. And the two enduring egalitarian unions—that is, the United States and Switzerland—have been considered model states. Unions may not fit the ideal of voluntary agreements, but they are as voluntary as international politics permits.

Every union relies on brawny arm-twisting; it is only a question of what kind of arm-twisting. Forced unions rely on large asymmetries in power to weld polities, unequal unions rely on the threat of conquest, and equal unions depend on the dangers of destabilizing security competition and foreign intervention. When relatively equal states like Virginia, wittingly or not, coordinate unification to compensate for security shortcomings, they act similarly to unequal states, like Piedmont or Prussia, annexing territory to balance against security threats.

Also of interest is a charge by Robert Keohane. He claims that realism "is better at telling us why we are in such trouble than how to get out of it."[3] As a good liberal, Keohane has his pet solutions, economic interdependence and international organizations, but many others have reached similar conclusions. Alexander

Wendt, Dani Rodrik, and Daniel Deudney all believe that a world state is the way of the future.

There are many ways to decrease conflict and violence, but arguably history's most reliable method is establishing a strong third-party enforcer and entering hierarchy. Union is the path out of anarchy, and this can be followed voluntarily or involuntarily. Few contest the supremacy of realism in explaining involuntary unions, but this work has gone farther, arguing that only realism offers a satisfactory explanation for voluntary unions.

So if by "trouble" Keohane means anarchy, his allegation falls flat. Realism is better than its rivals at telling us why we are in such trouble and how to get out of it, but its answer is not a Hollywood ending. Unification is rare, risky, and arduous. When unification was undertaken, it was more about running away from the clutches of some than running into the arms of others, and this logic runs counter to other paradigms. Voluntary union is unlikely to live up to the hopes of idealists (and realists, who are often jilted idealists), but it is still progress to learn the limits of an ideal.

IMPLICATIONS FOR POLICY

A book on state fusion may seem out of place in an era of political fission. But the examples above show that integration and disintegration are interrelated—if the findings are sound, they ought to be continually relevant. The overriding point is that security and unity antagonize each other. For now, the world is a relatively safe place, and that means that the marquee events will be stories of division. Below, I outline two, but the logic applies more broadly.

The Decline of Bipolarity

The breakup of the Soviet Union had far-reaching effects on world politics, making understanding why it dissolved all the more worthwhile. The Soviet Union faced intense great power threats from its inception, during World War II it paid an egregious human toll, and after World War II it faced a wary, nuclear-armed United States. As the Cold War wore on, it became increasingly clear that nuclear weapons made interfering with vital interests infinitely dangerous. After détente, the threat from the First World generally declined. Nonetheless, the USSR was slow to relax its ties. States, like all institutions, have high start-up costs, and when they are entrenched are seldom altered lightly.

Meanwhile, domestic causes eroded the Soviet Union.[4] Soviet oppression alienated satellites that felt an asymmetry between their interests and those of their great power sponsor. When threats decrease in intensity and symmetry, states become susceptible to disassembly. The openness of *glasnost* and *perestroika* paved the way for elites to challenge central authority, and internal factors completed the job that external factors started. Obviously, there is much detail lost at this altitude and much detail that my argument does not account for. Here I only claim that elements of my argument explain some of the Soviet Union's demise, and the evidence there is promising.

Unity in Unipolarity

At the same time, we ought to wonder why we live in a unipolar world. If unions only cohere when there is countervailing pressure, then the United States is ripe for disintegration. It has a hemisphere to itself, it is protected by two massive moats, and it is more powerful than any state or coalition that opposes it. Part of the answer is institutional inertia—discarding institutions that have served superbly in the past and may do so again in the foreseeable future would be insanity. A united Europe and/or a strong China are on the American foreign policy horizon, and are sufficiently threatening to sustain union for decades. If American policymakers want the country to stay together, they are in the awkward position of needing a rival's power to grow, but not too much.

Should these threats fail to materialize and nothing comparable take their place, the United States will become decreasingly united. Indeed, one can argue that we are witnessing the beginning of this process. As the gap between the United States and its largest enemy has grown, the American electorate has grown more polarized.[5] The United States is the most powerful state since Rome, but that analogy has a dark side. "Red" versus "blue" Americans evokes "blue" versus "green" Romans, and the divisions that split the Roman Empire. After Rome crushed its last peer competitor, Carthage, it continued on inertially for several decades, its factions growing deeper until a series of security crises, conspiracies, and cataclysmic civil wars shook Rome for generations. The Roman Empire held together for an impressive length of time, but only with a staggering amount of suffering and the establishment of the Eastern Empire. No peer competitor, no unified state, and other works on Rome's fall reach similar conclusions.[6]

Unity and security seldom cohabitate for long. Should Americans yearn for well-mannered politicians and cooperative citizens, they must have something resembling a peer competitor. Should Americans become enamored with their present level of power, and succeed in maintaining it, their unity will crumble. The United States was founded on the belief that cupidity correlated with capability, that concentrations of power corrupt, that tyranny followed mastery. By the Founders's logic, the greatest threat to the United States is American primacy.[7]

CONCLUSION

I have argued that unions are a matter of opportunity, fortune, and virtue, and tried in the process to break new ground. Still, the conclusions may be thought a letdown, a killjoy, an emotional disenchantment. Let us take a different position.

No story is more honeyed than the story of a nation's beginnings. This work has argued that even the loftiest origins are somewhat earthier, and grow out of foreign foes, force, propaganda, and stormy domestic politics. While this may offend cherished ideals, it need not. We are surrounded by oceans of relationships made possible by unification, and silk is no less beautiful because it comes from worms. A less illusioned understanding of union retains ample romance, and it beats the alternative: neglecting the causes of union invites unnecessary violence. In closing, the potential payoff of this work is to subvert Santayana.[8] Those who cannot remember the past cannot prudently repeat it.

The structure of *The Prince* has always been examined in the hope of finding a solution to the much debated question whether the Italian nationalism of the last chapter formed an integral part of Machiavelli's political outlook or whether it was merely a decorative conclusion—a rhetorical, humanist ornament. . . . I believe we have to accept . . . the last chapter, which is not prepared for by any hint in the preceding sections of the book, stands by itself, mainly intended as a concluding rhetorical flourish.

—FELIX GILBERT[1]

Appendix

MACHIAVELLI AND THE MISSING ROMULUS

ALONE AMONG REALISTS, Machiavelli left developed thought on how self-help behavior can unify relatively equal states—thought that has been lost. He foreshadows his ideas in *The Prince* here and there, but waits until the book's final chapter to tie them together. Then he uncorks a savage surprise ending. So I claim, anyway; determining Machiavelli's message is an inescapably messy matter. He admits that "for a long time I have not said what I believed, nor do I ever believe what I say, and if indeed sometimes I do happen to tell the truth, I hide it among so many lies that it is hard to find."[2] This chapter aims to rediscover his logic and show how my arguments differ from his.

I argue that *The Prince* ends with a darkly detailed death warrant. Through a neglected parallel in chapters 6 and 26, Machiavelli recommends Romulus as the best model of how to go about unifying the fractious states of Italy. Romulus is the most excellent example because he founds a state that unifies Italy by killing his uncle and brother. Dedicating the work to Lorenzo de' Medici and encouraging him to copy Romulus implies horrific undertakings, specifically murdering his uncle, Pope Leo X, and the college of cardinals. Machiavelli cannot openly suggest such actions without courting death and wrecking the chances of surprise attack.

I dissent from Machiavelli because my notion of voluntary union involves less homicide. For Machiavelli, the best way to change minds is to sever heads. His models of Romulus and Rome share with my explanation an emphasis on the balance of power and the importance of force and fraud in politics. We differ, however, on sources and substance. Machiavelli relies on sources that are essentially folklore—because nothing better existed—and his ideas hinge on a single, brutal case. Consequently, his conclusions are considerably more bloodthirsty than mine.

To develop these arguments, I first discuss the puzzles. The second section presents my logic in depth. In the third section, I show the strongest ways to overthrow my logic, and why none of them work. And the final section sums my points and addresses implications of the argument.

THE PUZZLES

The puzzles of this paper can be divided into practical and textual. The practical problem is how to unite Italy. Unification, says Machiavelli, is imperative for the safety and happiness of Italy. There is no question what keeps it divided and weak: the Church. Machiavelli argues:

> And no province has ever been united or happy unless it has all come under obedience to one republic or to one prince, as happened to France and to Spain. . . . Thus, since the church has not been powerful enough to be able to seize Italy, nor permitted another to seize it, it has been the cause that [Italy] has not been able to come under one head but has been under many princes and lords, from whom so much disunion and so much weakness have arisen that it has been led to be the prey not only of barbarian powers but of whoever assaults it.[3]

Although popes are the most powerful actors in the Vatican, cardinals also exert a divisive pull: "Nor will these parties ever be quiet as long as they have cardinals; for cardinals nourish parties, within Rome and without, and the barons are forced to defend them."[4] The problem is that popes create cardinals and vice versa. If a pope dies, cardinals can always select a new one, and popes can do the same for cardinals.

Then there are the semi-powerful Italian city-states to contend with. They stand in the way of unity by jealously guarding their autonomy, and they too would have to be brought under one rule if Italy was not to remain at the mercy of great powers.[5] In short, the practical puzzle is how to rid Italy of the Church's divisive influence and baleful Italian statelets.

But understanding Machiavelli's practical solution requires cracking his textual puzzle first. In the dramatic conclusion of *The Prince*, Machiavelli details the deplorable state of Italy to Lorenzo de' Medici, the young prince to whom the work is dedicated:

> And if, as I said, it was necessary for anyone wanting to see the virtue of Moses that the people of Israel be enslaved in Egypt, and to learn the greatness of spirit of Cyrus, that the Persians be oppressed by the Medes, and to learn the excellence of Theseus, that the Athenians be dispersed, so at present to know the virtue of an Italian spirit it was necessary that Italy be reduced to the condition which she is at present, which is more enslaved than the Hebrews, more servile than the Persians, more dispersed than the Athenians, without head, without order, beaten, despoiled, torn, pillaged, and having endured ruin of every sort.[6]

When Machiavelli remarks, "as I said," there is no ambiguity. The only other time that series occurs is in chapter 6, where he is extolling the "most excellent":

> For since men almost always walk on paths beaten by others . . . a prudent man should always enter upon the paths beaten by great men, and imitate those who have been most excellent, so that if his own virtue does not reach that far, it is at least in the odor of it. . . . I say that the most excellent are Moses, Cyrus, Romulus, Theseus, and the like.[7]

In chapter 6, Machiavelli actually recommends these four illustrious names as a group at least three times.[8] In the grand finale of the book, everyone else reappears, but Romulus disappears. This is a whopping omission. If the idea is to unify Italy, Romulus is the sole founder whose empire did it. Why would Romulus go missing when his example is the most relevant?

ARGUMENT

This section answers three questions: Who is the best example for Italian liberation? How does Machiavelli suggest this example? And why does he make the suggestion under his breath?

The first answer is that Machiavelli omits Romulus not because he is unworthy of recommendation but because he is supremely worthy of recommendation. Although all four founders have much in common, Romulus stands out because he rose to power by executing his uncle and consolidated power by killing his brother.

Applying Romulus's actions to his own situation, Lorenzo might see that by assassinating his uncle, Pope Leo X, and the college of cardinals, he could shatter their legitimacy. Lorenzo would then be free to reorganize the Church and begin conquering an Italian state that could compete with other great powers.

Second, Machiavelli uses a subtle pattern from Livy to pique Lorenzo's curiosity. Third, Machiavelli has to be quiet about his suggestion. The Medici have already singled him out for torture, he is clearly on their bad side, and his anti-papal, parricidal policy goes above and beyond evil. In addition, if Machiavelli's plan were accessible or public, surprise attack would be nearly impossible. Butchering a pope, cardinals, and perhaps also heads of state is easiest with unsuspecting victims. Advertising such a plan ruins it.

Who

Machiavelli's most excellent examples have a lot in common. All are rulers in search of states: Moses founds the spiritual empire that begets Judaism and Christianity; Cyrus creates the Persian Empire; Romulus and Theseus found cities that spawn military and cultural empires. All claim distinguished lineage despite being abandoned at birth by one or both of their parents, and, with the exception of Theseus, were exposed to the elements.[9] All are militarily successful and take upon themselves the task of establishing an empire, typically at a young age.[10] All die unfulfilled if not ignominiously. Moses expires at 120 overlooking the Holy Land he would never reach. Cyrus falls in battle, ironically from a Machiavellian perspective, against a woman, and his empire crumbles.[11] Theseus falls from power, is taken in by a false friend, and thrown from a rock. Romulus dies in a thunderstorm, mythically as if scooped up by the gods, but likely, says Livy, the Senate kills him.

Yet Romulus stands out because his opportunity most resembles Lorenzo's. The reasons are part geography, part heredity. Italy is not being unified so much as reunified, and Romulus's empire was the only one to bring Italy together.[12] As opposed to the other founders, Romulus had no preexisting people and had to create one from disparate groups. Of all the most excellent founders, Romulus alone attained and consolidated his power by assassinating family members.[13] Before founding his new principality, he had to murder his great-uncle Amulius and his brother Remus.

While all the most excellent examples used extraordinary modes to come to power, and all were responsible for many deaths, no one but Romulus founded a new principality directly through killing a near relative. This is not to say that any of the others were guilt free in the decline and fall of family members. Moses was "forced to kill infinite men,"[14] including the pharaoh, in whose house he had lived. Cyrus deposed his grandfather and deceived his uncle, though he did not kill them. Because he forgot to put up the white sail of victory, Theseus caused the suicide of his father. However, Romulus alone founded his state through parricide.

Applying the example of Romulus to Machiavelli's times, Lorenzo's opportunity is strikingly similar. Lorenzo too faces an Italy that is a "mixed" or "disparate" province.[15] If he murdered his uncle, Pope Leo X, and the cardinals (i.e., "brothers"), he could reorder the Catholic Church along civic religious lines, and found a new state unencumbered by the biggest obstacle to unity. Machiavelli is not the enemy of religion; he detests destroyers of religion in the strongest terms, but the Church used Christianity as an infantilizing influence and so should be reformed.[16]

No parallel is perfect, and the parallel between Romulus/Amulius and Lorenzo/Leo X is no exception. Romulus gained prominence violently; Lorenzo inherited his position peacefully. One gained by killing his great-uncle, the other could gain by killing his uncle. One benefited by murdering his blood brother, the other could gain by murdering priestly brothers (Lorenzo did not have a blood brother). But the similarities are striking given the available materials.

Originally, Machiavelli had intended to dedicate *The Prince* to Giuliano de' Medici, Leo X's brother. Giuliano died in 1516, but his family connections support the view that *The Prince* may have been conceived with a consistent conspiracy in mind. Both Giuliano and Lorenzo stood to gain the same prize by the same actions. Of course, the Medici are Machiavelli's best but not only hope to uncover a shortcut to Italian unification; he appeals to "anyone who understands."[17] In any event, Machiavelli, like other writers, tries to kindle curiosity, envy, and ambition in his readers to make them emulate the excellent.

The political roles of the Medici were often at odds with their familial bonds.[18] When Lorenzo was put in charge of Florence, Leo X gave him condescending instructions. Shortly thereafter, Lorenzo explicitly overruled his uncle's instructions on the Florentine governing council. Lorenzo was also put in the resentful role of scapegoat when Florentines did not receive their hoped-for papal patronage.

The flashpoints of further conflict were numerous: marital matches, competition to lead the army in 1515, who should rule Urbino and the Romagna, and Lorenzo's arrogance in governing Florence. Worse still, Lorenzo owed Leo X quite a bit of money, and Leo X accused Lorenzo of treacherous alliance formation, tilting too far toward France. When Lorenzo died, Cardinal Giulio de' Medici rushed to Florence to undo Lorenzo's policies with such haste that he skipped Lorenzo's funeral. Not only was it reasonable to guess at such family tensions, not only were such tensions present, but Machiavelli's correspondence reveals that he knew about these tensions.[19] Murder has happened over less, and Machiavelli could reasonably believe such motives would suffice.

Yet these intramural disputes are redundant. In the examples that Machiavelli provides in *The Prince*, there appears to be long-standing amity prior to the moment of hostility. Consistent with this argument, there are at least three favorable references to nephews increasing their power by deceiving their uncles. Cyrus attained greatness by deceiving his uncle Cyaxares. Giovan Galeazzo Visconti gained a state by killing his uncle Bernabo Visconti, and tried to become king of Italy. And Giovanni Fogliani was killed by his nephew Liverotto da Fermo, who thereby acquired his state. Discord is unnecessary; a glory-seeking prince can make his own opportunity as others have done.[20]

Equally to the point, Machiavelli praises potential papal assassination at least four times. First, in 1505 Machiavelli was present when Giovampagolo Baglioni had a golden opportunity to kill Pope Julius II and the cardinals. He bitterly denounces Giovampagolo's lack of nerve:

> So Giovampagolo, who did not mind being incestuous and a public parricide, did not know—or, to say better, did not dare, when he had just the opportunity for it—to engage in an enterprise in which everyone would have admired his spirit and that would have left an eternal memory of himself as being the first who had demonstrated to the prelates how little is to be esteemed whoever lives and reigns as they do; and he would have done a thing whose greatness would have surpassed all infamy, every danger, that could have proceeded from it.[21]

Similarly, Machiavelli wrote to his friend Vettori, "all the things that have been can, I believe, be again; and I know that pontiffs have fled, gone into exile, been pursued, suffered to the utmost, like temporal rulers, and this in times when the Church in the spiritual matters was more revered than she is today."[22]

Second, Machiavelli infamously details the exploits of Cesare Borgia, son of Pope Alexander VI. Jacob Burckhardt argues: "Unless we are much deceived, this is the real reason of the secret sympathy with which Machiavelli treats the great criminal; from Cesare, or from nobody, could it be hoped that he 'would draw the steel from the wound,' in other words, annihilate the papacy—the source of all foreign intervention and of all the divisions of Italy."[23] Machiavelli also describes Cesare's unification of the Romagna in language that could easily describe unification of Italy: "It had been commanded by impotent lords who had been readier to despoil their subjects than to correct them, and had given their subjects matter for disunion, not for union." So too Machiavelli's admiration of Cesare's cruelty could be instructive to a would-be Italian unifier. For it was Borgia's cruelty that "restored the Romagna, united it, and reduced it to peace and faith."[24]

When cataloging Cesare's virtues in chapter 7, Machiavelli counts among them that "he could have kept anyone from being pope,"[25] leaving ambiguous whether Cesare merely held veto power over pontifical ascension or could eliminate the pope and cardinals altogether. Further, in chapter 8, Liverotto da Fermo gains his patrimony through parricide and Cesare enlarges his by killing Liverotto. The reader may fairly wonder: What benefits would Cesare reap by becoming a parricide like Liverotto? Ultimately, Borgia depends too much on his father, loses his prudence, and meets his political demise. But Borgia began to fulfill Machiavelli's unifying project and his mistakes are educational.

A third instance is in *Florentine Histories* VI.29, when Machiavelli writes an apologia for a would-be assassin of the pope. Stefano Porcari, "a Roman citizen, noble by blood and learning, but much more so by the excellence of his spirit" seeks to kill the pope and restore his fatherland to its ancient form of life. Porcari becomes suspect and is banished to Bologna. Nonetheless, he still undertakes the conspiracy, which is exposed and fails the night before its execution. Machiavelli closes the section ruefully: "The intention of this man could be praised by anyone, but his judgment will always be blamed by everyone because such undertakings, if there is some shadow of glory in thinking of them, have almost always very certain loss in their execution."[26]

Fourth, Machiavelli flatters Gaston de Foix, Duke of Nemours. De Foix, the nephew of Louis XII, is given great credit for his audacity and military exploits throughout the *Discourses*. His untimely death in the Battle of Ravenna was a crushing blow to his army, and turned back an assault on the pope. Prior to the battle, the Duke harangued his troops promising booty in Rome "where the boundless riches of that wicked court . . . will be sacked by you. . . . [de Foix calls for] divine justice to punish . . . the pride and enormous vices of that false Pope Julius. . . ."[27] If title dictated behavior and the duke of Nemours remained an enemy of the pope, the position could have been auspicious. After de Foix, the dukedom of Nemours went to Giuliano de' Medici, the original dedicatee of *The Prince*.

How

Machiavelli may be imitating his favorite historian, employing a Livian pattern of silent but superlative praise. To argue that Machiavelli smiles on instruction by omission, some point to *Discourses* II.10. In this chapter Machiavelli calls Livy a "truer witness than any other" for the opinion that money is not the sinew of war perhaps because "he comes to his conclusion without ever mentioning money."[28] That is, Livy sets his conclusions off in bold relief by conspicuous omission, and Machiavelli is disposed to follow him. Yet I contend this is the wrong model. In *Discourses* II.10, what is obvious and omitted is frowned upon. Scholars have overlooked a better model, where Livy impregnates silence to signal supremacy.

If Machiavelli is looking for a template, Livy provides him with a precise pattern of how to name three individuals while ranking four. Livy tells a story of Hannibal meeting with Scipio after the Second Punic War. Scipio asks Hannibal to rank his top three generals. Hannibal replies that first is Alexander, second is Pyrrhus, and third is himself. Laughing heartily, Scipio inquires where Hannibal would rank himself had Scipio not beaten him. "I should certainly put myself . . . before all other generals!" was Hannibal's response, implying with "Punic subtlety" that Scipio was in a league of his own. So much did Scipio outrank all the greatest generals that Hannibal considered him worthy "beyond calculation."[29]

Why

Machiavelli must suggest his plan stealthily because he risks rebuke by suggesting odious actions openly, strategic surprise aids assassination, and cloaking who the initial targets of Italian unification would be dulls the strength of a balancing coalition.[30] For anyone wishing to retain flexibility or sound out another's position, ambiguity is practically a reflex. And Machiavelli was not just anybody; he was a seasoned diplomat and a sought-after conversationalist—indiscretion was not his wont. With the stakes at lethal levels, ambiguity was a necessity.

Rising to greatness requires fraud, and Lorenzo needs deception just as Machiavelli does. Characteristically, he praises the early Romans for their fraud: "The Romans therefore are seen in their first increases not to be lacking even in fraud, which it is always necessary for those who wish to climb from small beginnings to sublime ranks to use and which is less worthy of reproach the more it is covert, as was that of the Romans."[31]

With regard to plausible deniability, Machiavelli is in a delicate situation advising Lorenzo to kill his uncle. The Medici had previously exiled and tortured him, and the suggestion would horrify most people. Machiavelli needed to be cautious in his counsels, and period sources suggest that he was quite hesitant about circulating *The Prince*. But by setting the agenda, Machiavelli can lead the reader to a door and have the reader enter on his own.[32] Indeed, the structure of *The Prince* can be read as an exercise in reticence. Machiavelli starts the book with a series of apparently neutral classifications, and then ends up by focusing only on virtuous new princes—a poor fit if the book aims to help the already-established

Lorenzo. The final chapter calls for the redeeming of Italy, a great task for a new prince.

With regard to strategic surprise, although it is unclear who the actual readership of *The Prince* was, overtly suggesting papacide would increase the chances that the audience would be exposed and suffer the same fate as Porcari. So too executing the pope and cardinals and announcing oneself as a new Romulus would quickly create a formidable balancing coalition against the new prince. The first targets of incipient Italian political union would be other Italian states, and they could not be expected to await slaughter like lambs. Ancient Rome had to lull its neighbors into thinking it unthreatening and defeat them sequentially to unify Italy.[33] A new Romulus would have to do the same.

On this reading, the bright tone in the final chapter may be employed to disguise or diminish Machiavelli's devilish intent, and the "barbarians" of chapter 26 (and *Discourses* I.12) may be some combination of the pope, the cardinals, and other Italian powers. It could be that the deficiently learned non-Italians were also barbarians, but a precondition to beating those barbarians was beheading the Italian barbarians first.

To close, Machiavelli hid cold-blooded policy recommendations in his *Prince*. By killing his uncle Pope Leo X and the college of cardinals, Lorenzo could begin to unify Italy and aggregate enough power to contend with Europe's great powers. This would spare Italy from the agonies of outside interventions. Machiavelli is forced for tactical and strategic reasons to offer his suggestions quietly, so he employs Livy's pregnant silence to advocate for the emulation of Romulus.

ALTERNATE EXPLANATIONS

The two strongest ways to disprove my argument are to make light of Romulus's disappearance or to come up with a better explanation for the finale of *The Prince*. No argument is airtight, but reigning arguments have to answer compelling puzzles and be better than the best rivals. This section takes the most promising routes to debunk my argument and finds that they come up short.

Puzzle Problems

As Felix Gilbert's epigraph testifies, the meaning of the last chapter of *The Prince* is the biggest puzzle in the most read book on politics. This is not hunting small game; readers have furrowed brows at this issue for five centuries. But these facts are a first line of attack. Just like one almost never sees a real hundred dollar bill on the sidewalk, if the missing Romulus were a real puzzle someone like Gilbert would have noticed it by now.[34]

The trouble with this criticism is that others have noticed Machiavelli's missing Romulus. While most writers appear to be unaware of the missing Romulus—and one scholar even imagines that Romulus shows up in chapter 26[35]—those that have caught the omission are no lightweights. In his book on Germany and international politics after World War I, Friedrich Meinecke recreates Machiavelli's pattern for Romulus but singles out Theseus instead, which suggests that he envisioned post-war Germany as an Athens-like cultural empire. J. H. Whitfield slyly recycles Machiavelli's orderings of the most excellent examples in his work (on which more in table 10.1). And Leo Strauss raises the absence of Romulus and then footnotes a reference to Stefano Porcari's attempt on the pope's life.[36]

Clearly, I am not the first to notice the missing Romulus, nor the first to suggest that Machiavelli advocated papal assassination. Why did predecessors not develop the argument? I cannot speak for them, and they are now in no position to speak for themselves. My hunch is that they graciously chose not to spoil a surprise ending. Were we discussing a cliffhanger movie with a twist at the end, this course of action would be tactful. But in my view many people are missing the culminating point of Machiavelli's celebrated work right before the curtain falls. In particular, realists have lost part of their patrimony because some scholars treated the missing Romulus as a private preserve.

To this point my defense sounds like an appeal to authority, but there is more behind it. A typical response would be that Romulus's absence is accidental. Everyone makes mistakes; authors are absent-minded; manuscripts are miscopied. What evidence is there that the missing Romulus is not just a product of random chance or error? For starters, it is incredibly implausible to think that someone smart enough to write the most famous book on politics would forget such an obvious example in a forehead-slapping fit of forgetfulness. Machiavelli's prose is legendarily lapidary, Roman-obsessed, and absorbed by conspiracy—the longest chapters in both *The Prince* and *Discourses* are on conspiracies.[37]

Moreover, chapter 26 is not missing the lone word "Romulus," but, to maintain symmetry, it is missing a whole phrase referring to Romulus's opportunity. Therefore, a massive, mid-sentence copy error would have had to surgically remove the whole phrase referring to Romulus and nothing else. More importantly, if Romulus's placement is accidental, prior orderings would be either unchanged or random. However, Machiavelli draws our attention to Romulus by changing his placement in the order and no one else's (see table 10.1).

Through the listings, Moses, Cyrus, and Theseus always stand meticulously in the same relation to each other; only Romulus moves. What are the odds? That

TABLE 10.1

Machiavelli's Most Excellent Examples

Listing	Chapter	Order
1	6	Moses, Cyrus, **Romulus**, Theseus
2	6	Moses, **Romulus**, Cyrus, Theseus
3	6	Moses, Cyrus, Theseus, **Romulus**
4	26	Moses, Cyrus, Theseus

depends on how one parses the probabilities, but assume we frame the problem in the most permissive way. What are the odds that any name would shift position four times by chance while the others stood in the same relation?[38] Less than half a percent—effectively zero.[39] We can be 99.54 percent sure that Machiavelli was up to something between chapters 6 and 26. The last chapter is prepared for by hints in the preceding sections of the book; Gilbert is wrong.[40]

Rival Views

The puzzle of chapter 26 is unavoidable—is there a better explanation for it? There are three contenders: Hans Baron, Sebastian de Grazia, and Mario Martelli. First, Baron does not notice the disappearing Romulus, but that is no reason to evade his vaunted interpretation. He argues that the last chapter of *The Prince* was a late addition, tacked on sometime between December 1514 and September 1515. Circumstances at that moment augured well for Leo X to set up a *nepote* state for Giuliano de' Medici in the North to keep the French at bay. Baron sweepingly proclaims his conclusions as "definitive," and promulgates that the "incubus" of the nationalist interpretation of *The Prince* "will never have the power to make a comeback."[41]

While I admire Baron's earlier scholarship and his aversion to noncommittal, numbing prose, we flatly contradict each other on this point. We clash because he does not notice Romulus's absence; he does not see chapter 26 as an essential part of *The Prince*; he soft-pedals deceit and duress; and he makes Machiavelli's plans too dependent on fortune. In a word, Baron's view is anti-Machiavellian.

I agree that conditions in Italy influenced Machiavelli to write what he did, and revisions were made over time. Where Baron and I part company is how big the window of opportunity was, and how transformative revisions were. I find it dubious that Giuliano de' Medici at the head of a paltry balancing coalition to keep the French out of Milan in 1515 would ignite Machiavelli's imagination, race his pulse, and sway him to append an emotional conclusion to an ostensibly dispassionate finished work.[42]

Baron is textually tin-eared. He uses chronology as a divining rod when Machiavelli's writings offer signage toward authorial intent. Baron's belief that Italian liberation depends on a delicate constellation of political factors is anathema to what *The Prince* preaches over and over. *The Prince* is the first great self-help book; Machiavelli makes clear that one does not need much opportunity. While ultimately Lady Fortune's preferences are the final arbiter—she "lets herself be won"[43] hy the bold—virtue is a fair match to fortune. He lays this out especially in chapters 25 and 26. Although "these men are rare and marvelous, nonetheless they were men, and each of them had less opportunity than the present; for their undertaking was not more just than this one, nor easier, nor was God more friendly to them than to you."[44]

The most excellent examples all founded great states despite probably being lowly, bastard children with felonious criminal records. They are great because they overcame things beyond human control, simply put, *fortuna*. Machiavelli approves of men who did not need to be related to the pope to have the opportunity to kill him and the cardinals, and he frowns on Cesare Borgia for his dependence on the pope. Machiavelli appeals to "anyone"[45] to widen the application of his ideas. It would be contrary to the letter and spirit of his work to be so sensitive to the garden-variety vagaries of politics. It is improbable that in an evergreen text like *The Prince,* events inspired and invalidated the capstone chapter in less than a year.

Baron claims that Machiavelli does not expect or even wish for a "redeemer" of Italy to use force of arms. This claim is based on a single passage in chapter 11, where Machiavelli hopes Leo X's "goodness and infinite other virtues" can make the pontificate very "great and venerable."[46] Thinking about the matter in a commonsense manner, how would one free Italy from barbarians without recourse to force? Would Machiavelli of all people think an unarmed policy possible, preferable, or stable? To the best of my knowledge, Baron is the sole scholar to portray Machiavelli as Gandhi's grandfather.

Machiavelli is likely alluding to other instances where he used similar language to make a broader, bloodier point. The only other time he uses the phrase "infinite virtues," chapter 17, is in the context of Hannibal's inhuman cruelty, which made him "venerable and terrible." Machiavelli uses "infinite" with reference to two other individuals, also when discussing cruelty. One is Agathocles for his "savage cruelty and inhumanity, together with his infinite crimes . . ." and "infinite betrayals and cruelties" in chapter 8. The other is Antoninus [Caracalla] for his "infinite individual killings" in chapter 19.[47] These references relate back to cruelties well or badly used. Cruelties well used are those done at a stroke, like the acts of Agathocles, who killed the wealthy and senators of his city at once in order to assume power. Having "infinite virtues" in this sense is a suggestion: to kill many important people quickly, then stop, and turn the deed to public advantage. Such vicious power consolidation fits with my interpretation of an activist Machiavelli, but not with Baron's passive, pacifist view.

Second, de Grazia contends that Romulus is not in chapter 26 for religious reasons: "perhaps because to Romulus . . . 'the authority of God was not necessary.'"[48] The text does not support this view. In chapter 6, Machiavelli makes clear that although Moses was a "mere executor" of things ordered by God, if one examines the other three founders, "they will appear no different from those of Moses, who had so great a teacher."[49] The authority of God was not necessary for any of them to found their states. And the biblical grounds de Grazia adduces to substantiate his point only support Moses and Cyrus—there are no reasons for supposing that Theseus too should not have been omitted. Moreover, if religion is important, why is Numa Pompilius, Rome's second king, who founds its religion, never mentioned in *The Prince* but praised highly in the *Discourses*?

Third, Martelli speculates that Romulus may be disqualified because he is the only one who does not have an oppressed people. This is true but ignores that Machiavelli presents oppression as uninformative when explaining political change.[50] Although in chapter 19 Machiavelli claims that if princes avoid being hated and are not oppressive then they will not be overthrown, his examples mischievously counter his claim. He recommends a prince who is not hated yet is still killed in conspiracy, Nabis the Spartan, as well as a prince who is hated but is not killed in a conspiracy, Severus. So too in the *Discourses* (III.6), Machiavelli undermines the same point in the same way with two counterexamples: Spurius Cassius and Manlius Capitolinus.

Of 15 major conspiracies that Machiavelli chronicles in his *Florentine Histories*,[51] hatred of the rulers predicts nothing. In the nine cases where the ruler was hated, four conspiracies were strategically successful; in the six cases where the ruler was not hated, three were strategically successful. Across his works, Machiavelli's examples point to the minimal effect that oppression has on effecting political change. He therefore could not have believed that an oppressed people was a requisite or even significantly interesting condition for a would-be founder.

To conclude, no prior treatment of Romulus's disappearance has been satisfying. An accidental omission is vanishingly unlikely, and Baron, de Grazia, and Martelli's explanations do not measure up. While a watertight explanation is too much to expect with so fluid an author, no rival view solves the practical problems of Italian unification or the case of the missing Romulus.

CONCLUSION

In summary, the dramatic conclusion of *The Prince* is a surprise ending. Romulus goes missing in the final chapter because he is the crowning example for Italian unification. He kills his uncle and brother to unify power, unite disparate peoples, and found a mighty empire, not coincidentally on the Italian peninsula. In Machiavelli's day, few individuals were as well positioned as Lorenzo de' Medici to kill the pope and cardinals, reorder the Church, and reunify Italy. *The Prince* represents Machiavelli's effort to imply the undertaking through his parallel constructions in chapters 6 and 26. Against Gilbert and Baron, *The Prince* is a more cohesive document than they know.[52] But Machiavelli cannot commend Romulus's example openly. Without plausible deniability, an offended audience would retaliate, deprive the plan of surprise, make the targets harder to destroy, or increase the probability and strength of a balancing coalition.

If the above is correct, my arguments overlap with Machiavelli's. The balance of power is central in both accounts, small states must copy great powers or suffer their depredations, and force and fraud are critical ingredients in unification. With Romulus as the exemplar of how to unify Italy, both accounts share an ambivalent view of democracy in unification.[53]

For all our similarities, Machiavelli's plot to unify the relatively equal states of Italy looks violently different from my general argument on voluntary union. His account stresses decapitation strategies; mine stresses equitable bargaining. Our differences stem, I suspect, from our source material. Machiavelli was forced to rely on early historians, who, despite their transcendent talents, provided historical information in small quantity. Classical states may have voluntarily unified, for example Athens, but literacy was not widespread enough to chronicle it in any detail contemporarily. This makes sense given that voluntary unions are prone to happen on the political periphery, where wealth and culture are less concentrated.

The ancient and modern states that Machiavelli had solid evidence on were dominated by violence; uniting without fighting was unknown. As a result, Machiavelli sings the realist refrain: autonomy is too precious to give up without a fight; states seek friends, but never spouses. Nevertheless, unlike other realists, Machiavelli had a well thought out plan to get around interstate jealousy. For him, merging equal states is possible, but compels conspiracies with high body counts. My project seeks to show that this is not necessarily so. Unifying elites may threaten instability, but ultimately their goal is a fair marriage, not a triumphant bloodbath. While my policy recommendations have their downsides, Machiavelli's are worse. Even had his scheme succeeded, its perpetrator would have been hard to envy.

NOTES

CHAPTER 1

1. Thucydides 1982, 96–97 [II.15]. On Greeks and unification, see also Sealey 1976; Plutarch 1992, 1:14–15; Polybius 1922, 1:335–347 [II.37–II.45].

2. Fazal 2004, 319.

3. See Deutsch et al. 1957; Haas 1964; Etzioni 2001; Wendt 2003; Deudney 2007, chap. 9. See also Carr 1964, chap. 13; Olson 1965.

4. I treat states as unequal when the ratio of their population and GDP are, on average, greater than three. I do this for the somewhat arbitrary but parsimonious reason that the conventional superiority thought necessary for major offensives is three to one. States with this size differential can credibly threaten conquest in the unification process. Naturally, my line is only a guide; the factors of net assessment are my underlying interest. For as much precision as net assessment admits, see Biddle 2004; Rosen 1991; Fearon 1997b; Lynn-Jones 1995.

5. The reunification of Germany is the duck-billed platypus of this study. While it has elements of self-help and equality, it is essentially a product of outside interests and not a partnership of equals. See Zelikow and Rice 1995; Maier 1997. Czechoslovakia is excluded less because it was a creature of the Versailles Treaty than because it was a union between unequals. See Stein 1997, 25; Leff 1988, 11, 24–25, 31, 138–139, 151; Leff 1997, 9, 19, 25; Kalvoda 1989, 11, 20; Kohn 1953, 12; also Mametey and Luza eds. 1973.

6. On political power, see Hintze 1975, chaps. 4–5; Morgenthau 1993, chaps. 3, 9; Baldwin 1985, 18–24; Schmitt 1996, 22–34; Deudney 2007, 49. Optimal size means a competitive amount of power centralized in a political unit, which is related to but distinct from geographic extent.

7. I breed definitions of M. Weber (1958, 78) and Mearsheimer (2001, 5): to qualify as a state, a group must have sufficient military assets to uphold legal supremacy within its borders; cf. Goertz and Diehl 1991, 53–54.

CHAPTER 2

1. Machiavelli 1996, 218 [III.6]. A more accurate title of this chapter might read "Hypotheses on Self-Help Political Unification between Relatively Equal States," but this is ungainly.

2. For realist views on integration, see Thucydides 1982, 96–97 [II.15]; Hobbes 1985, chaps. 11, 13; Carr 1945, 47, 51–59; 1964, chap. 13; Kennan 1954, 106–107; 1993, 190, 234, 245; 1996, 121, 217; Morgenthau in Mitrany 1966; Morgenthau 1993, chaps. 22–25; Haslam 2000, 88–89; Waltz 1979, 180; Walt 1996, 269–272. See also Tuck in Grotius 2005, 1:xxxiii; Grotius 2005, 1:356–358; 2:434–435, 568–570; Forsyth 1981, 160, 206–208.

3. For realist flavored accounts of integration, see, for example, Amar 2005; Riker 1964, 12–13; 1987, 3.

4. On political entrepreneurs (i.e., individuals, whether heads of groups or not, pitching novel policies in the political marketplace) and the tipping models that accompany them, see Schelling 1978; Kuran 1997; Sunstein 1997; Laitin 1998; DeFigueiredo and Weingast 1999. Here I focus on the subset of entrepreneurs seeking to revise the fundamental locus of power. These are political entrepreneurs in the purest form, as individuals advocating relocation of the community's membership boundaries. See Schmitt 1996. On the relationship between threat and cooperation, see Stein 1976.

5. In short, I adapt prior scholars' work on measuring and perceiving threats. See Christensen 1996, 27–28; Walt 1987; Waltz 1979; Wolfers 1991; Olson and Zeckhauser 1966; Wagner 1993; Edelstein 2002. One could think of perceived threats as Bayesian updating, a sort of lag effect of prior distributions of power.

6. Cha (1999, 37) points out, citing Glenn Snyder, that realism misses much of the gray area in alignment behavior. On differences and ambiguities of threat, see Buzan 2007, 119–123. Related to bandwagoning is, as Paul Schroeder (2004) points out, hiding, where small powers do not so much align with great powers as try to avoid their attention. In either case, the result is still asymmetric relations.

7. Tainter 2005, 32. This is a restatement of Simmel 1955; see also Spykman 1965; Coser 1964.

8. Grieco in Baldwin ed. 1993, 335; cf. Grieco in Mansfield and Milner eds. 1997, chap. 7; cp. Stein 1983, 136–139. For the literature on weakness of the will (*akrasia*), discount rates, and cooperation, see Schelling 1978b; 1984a; 1984b; 1985; Strotz 1955; Thaler 1994; E. Posner 2002; cf. *Federalist* nos. 3, 22 (Jay and Hamilton, respectively) in Hamilton et al. 1987, 94, 177.

9. Here I borrow from Keohane and Nye 1989, 8–13; Cha 1994, 5, 47–64; cf. Kissinger 1995, 53, 90–91, 246–250; Mearsheimer 1998b, 433–434. Symmetry is not the same thing as equality of power, though the two are related. Many states have comparable power, yet few unify. Symmetry is the similar fear of abandonment (see Cha 1999, 46–47), which is somewhat more likely if they have relatively equal power.

10. A note on water, my argument is more Mearsheimer (2001, 83–84) than Mahan (1987, 25).

11. See Olson 1965. On German politics after the Thirty Years' War, see Holborn in Paret ed. 1986; Craig 1978, chap. 1. Critics could object that when numbers are lower the risk of exploitation is greater because a single defection could be fatal. This is true but neglects the nature of the threat; if it is dire and symmetric then, by standard balancing logic, bandwagoning is the riskier option. See Walt 1987, 18–33.

12. Crises are imperfect eye-openers that can cause punctuated equilibrium. As Aaron Friedberg states (1988, 287): "Crises were catalytic rather than simply causative; they did not abruptly change minds but instead opened them up, if only briefly . . ." See also Taylor 2003,

166, 221, 225; Quester 1988; Farnham 1997, 135–136; Spruyt 1994a, 22–25; Zakaria 1998, 11, 104; Jervis 1976, 308–315; Gilpin 1981, 47–49; Legro 2005, 13–16.

13. See Schlesinger 1999, 435; Spruyt 2005, 4–7.

14. See Lippmann 1997; 1999; Dewey 1988, 213–220, 235–372; Kuran 1997; Fogel 2000; Kaufmann and Pape 1999.

15. 2000, 56. See also Snyder and Ballentine in Brown et al. eds. 1996–1997; Page and Shapiro 1992; Becker 1998b, chap. 10; Becker in Stigler ed. 1988, chap. 2; Habermas 1989; Kennan 1984, 62.

16. See Schelling 1960, 196; cf. Jervis 1989; E. Posner 2002.

17. See Bachrach and Baratz 1962; Riker 1996.

18. In the above, I allude to Waltz's sameness effect (1979, 127). On institutional selection, evolution, and duration, see Spruyt 1994a, 29–33; Tilly 1993; Brooks and Wohlforth 2000/2001. On luck being proportionate to skill, see Machiavelli 1996; 1998; Will 1991, Grant 1999, ix; Carr 1961, 130.

19. As with any two-by-two table, there are borderline cases that blend characteristics of ideal types. For instance, Western Europe faced high threat for at least 15 years after World War II, and key states created institutions that had unified command structures like a union, but room for national prerogatives, like an alliance. See Rosato 2011.

20. See Parent 2007.

21. Quoted in Hofstadter 1973, 89.

22. The main logic I engage here derives from Adler and Barnett eds. 1998; Wendt 1999; 2003. On constructivism generally, see Etzioni 2001; Barnett and Duvall 2005; Finnemore 1996; Finnemore and Sikkink 1998; Habermas 1984; Mueller 2004; Katzenstein ed. 1996; Cronin 1994; Bull 1995; Merritt and Russett eds. 1981, 151–156.

23. On Deutsch's view see Deutsch et al. 1957, 46–58; 1963, 176–178; 1963 ed.; 1967; 1976. For Adler and Barnett's views, see their 1998, chaps. 2, 13. For Alexander Wendt's views, see his 2003. Adler and Barnett's argument can subsume similar work by Cronin (1994; 1999), Finnemore and Sikkink (1998), and Fligstein (2009). While there are material conditions that help integration, the argument is not material—community forms for reasons "beyond political expediency" (Cronin 1999, 3).

24. Adler and Barnett 1998, 38–39; cf. Kupchan 2010, 6, 35, 66–67.

25. Karnes 1961, 247. With a strict definition of culture, Erik Gartzke and Kristian Skrede Gleditsch (2006) find that, other things equal, conflict is more likely between culturally similar states.

26. On culture as tool kit, see Swidler 1986. On political entrepreneurs working with a lumpy distribution of semi-malleable identities in particular institutional contexts, see D. Posner 2005. On shifting distributions of power, behavior, and trust, see Erikson and Parent 2007; Parent and Erikson 2009; Parent 2009a.

27. On interdependence, see L. Lindberg and Scheingold 1970; L. Lindberg and Scheingold eds. 1971; Scheingold 1970; Nye ed. 1968; D. Friedman 1977; cf. Waltz 1970. On the functionalist approach, see Mitrany 1948; 1971; 1975. On neofunctionalism, see Haas 1956; 1958; 1964; 1968; 1970; 1975; Haas et al. 1977; 1990; Stone Sweet, Sandholtz, and Fligstein 2001; cf. Haslam 2002, 202–203; Mattli 1999, 25–28; Acharya and Johnston eds. 2007, 2–15.

28. On the vicissitudes of neofunctionalism, see Mattli 1999, 28. On regional integration, see, for instance, Nye 1965; Nyong'O 1990; Nyerere 1978; Gambari 1991; Bora and Findlay eds. 1996; L. Lindberg and Scheingold eds. 1970. Realists are not immune to the charms of technocratic government either; see Lippmann 1999; Kennan 1993.

29. See Rodrik 2000, 183, also 180.

30. On the high-low politics distinction, or lack thereof, see Keohane and Nye 1989, 27–29; Milner 1997, 181.

31. On trade flows as cause and consequence of integration, see Mansfield and Milner eds. 1997; Anderson and Blackhurst eds. 1993; Mansfield and Pollins eds. 2003; Gowa 1994.

32. For other internal explanations of integration, see Hale 2004; Rodden and Wibbels 2002; Ziblatt 2004.

33. On institutional explanations of integration, see Niou and Ordeshook 1998; Alesina and Spolaore 2003; Riker 2005a; 2005b; Lake 1997; 1999; 2003; 2004; 2009; K. Weber 1997; Cooley 2005, esp. 51; Cooley and Spruyt 2009; C. Rector 2003; 2009; cf. Mearsheimer 1998b; 2004b; MacDonald and Lake 2008. This work is often based on the transactions cost literature in economics, see Coase 1990; Williamson 1983; 1985; Williamson and Winter eds. 1991; North 1999; cf. Lake 1999; Hirschleifer 2001.

34. Kupchan 2010, 3, 181, 214.

35. See, for example, Hendrickson 2003; Moravcsik 1998; Kupchan 2010. Alas, there are too many stimulating arguments on integration to give full attention to them all. Nonetheless, I integrate Hendrickson into the American chapter and Moravcsik into the European chapter to compensate for this misfortune. Kupchan's thoughtful, eclectic book poorly matches the scope of the present work, and "does not advance a theory of when and why states advance along this [anarchy/hierarchy] continuum . . ." (Kupchan 2010, 68). However, I engage his provocative observations passim.

36. On binding arguments, see Mill 1991, chap. 17; Riker 964, 12–13; Schroeder 1994; 2004, chap. 9; Weitsman 1997; Wallander and Keohane 1999, 23–25; Cronin 1999, 4; Hendrickson 2003; Jones 2007; Deudney 2007. Deudney's argument that weapons technology change is driving integration was anticipated by Kenneth Boulding (1962, 228, cf. 272–273). Full disclosure: much of what became this work was written while rooming with Josh Baron, my ingenious friend, frequent discussant, subsequent coauthor, a former student of Deudney's, and an ardent believer in binding arguments.

37. Etzioni 2001, xlviii.

38. See Jervis 2005, 52; Waltz 2002, 353; cf. Mueller 2006.

39. On the political responses to environmental pressures, see Kahl 2006, chap. 5; Diamond 2006, 497; Rotberg ed. 2004.

40. 2001, xx, 142; cf. Schlesinger 1999, chap. 2; Hirschman 1997, 132; Croce 2000, 58.

41. See Herodotus 1987, 203, 518; Thucydides 1998, 47, 130, 136, 262, 345; Xenophon 1972, 258–259 [V.8]. For cursory prior treatments, see Hobbes 1985, chaps. 11, 13; Carr 1945, 47, 51–59; Waltz 1979, 180; Walt 1996, 269–272; Forsyth 1981, 160, 206–208. For my differences with Machiavelli, see appendix.

42. See Walt 1996, 15–16; King, Keohane, and Verba 1994, 85–86, 225–228.

43. See Collier 1995, 464; Caporaso 1995; Rogowski 1995; Laitin 1995; Gerring 2007, 104–105; Goertz 2006, chap. 7.

44. Economic elites are defined as individuals in the top 10 percent of a state's wealth distribution. Social elites are those individuals occupying the most prestigious 10 percent of the social hierarchy. Political elites are those occupying the top 10 percent of the governmental hierarchy. On measuring how elites spend political capital, see Krasner 1978, 14.

45. See Kaysen 1990; Mueller 2004; Spruyt 2005.

46. See Waltz 1979, 118–119.

47. As opposed to say, Kennan (1993, 144–145), who opposes bigness, and others, e.g. Gibbon (1993, 1:90 [chap. 3]) and Tainter (2005, 6, 39–40), who appreciate the association between large polities and developed cultures.

CHAPTER 3

1. Hamilton in Hamilton et al. 1987, 87–88. The beginning of *The Federalist Papers* bears an uncanny resemblance to another work of political theory. See Plato 1991, 3–6. "Publius" takes a middle way, spending many of the essays reasoning about force.

2. See Morgenthau 1993, 344–347; Walt 1996, 270–272; Riker 1996; Niebuhr 1972, 166–167.

3. The conventional wisdom can be seen in Beeman 2009, esp. 9; cf. Wood 2009, 11–18. See also Dewey 1985; Lippmann 1999; Ienaga 1996; Cruz 2000. Madison is technically James Madison, Jr., but I drop the "Jr." throughout to stick with common parlance.

4. Bailyn ed. 1993, 1:888. See also Huntington 1997. Quotes such as Huntington's could be multiplied many times over, see Bailyn ed. 1993:2, 521, 589; Farrand 1968, 62. Hannah Arendt (1965, 134–135) claims that the French Revolution, with its more typical revolutionary excess, was the more exported example. All the cases in this study run counter to her claim.

5. Madison 1999, 158. Spain also irritatingly projected its power into Florida and the Mississippi, and Britain across the seas and into Canada, of which more later. On state violations of Congressional authority, see E. Morgan 1956, 125. There was talk of political union between the American colonies and Britain at the time of the American Revolution, most notably by Adam Smith and Benjamin Franklin, but London never seriously considered it. See R. Smith 2002, 23, 38; Franklin 1987, 820.

6. On the economic performance of the thirteen colonies see Arendt 1965, 68, 157; Wood 1998, 395; 1993, 3–4, 169; Middlekauff 1982, 591; Jensen 1962, 235; E. Morgan 1956 113, 118, 120; North 1961, 19. On the population growth of the thirteen colonies see McCullough 2002, 395. The American experience was typical in that objective conditions poorly predicted revolution, see Gurr 2000, chap. 3–4; Connor 1994, chap. 6. On the Continental Army disbanding and the military threat the states saw in the Constitution, see Carp in Greene ed. 1987, 31, 34; cf. Schwoerer 1974, 2, 5, 197–198; Schwoerer in Pocock ed. 1980, chap. 6; Pocock in Pocock ed. 1980, 285. On the Articles's success, see Jensen 1962, 347, 360, 382, 388; cf. Farrand in Hall ed. 1987, chap. 9; Elkins and McKitrick in Levy ed. 1987, 229–230.

7. Washington 1997, 602; Franklin quoted in Beard 1941, 47; cf. Pinckney quoted in Greene 1993, 177. Franklin makes a similar statement the prior year as well, see Franklin 1987, 1161. On mass opinion, see Hyneman and Lutz 1983, 646–647; Bailyn ed. 1993, 1:443; 1993, 2:106, 625–626.

8. Rakove 1996, 28–29; E. Morgan 1956, 88, 145; Wood 1993, 12. The argument that the crisis that resulted in the Constitution was constructed has a longer history and goes back, according to Beard (1941, 48), to 1871, when Harry Dawson made it in *The Historical Magazine*, vol. IX, second series, pp. 157 ff. Merrill Jensen (1962, xiii) also makes a similar case much later.

9. Marks 1973, 48; Antifederalist quoted in Wood 1998, 500; see also Sharp in Boyd ed. 1985, 120; Wood 1998, 356.

10. Scudiere in Conley and Kaminski eds. 1988, 14; Levy in Levy ed. 1987, xxxiii; Beard 1941; Dinkin 1982; Riker 1996, 25, 255; on the general volatility of elections see E. Morgan 1989, 303–304. On apportionment under the Articles, see Roll in Hall ed. 1987, chap. 27. For the fragmentary evidence we have on early American voting, see the American Antiquarian Society's "A New Nation Votes" database, which is available at: http://elections.lib.tufts.edu/aas_portal/index.xq.

11. The character sketches that follow draw on Rakove 1996, 36–39; McDonald 1979, 262–263; Madison 1999; Wood 1993, 197–199, 205; Middlekauff 1982, 622; Farrand 1968, 17; Beard 1941, 125; J. Ellis 2002, 53–54.

12. The title of this section plays off J. G. A. Pocock's famous book and refers to two related questions: when and how. In one sense, it refers to the actual moment when a politician publicly enters the unification fray, the *Schwerpunkt* of constitutional change. In another sense, the Madisonian moment is a way of creating the state as an entity resistant to morbidity and mortality. I part company from Rakove 1996, chap. 3; see also Tocqueville 1988, 31, 49.

13. I use the term "Federalist" to mean those who sympathized with the nationalist policies embodied in the Constitution and "Antifederalist" to mean those who prioritized states' power over national power.

14. 1984, 23–24.

15. Bailyn ed. 1993, 1:962; cf. Dougherty 2001, 26–32, 83.

16. Rakove 1996, 25–31; Rakove in Greene 1987, 82, 92; Madison 1999, 20; *Federalist* no. 18; Elkins and McKitrick 1993, 101.

17. On Morris's machinations, see Ferguson in Hall ed. 1987, 188–194; McDonald 1979, 49–57.

18. For population data, see Conley and Kaminski eds. 1988, xii; J. Ellis 2002, 79; Beard 1941, 36. Beard's data is from 1795. On Virginia's weakness as hegemons go, see Onuf 1983, 89; Washington 1997, 563, 661; Banning in Gillespie and Lienesch 1989, 276.

19. See Dougherty 2001, 156; McDonald 1979, 236–237. On the need for radical reform, see Madison 1999, 51, 80; Washington 1997, 648. This was not the only transportation cooperation at the time; see Jensen 1962, 342–343.

20. Farrand 1968, 8; Risjord 1978, 257–259. For eighteenth-century Americans, conventions were regarded as "legally deficient bodies existing outside of regularly constituted authority." Wood 1998, 312; see also E. Morgan 1989, 107. But they had yet to get a bad reputation from the French Revolution.

21. Quoted in Briceland in Conley and Kaminski eds. 1988, 204. For Madison's perspective on this, see his 1999, 47–50. On the call to Annapolis, see also McDonald 1979, 237–238.

22. Monroe and Madison quoted in Feer 1969, 391–392.

23. Jefferson 1984, 882–883. Washington had predicted this in 1784, see Wood 2009, 114. For elite concerns about river navigation, see Madison 1999, 14–16, 25–29, 55–56, 60; Washington 1997, 560–562, 570–571, 575, 581, 586–587, 592, 663; Hamilton 2001, 856, 914; Rakove in Greene ed. 1987, 91.

24. Farrand 1968, 9; also ibid., 54. On New Jersey's singularly broad instructions, see Middlekauff 1982, 600. Other states were known to have delegations en route when Annapolis disbanded hastily; see Risjord 1978, 265–266.

25. Hamilton 2001, 143–144.

26. Farrand 1968, 39, see also 20, 24, 26. Congress's reaction to the Annapolis convention had been flat. "It referred the proposals to a committee of three, which referred it to a committee of thirteen, which Congress never appointed. In short, the grandiose proposal was not even allowed to lie and die on the table." McDonald 1979, 247.

27. Bailyn ed. 1993, 1:1076. On the instructions given to delegates, see Ackerman 1998, 35–36.

28. See Briceland in Conley and Kaminski eds. 1988, 209; Madison 1999, 66; Beeman 2009, 92.

29. See Beard 1941, 64, 149; McDonald 1979, 35; cf. Marks 203; Riker 1996, 18, 148.

30. 1948, 94; cf. Marshall 2001, 322.

31. See Parent 2010. On records of participation, see Richards 2002, 60–88; also Brynner 1993, 83–91, Szatmary 1980, 100.

32. Quoted in Beeman 2009, 290; cf. Carp in Greene ed. 1987, 32; Dougherty 2001, 103–105, 128. On tax relief, see Richards 2002, 119. On the minimal Constitutional impact, see Feer 1969; Brynner 1993.

33. Washington 1997, 631–632; Madison quoted in Marks 1973, 102. For the long-standing fears about British intrigue and efforts to hurt the former colonies, see Madison 1999, 38, 48; Washington 1997, 527, 539, 552, 563–564, 597, 630; McDonald 1979, 244–251. This conspiratorial puppetry motif in American foreign policy later led George Kennan (1984, 164) to investigate "this tendency of ours to insist on seeing as blind puppets of some other great power weaker or smaller factions or regimes whose relations with that great power are actually much more complicated and much less sinister than that." On the provenance of political paranoia, see Parent 2010.

34. *American Historical Review* 1897, 694. Reliable sources of information also include Chief Justice of the Berkshire County Court, William Whiting, Washington's former drill master Baron von Steuben, and Noah Webster. See Richards 2002, 14, 15–16, 80.

35. In the run-up to Philadelphia, Madison had been hard at work preparing. See Madison 1999, 69–80, 896–897; cf. Harrington 2001; Hume 1998, 228; Rakove in Greene ed. 1987, 95–97.

36. Beeman 2009, 70.

37. Bailyn ed. 1993, 1:632. See also Farrand 1968, 58; cf. Kant 1995, 186–187. For Madison and Washington's defense of this policy see Elster 1999, 109–110; Sunstein 1993, ix, 22; Madison 1999, 24, 51; Washington 1997, 636.

38. Bailyn ed. 1993, 1:1081.

39. See Madison in Wood 1998, 593.

40. Bedford quoted in Saladino in Gillespie and Lienesch eds. 1989, 39, cf. 50; McDonald 1979, 282; Saye and Fox in Conley and Kaminski eds. 1988, 85, 120; Dicksinson quoted in Roche in Levy ed. 1987, 191. The Morris quote is from Middlekauff 1982, 640. The Madison quote is from Amar 2005, 120, and is followed by a similar quote by Ellsworth. Madison noted that Wilson's suggestion of partial union by a plurality of states was "probably meant in terrorem to the smaller states of N. Jersey and Delaware." Quoted in Rakove 1996, 104; see also Beeman 2009, 176, 204.

41. Farrand 1968, 128; Hamilton et al. 1987 [no. 45], 296; Amar 2005, 27; Wood 1998, 615; Machiavelli 1996, 61 [I.25]; Madison 1999, 80–82. Antifederalists realized the switch, see Bailyn ed. 1993, 1:40; cf. Kratochwil in Falk et al. eds. 1985, 238–239; Deudney 1995.

42. Randolph quoted in Beard 1941, 219; cf. Amar 2005, 311. True to form, Madison had such ideas early, see Madison 1999, 83.

43. Kurland and Lerner 1987, 4:654; cf. Wolfers 1991, 13. *Federalist* no. 43 makes an identical case, appealing to "the absolute necessity of the case; to the great principle of self-preservation . . ." Hamilton et al 1987, 285. Washington uses the "house on fire" metaphor as well in February 1787, see Washington 1997, 635.

44. See T. Anderson 1993, 165; Farrand 1968, 3, 158–159. On a somewhat related note, the abhorrent number that blacks count as three-fifths of whites also has pre-Constitutional origins. The figure was a focal point because it was used in a Congressional revenue request in 1783. See ibid. 5, 108; Amar 2005, 95.

45. Kurland and Lerner 1987, 4:657.

46. Kurland and Lerner 1987, 4:657. See also Farrand 1968, 192; Madison 1999, 190–192; Washington 1997, 666, 669.

47. The idea appears to have been Gouverner Morris's, though. See Beeman 2009, 361.

48. A claim that was still very much contested. See, for example, Bailyn ed. 1993, 2:3, 108, 297, 378, 596. For others' arguments on how the Federalists prevailed, see T. Anderson 1993, 174–175; Hendrickson 2003, 251–252; Bailyn ed. 1993, 2:460; Wood 1998, 486–487.

49. It is hard to overstate how littered period literature is with references to Washington and Franklin, and how they could do no wrong. See, for example, Bailyn ed. 1993, 1:54, 78, 102, 162, 378, 688, 727, 938; Bailyn ed. 1993, 2:16, 81; Rakove 1996, 135. Economic growth had gathered steam by the time the Constitution was ratified, giving the document a well-timed boost. It seems initially that growth was good for the Constitution, not the other way around. See Farrand 1968, 210.

50. See *Federalist* no. 37; Franklin in Bailyn ed. 1993, 2:404–405; Rush in Bailyn ed. 1993, 1:869.

51. See Jensen 1962, cf. Pincus 2009, 302. Indeed, Antifederalist ideas would be very popular in American politics for some time once they were rebranded as "republican" (and, in poetic justice, their opponents branded as "anti-republican"). See Wood 2009, 151.

52. See Beard 1941, chap. 5; McGuire and Ohsfeldt in Grofman and Wittman eds. 1989, 175, 199; Main 1964. See also Fink and Riker in Grofman and Wittman eds. 1989, 221; Jensen 1962, 20, 178.

53. Hamilton in Bailyn ed. 1993, 1:9–10; Madison in Bailyn ed. 1993, 1:204–205; Comte de Moustier in Bailyn ed. 1993, 2:356. For Washington and Madison's assessments of success, see Washington 1997, 664, 682; Madison 1999, 154, 158. Antifederalists cast a darker complexion on the public's reception of the Constitution. See Bailyn ed. 1993, 2:295.

54. Bailyn ed. 1993, 1:420–421. This is why Riker's (1996, 21) statement that the choice was between the status quo and the Constitution is incorrect. He undermines his point himself, see Ibid. 81–82, 149; cf. Riker 1987, 3.

55. For the Federal Farmer quote, see Bailyn ed. 1993, 1:250. For other essays, see Bailyn ed. 1993, 1:103, 250, 424, 494, 526, 687; 1993, 2:81–82, 243.

56. Bailyn ed. 1993, 1:415; Ackerman 1998, 38; Jefferson 1984, 913. For Jefferson's view of the minor problems that the Articles presented, see Jefferson 1984, 575–579.

57. Hancock in Conley and Kaminski eds. 1988, 31; also ibid. 32–35; Saladino in Gillespie and Lienesch eds. 1989, 41; Goldstein 2001, 49.

58. On Pennsylvanian politics, see Doutrich in Conley and Kaminski eds. 1988, chap. 3; Ackerman 1998, 55; E. Morgan 1956, 92, 150; McDonald 1979, 335–336; R. Smith 1909; Benton in Hall ed. 1987, chap. 4; Boyd in Hall ed. 1987, chap. 5.

59. See Riker 1996, 172.

60. Wilson in Bailyn ed. 1993, 1:798.

61. Bailyn ed. 1993, 1:526–531, see also 582. In fact, only after ratification did Antifederals get into gear, see Graham in Gillespie and Lienesch eds. 1989, 67–68. Please note that Pennsylvania is unicameral with an unusual quorum rule requiring a two-thirds supermajority to form a quorum.

62. Murrin in Conley and Kaminski eds. 1988, 73. See also Shumer in Gillespie and Lienesch eds. 1989, 77, 86–87.

63. Quoted in Saye in Conley and Kaminski eds. 1988, 86–87; cf. McDonald 1979, 123; Marks 1973, 4; Cashin in Gillespie and Lienesch eds. 1989, 94, 108.

64. Quoted in Collier in Conley and Kaminski eds. 1988, 101. The speaker is William Samuel Johnson, the soon-to-be delegate at Philadelphia. See also McDonald 1979, 185–194; Gerlach in Hall ed. 1987, chap. 13; Lutz in Gillespie and Lienesch eds. 1989, 117–118, 125.

65. Nevins 1927, 546.

66. Collier in Conley and Kaminski eds. 1988, chap. 5. In his otherwise fine work, Riker (1996, 178–179) misses these finer details.

67. Sherman quoted in Conley and Kaminski eds. 1988, 105; Ibid., 106.

68. Collier in Conley and Kaminski eds. 1988, 106–107.

69. Collier in Conley and Kaminski eds., 107. See also Lutz in Gillespie and Lienesch eds. 1989, 128.

70. Bailyn ed. 1993, 2:8.

71. A reputation that the state would proudly maintain for some time, see Saxon 1989; Barnum 2000. Connecticut calls itself the "Constitution State," but not for this chapter in its history. Historians argue that the 1638–1639 Fundamental Orders were the first real written constitution in history, and provided a model for the U.S. Constitution.

72. This section draws on Fox in Conley and Kaminski eds. 1988, chap. 6; also McDonald 1979, 217–226, 343–344, 365; Dougherty 2001, 128.

73. For the Dawson quote, see Richards 2002, 150. For the Minot quote, see Brynner 1993, 243–244.

74. To say nothing of being meretricious. In October of 1788, Madison described Hancock to Jefferson as *"weak ambitious a courtier of popularity given to low intrigue"* Madison 1999, 419, emphasis in original; cf. McDonald 1979, 365. Gillespie (in Gillespie and Lienesch eds. 1989, 155) casts reasonable doubt on Hancock accepting a political bribe.

75. Maryland Senate quoted in Stiverson in Conley and Kaminski eds. 1988, 139. On Maryland's ratification drive, see Eavey and Miller in Grofman and Wittman eds. 1989, 214–217; McDonald 1979, 157–171, 347; Risjord 1978, 272–273, 279; Hoffman 1973; Onuf in Gillespie and Lienesch eds. 1989, 176–177.

76. Quoted in E. Morgan 1989, 185–186. See also Stiverson in Conley and Kaminski eds. 1988, 150; Risjord 1978, 285, 293.

77. See Nadelhaft in Conley and Kaminski eds. 1988, chap. 8; McDonald 1979, 171–181, 347; Weir in Gillespie and Lienesch eds. 1989, 224–225; Beeman 2009, 243.

78. See Daniell in Conley and Kaminski eds. 1988, 188, 191. For background on New Hampshire politics of the period, see McDonald 1979, 194–204, 348, 354.

79. Daniell in Conley and Kaminski eds. 1988, 194. Sullivan, for one, was no stranger to venality, having been bribed by the French in the American Revolution. See McCullough 2002, 260; Jensen 1962, 56.

80. Daniell in Conley and Kaminski eds. 1988, 195, also Yarbrough in Gillespie and Lienesch 1989, chap. 9.

81. Marks 1973, 3–4.

82. Hamilton 2001, 486.

83. Washington in Bailyn ed. 1993, 2:421; Washington in ibid., 1:612; Washington in ibid., 2:180. On Virginia politics of the time, see McDonald 1979, 123, 132–136, 355.

84. Pendleton quoted in Briceland in Conley and Kaminski eds. 1988, 214–215. See also Risjord 1978, 293–306.

85. Washington in Kurland and Lerner 1987, 4:661.

86. Randolph in Bailyn ed. 1993, 2:717; Randolph quoted in Banning in Gillespie and Lienesch eds. 1989, 285–286; McDonald 1979, 339–340; see also 1979, 264–265; Kaminski in Conley and Kaminski eds. 1992, 36.

87. Briceland in Conley and Kaminski eds. 1988, 220.

88. Kaminski in Conley and Kaminski eds. 1988, 234; McDonald 1979, 351, 360–363.

89. Quoted in Kaminski in Conley and Kaminski eds. 1988, 242; quoted in ibid., 246; quoted in ibid., 243.

90. Quoted in ibid., 244.

91. Dane in Bailyn ed. 1993, 2:845–846. Smith in Bailyn ed. 1993, 2:851. Dane and Smith appear early in Madison's correspondence as Federalist opponents, see Madison 1999, 137, 138, 155; cf. Marks 1973, 198. On Melancton Smith, see Brooks in Hall ed. 1987, chap. 6.

92. Bailyn ed. 1993, 2:852. Cecil Eubanks makes the compelling argument that Madison's letter to Hamilton at this time (warning that "the Constitution requires an adoption *in toto* and *for ever . . . any condition* whatever must viciate [sic] the ratification") ultimately convinced Smith to switch his position. Smith remarked on July 23, "'reasonings . . . from persons abroad . . .' had led him to conclude that conditional ratification of any kind would unacceptable to the nation and dangerous to the interests of New York." Eubanks in Gillespie and Lienesch 1989, 327–328; cf. Madison 1999, 408. On the capital and impost, see Kaminski in Conley and Kaminski eds. 1988, 246.

93. See Watson in Conley and Kaminski eds. 1988, 263–265; Ackerman 1998, 58; cf. McDonald 1979, 136–149; Crow 1980, 101; Newsome in Hall ed. 1987, chap. 24; Lienesch in Gillespie and Lienesch eds. 1989, 343, 348–349, 363–364.

94. Quoted in Conley in Conley and Kaminski eds. 1988, 269–270. Threats to Rhode Island started early, see Kaminski in Gillespie and Lienesch eds. 1989, 377, 380, 385.

95. Ellsworth and Huntington, quoted in Conley in Conley and Kaminski eds. 1988, 287.

96. William Maclay quoted in Conley in Conley and Kaminski eds. 1988, 289.

97. Providence delegates quoted in Conley in Conley and Kaminski eds. 1988, 287.

98. *Federalist* no. 49 quote is Madison in Hamilton et al. 1987, 314. The Washington quote is from Gillespie in Gillespie and Lienesch eds. 1989, 153.

99. Quoted in Kaminski in Conley and Kaminski eds. 1992, 43. At the time, Madison explained his views thus (1999, 471–472): "The nauseous project of amendments has not yet been either dismissed or dispatched. . . . [a bill of rights] will kill the opposition every where, and by putting an end to the disaffection of the Govt. itself, enable the administration to venture on measures not otherwise safe." See also Madison 1999, 420–421, 427–428.

100. Bowling in Conley and Kaminski eds. 1992, 50.

101. Washington quoted in Bowling in Conley and Kaminski eds. 1992, 52. Amar (2005, 318) makes a compelling case that Washington's support and enthusiasm for the Bill of Rights were larger than Bowling portrays them. The Antifederalist sentiment is William Grayson's, see Bowling in Conley and Kaminski eds. 1992, 54. See also Elkins and McKitrick 1993, 61–62. To Samuel Johnston on June 21, 1789, Madison commented that his amendments aimed, "at the twofold object of removing the fears of the discontented and of avoiding all such alterations as would either displease the adverse side or endanger the success of the measure." Madison quoted in Risjord 1978, 340.

102. Jefferson quoted in Bowling in Conley and Kaminski eds. 1992, 55. Madison and Hamilton continued to entertain grave doubts about their creation, see Rakove 1996, 189; E. Morgan 1989, 276.

103. On powers of war and peace, see Amar 2005, 22–26, 106, 114–118, 242, 299–300; Nevins 1927, 658–660; Marks 1973, 123. On revenues and expenditures, see Wood 2009, 103.

104. Amar 2005, 37.

105. On the South's odds of victory, see McPherson 1996, 114; H. Adams 1990, 110–112, 144–158; H. Jones 2010.

106. For the Madison statement, see Beard and Beard 1933, 2:50. On Shellabarger and the Supreme Court, see McKitrick 1960, 93–116. For views different from mine, see Deudney 1995, 193; Kupchan 2004/2005, 103–120.

CHAPTER 4

1. Adams in Merrill and Paterson eds. 2005, 32; Madison 1999, 20; cf. Washington 1997, 975; J. Q. Adams in Bemis 1949, 182, 417.

2. Bemis 1926, 83.

3. For houses on fire, see Kurland and Lerner 1987, 4:654; Washington 1997, 635; cf. Wolfers 1991, 13. On generalship in the Revolutionary War, see C. Adams 1911, 1–173. For the long-standing fears about foreign intrigue, see, for example, Madison 1999, 38, 48; Washington 1997, 527, 539, 552, 563–564, 597, 630–632; McDonald 1979, 244, 246, 251; Madison quoted in Marks 1973, 102; Franklin 1987, 1093; Hamilton 2001, 124; Jefferson 1984, 663.

4. On the pessimistic perceptions of American federalism before and after union, see Dull in Greene ed. 1987, 151; Onuf in Greene ed. 1987, 189–190, 196; Marks 1973, 7, 188; E. Morgan 1956, 5; Ritcheson 1969, 33–34; Slaughter 1986, 191. England and France had asked for thirteen ambassadors, see Marks 1973, 123.

5. *Federalist* no. 43 is Madison in Hamilton et al. 1987, 285. Few words are more ubiquitous during the late 1700s than "necessity." See Arendt 1965, 13, 39–40, 47–48, 59, 63–64; Hamilton et al 1987, 216, 232, 247; Beard 1941, 232–233. See also Thucydides 1982, 23 [I.37]; Dover 1974, 109; Ober 1998, 75–76, 142; Livy 1982, [IX.I.10]; Tacitus 1942, 207, 340 [VI.22, XIV.35]; Hume 1992 [I.III.14, II.III.1–2]; Croce 2000, chap. 4; Carr 1961, 130–134. For the *Federalist* reprint data, see Amar 2005, 43–44.

6. On the sameness effect and America copying the English unifying example, see Waltz 1979, 127; Amar 2005, 30–31, 36, 45, 49, 472; cf. Pincus 2009, 475–476. Amar (2005, 46–51, 242) also argues that geopolitical concerns left marks on almost every article of the Constitution.

7. Washington quoted in Wood 1998, 472; Madison quoted in Rakove 1996, 167; Madison, Hamilton, and Jay quoted in Amar 2005, 38; cf. Madison 1999, 408. Even after the ratification, the United States worried about being strangled in the cradle, in Hamilton's (2001, 817) allusion: "If a Hercules—a Hercules in the cradle." Madison never abandoned his rejection of nullification. See Beard and Beard 1933, 2:50.

8. Quoted in Wood 2009, 86. On defense expenditures, see Dougherty 2001, 35. On the dislike triangle between the United States, foreign powers, and Native Americans, see Bemis 1926, 48, 52, 64–67, 136, 206; Merrell in Greene ed. 1987, 203; Marks 1973, 20–21, 36; Ritcheson 1969, 166–170; Whitaker 1927, 62. On America's credit problem, see Rakove in Ferejohn et al. eds. 2001, 61; Rakove in Greene ed. 1987, 90–91; Onuf in Greene ed. 1987, 189–190; Marks 1973, 45; Hamilton 2001, 109, 635, 863; McDonald 1979, 45–47; Amar 2005, 47, 107, 271. Native Americans were not the only ones on the take, John Jay received a Spanish stallion free of charge (with Congressional approval) and Henry Lee received a large sum of money from the Spanish (without Congressional approval), never repaid. See Bemis 1926, 81, 107.

9. Madison 1999, 143.

10. On the problems of the Mississippi, see Bemis 1926, 52, 93, 101; Ritcheson 1969, 30, 44; McDonald 1979, 243–244; Nevins 1927, 565–568. For elite concerns about river navigation, see Madison 1999, 14–16, 25–29, 55–56, 60; Washington 1997, 560–562, 570–571, 575, 581, 586–587, 592, 663; Jefferson 1984, 882–883; Hamilton 2001, 856, 914. On secessionist movements in Maine, Vermont, Tennessee, Kentucky, Pennsylvania, North Carolina, Nantucket, and more,

see Bemis 1926, 122–204; Elkins and McKitrick 1993, 218; McDonald 1979, 108, 143; Jensen 1962, 336–337; Slaughter in Boyd ed. 1985, 25; Dull in Greene ed. 1987, 156; Horsman 1985, 32–33; Marks 1973, 104, 130; Richards 2002, 34; Risjord 1978, 230–243; Ritcheson 1969, 152–158; Whitaker 1927, 90, 108–113, 115–119, 209–213; Wright 1975, 32–33.

11. The quotes are from Jensen 1962, 170, 336–337. On the covert action links between foreign powers and Native Americans, see Nevins 1927, 600–601; Bemis 1926, 48, 52, 64–67, 136, 206; Merrell in Greene ed. 1987, 203; Marks 1973, 20–21, 36; Ritcheson 1969, 166–170; Whitaker 1927, 62. On Spanish agents in the American government, see H. Adams 1986a, 784, 838; McDougall 2004, 561. Because of the Native American–foreign power nexus, John Jay thought war with Spain inevitable (Nevins 1927, 601.)

12. From 1964–1971, there were 750 riots that killed 228, injured 12,741, and did enormous economic damage that lasted for a generation. See Postrel 2004. On antebellum disturbances, see Shy in Greene ed. 1987, 77; Szatmary 1980, 124–126; cf. Pencak et al. eds. 2002.

13. See Feer 1969; Brenner 1993.

14. Ellsworth quoted in Bailyn ed. 1993, 1:241.

15. Hamilton in Madison et al. 1987, 174 (no. 21).

16. See Parent 2010.

17. The timing and geographic extent of the original United States was not inevitable. Union was suggested as early as 1754, but the crown rejected it. See Franklin 1987, 383–401, 444, 1430–1431. In 1775, invitations were sent out to Quebec, St. John, Nova Scotia, Georgia, East Florida, and West Florida; Canada was offered equal terms in the Articles—all to no avail. See Amar 2005, 22, 50, 274.

18. Warren 1905, 64. On Knox's popular hysteria, see McDonald 1979, 250–251.

19. See R. Smith 2002, 56, 61; McDonald 1979, 319.

20. Antifederalist quoted in Wood 1998, 486–487; Merritt in Deutsch et al. 1963, 65; Morgan 1956, 151; Franklin 1987, 47; cf. Pole in Jeffreys-Jones and Collins eds. 1983, 4; Riker 1996, 27–28. On Knox's duplicity, see Brynner 1993, 133; Marks 1973, 16–17; Szatmary 1980, 127.

21. On patronage networks, information networks, and voting patterns, see Wood 1993, chap. 4, esp. 87–88; McDonald 1979, 72–75, 319; Risjord 1978, 350. On tampering with the public mail, see Main 1964, 250; Brynner 1993, 243–244. On systematic bias in the press, see Main 1964, 251–253.

22. Ability to prosecute a war should not be conflated with intention to prosecute a war, and Washington's intentions were hard to read. On defense dominance in North America, see Franklin 1987, 635. On the army in early American history, see Katznelson in Katznelson and Shefter eds. 2002, chap. 4.

23. For these quotes and others like them, see Madison quoted in Rakove 1996, 104; Bedford quoted in McDonald 1979, 282; Morris quoted in Middlekauff 1982, 640; Madison quoted in Amar 2005, 120. For ultimate decision by the sword quotes, see Kurland and Lerner 1987, 4:657; Farrand 1968, 192; Madison 1999, 190–192; Washington 1997, 666, 669; Randolph in Bailyn ed. 1993, 2:717; Randolph quoted in Kaminski in Conley and Kaminski eds. 1992, 36.

24. In one sense, most politics is procedural manipulation. But that does not mean all manipulations are consonant with minimal standards of deliberative democracy. It is these violations that I intend by the term "procedural manipulations."

25. See McDonald 1979, 319; McDougall 2004, 565; cf. Riker 1996, 25, 129, 255; Scidiere in Conley and Kaminski eds. 1988, 14. Scholars estimate that it would be generous to say 25 percent of adult white males voted in the ratification elections. Earlier elections had high variability in turnout but were generally higher than ratification's turnout. Compare Dinkin 1982,

129–130 with Dinkin 1977, chap. 7; also Main 1964, 249; Elkins and McKitrick 1993, 521; Levy in Levy ed. 1987, xxxiii. For the fragmentary evidence we have on early American voting, see the American Antiquarian Society's "A New Nation Votes" database, which is available at: http://elections.lib.tufts.edu/aas_portal/index.xq.

26. Morris quoted in McDonald 1979, 346. The example *par excellence* was Washington. He died arguably the wealthiest American of his era, nearly twice as wealthy as Hancock at his death and more than three times wealthier than Franklin at his. To get a better sense of Washington's wealth, compare his net wealth at death (1799) to U.S. federal government outlays and total U.S. GDP and contrast his figures to those of other wealthy Americans: John D. Rockefeller at the height of his wealth (1913) and Bill Gates in 2005 (note: the relative size of the U.S. government increases over time.) Washington's wealth was 10 percent of federal outlays and 1 percent of GDP; Rockefeller was 125 percent of federal outlays and 3 percent of GDP; Gates is 2.5 percent of federal outlays and 0.5 percent of GDP. See R. Smith 2002, 84–88; Chernow 1998, 557. My thanks to Ryan Parks for discussion on this point.

27. Washington 1997, 635.

28. See Ackerman 1998, 38; Riker 1996, 9; Ferejohn et al. 2001, 29; Young in Wilentz ed. 1992, 57; Amar 2005; cf. Tilly 1984, 56–59.

29. Hendrickson 2003, xii. Other claims of his will be treated in the binding section to follow.

30. Adams in Abramson 1994; cf. Wood 1993, 12. See Merritt in Deutsch et al. 1963, 57; 1957; Merritt 1966; Cronin 1994; Bukovansky 1994; 1997.

31. More than 40 percent of adult white males voted, more than any other state. Though evidence is fragmentary, we know about 27 percent turned out in Virginia and Massachusetts, 24 percent in Rhode Island, 17 percent in Pennsylvania, and 15 percent in Maryland. See Dinkin 1982, 129; Kaminski in Conley and Kaminski eds. 1988, chap. 11; Riker 1996, 129; cf. Dinkin 1977, chap. 7. On material conditions and resonant ideas, see Deudney 1995, 225.

32. Rousseau 1979, 458. On realist views of international law, see Mearsheimer 1998b; Carr 1964, chaps. 10–14; Machiavelli 1998, chap. 18; Morgenthau 1993, chaps. 7, 14–17.

33. Quoted in Tuck 2001, 85. See also Tuck 2001, 89, 108. Grotius also argued that where the law provided an end, it also provided the means to attain that end. Quoted in Latin in Sidney 1996, 529. For contrasting viewpoints, see Lauterpacht and Falk in Falk et al. eds. 1985, chaps. 1–2.

34. See Bailyn ed. 1993. Onuf and Onuf (1993), Onuf (1998), and Amar (2005, 27) claim Vattel as influential, and Hendrickson (2003, 52–53) claims Grotius as key. For contrast, Machiavelli is never cited, Adam Smith once, Don Quixote twice, Homer three times, David Hume five times, and Montesquieu at least thirty-five times.

35. See Beard 1941. For kitchen sink approaches, see Middlekauff 1982, 627–628; McDonald 1979, 231; Wood 1993, 122, 308, 311, 337; Nevins 1927, 570; Hendrickson 2003, 170; cf. Haslam 2002, 47–50. For critiques of Beard, see, for example, Elkins and McKitrick 1993, 4; Hofstadter 1950, 195–213; Amar 2005, 159, 279n; Brown, McDonald, and Main in Levy ed. 1987, chaps. 5–7.

36. Zakaria 1998, 56–58, 82–83, 180; LaFeber 1998, 32–34, 112–114.

37. Washington 1997, 592.

38. Deudney 2007, chap. 6, esp. 163; see also Onuf 1983; Hendrickson 2003, 263–264.

39. Deudney 2007, 165.

40. *Federalist* no. 4 is Jay in Hamilton et al. 1987, 99–100; no. 5 is Jay in Ibid., 103; no. 7 is Hamilton in Ibid., 113.

41. Grant 1999, ix. See also Scipio's lament in Polybius 2000, 437 [XXXVIII.21]; cf. 2000, 77–79 [XXIX.20–21]; Juvenal 1967, 137 [VI.290–291]; Gibbon 1994, 4:119–124; Gaddis 1994;

Amar 2005, 299; Livy 1971, 34 [I.1]; Herodotus 1987 [I.32]; Smith 1984, 158. For early Americans' views on concentrations of power, see Ackerman 180; Arendt 147, 175; Bailyn ed. 1993, 1:6, 123, 170, 306, 726, 938; Beard 1941, 173; Wood 1998, 108, 411, 571. Washington opined, "I do not think we are more inspired, have more wisdom, or possess more virtue, than those who will come after us." Bailyn ed. 1993, 1:306; cf. Jefferson 1984, 1428; Wood 1993, 222; Schlesinger 1999, chap. 3.

CHAPTER 5

1. 1948, 3. The *Staatenbund* expression can be found in McCrackan 1901, 336.

2. The Welles reference is to *The Third Man*; the Deutsch references can be found in Deutsch 1976; Deutsch et al. 1957, 44–45.

3. Lunn 1952, 20–21. This is not entirely true. Presumably they hail, like everyone, from Africa, but the first family member we catch a glimpse of is the Alsatian Bishop Werner of Strasbourg. He built a bastion, the *Habichtsburg*, or castle of the hawk, to protect lands in his family since the tenth century, near the intersection of the Aare, Reuss, and Limmat rivers. The fortress gives the family its name. See Bonjour et al. 1952, 66. Ironically enough, the Swiss flag descends from Rudolf's imperial banner, a symbolic grant made to Schwyz in 1289. See Martin 1931, 35. On early Swiss history, see Bonjour et al. 1952, 69–142; Colton 1897, 21–140; Gilliard 1955, 14–39; Herold 1948, 3–25; Lunn 1952, 25–47; Martin 1931, 33–49; Planta 1807; Steinberg 1976, 6–21.

4. On the confederation's persistent balancing behavior, see Lunn 1952, 25, 29; Thürer 1971, 33; Bonjour et al. 1952, 83. The Tell myth is not the only Swiss independence legend. The tale of Arnold von Winkelried also survives, but, perhaps because the name does not lend itself so well to heroism, it is not as well known.

5. On Stüssi and the Toggenburg War, see Thürer 1971, 36–39; Bonjour et al. 1952, 115–118. Although it was particularly ungrateful of Zürich to call in Austria (the city had been besieged by the Habsburgs three times between 1351 and 1355, only to be rescued by the forest cantons), this was not the first time the Austrians had been called in. In 1403, St. Gallen called in Austria to help defeat a much smaller Appenzell and Schwyz army. Predictably, Austria and St. Gallen lost. See Bonjour et al. 1952, 92, 110.

6. Machiavelli 1961, 130.

7. Bonjour et al. 1952, 142; Morgenthau (1993, 344–345) makes a like case. For this section I draw on Bonjour et al. 1952, 158–243; Colton 1897, 141–251; Gilliard 1955, 39–71; Herold 1948, 25–37; Lunn 1952, 44–60; Steinberg 1976, 21–27.

8. Gilliard 1955, 39. On the Reformation in Switzerland and Zwingli, see Thürer 1971, 56–69; Bonjour et al. 1952, 150–162.

9. Steinberg 1976, 24. On perceptions of threat and foreign incursions into Switzerland during the Thirty Years' War, see Thürer 1971, 65; Bonjour et al. 1952, 183–184.

10. On bears as booty, see Lunn 1952, 55; Thürer 1971, 84. On how France abused Switzerland, see Bonjour et al. 1952, 221, 224, 234; Thürer 1971, 88–89, 93–94.

11. William Martin quoted in Schroeder 1994, 492. This section draws broadly on Bonjour et al. 1952, 245–272; Colton 1897, 252–280; Gilliard 1955, 82–94; Herold 1948, 39–41; Lunn 1952, 64–65; Martin 1931, 241–246; McCrackan 1901, 323–336; Steinberg 1976, 32–35; Thürer 1971, 97–113.

12. As an interesting historical note, according to Webster's dictionary, the word "putsch" was introduced to standard German through reports of Swiss uprisings in the 1830s, and especially the Zürich revolt of 1839.

13. Colton 1897, 273. The statement is a half-truth. The Diet did not have the authority to oppress their confederate brothers, but it did desire and in fact went a long way toward nullifying cantonal sovereignty by forcing a change in the confederate compact. See Tilly 2004, 204–205.

14. Quoted in Lunn 1952, 65. For similar quotes, see McCrackan 1901, 330; Mackenzie 1899, 503.

15. Steinberg 1976, 32. On the gathering chaos in Switzerland and how close the Sonderbund came to receiving foreign aid, see Thürer 1971, 100–109; Schroeder 1994, 795–796.

16. See Steinberg 1976, 35; Thürer 1971, 113; Tilly 2004, 205; Riker 1964, 35.

17. In this section I draw on Bonjour et al. 1952, 278–313; Colton 1897, chap. 24; Gilliard 1955, 97–105; Herold 1948, 68; Thürer 1971, 122–137.

18. On the disputes involving Ticino and Neuchâtel, see Thürer 1971, 136–137. On the increasing governmental centralization in Switzerland after 1874, see Bonjour et al. 1952, 313; Gilliard 1955, 105.

19. On outside powers forging Switzerland, see Bonjour et al. 1952, 209, 280. On the variation over time of perceived threats, see Bonjour et al. 1952, 131, 142, 183–184; Gilliard 1955, 97–100; Herold 1948, 68; Steinberg 1976, 30.

20. Bonjour et al. 1952, 260. On the economic and social causes of union, see Thürer 1971, 102.

21. Thürer 1971, 114.

22. See Blainey 1988, chap. 8. On the nationalist shooting clubs, see Bonjour et al. 1952, 259.

23. See Deutsch et al. 1957, 46–58.

24. See Deutsch 1963, 177–178.

25. See Steinberg 1976, 165; cf. Gartzke and Gleditsch 2006.

26. See Bonjour et al. 1952, 258–259.

27. The Swiss and the American cases intersect in several places. In *Federalist* no. 19, Hamilton derides the Swiss confederation as weak and not a true state. The Swiss quite deliberately copy the American Constitution to solve some of their institutional dilemmas. See McCrackan 1901, 336; Herold 1948, 31; Bonjour et al. 1952, 281; Tilly 2004, 175.

CHAPTER 6

1. Letter to the King of Norway, 19 May 1814, quoted in Derry 1957, 135.

2. Interested parties may learn more on such issues in Stomberg 1970, chaps. 1–7; Scott 1988, chaps. 1–4; Keilhan 1944; Oakley 1966, chaps. 1–4; Derry 1957, chap. 2, 68; Gjerset 1969, 1:chaps. 1–74; 1969, 2:chaps. 1–15; Anonymous 2000a; Anonymous 2000b; Hume 1983, 1–2; Miller 1990. A note on sources: information on Sweden and Norway's union in English is evidently not a high scholarly priority. One indication of this is the paucity of publications in history and political science journals over the last hundred years. Several searches in JSTOR's archives divulged a single match on the subject, and the article was four pages long.

3. On the Kalmar Union, see Boyesen 1886, 469–470; Oakley 1966, chap. 5; Stomberg 1970, chaps. 7–8. On failed Norwegian uprisings against Denmark, see Boyesen 1886, 481–482; Derry 1957, chap. 4.

4. On border strife between Norway and Sweden, see Scott 1988, 312; Stagg 1956, 122–123, 126–129, 140–141, 160; Stomberg 1970, 585; Boyesen 1886, 496, 502–504; Gjerset 1969, 2:chap. 32.

5. This action named a trend. Nelson and the English fleet presented Denmark with the choice of surrendering its fleet so it could not fall into Napoleon's hands or having their ships violently taken from them. Denmark chose the latter and England sunk or requisitioned the Danish fleet in Copenhagen harbor. Henceforth, "Copenhagening" as a verb would mark British plans or fears of British plans to neuter challenging navies—e.g., Germany in World War I and France in World War II. I thank George Quester for the point. For the details of Scandinavian alignment in the time of Napoleon, see Scott 1988, 293; Stomberg 1970, 598–600. On the damage Danish policy caused to Norway, including famine and the eating of "bark bread," see Gjerset 1969, 2:388–390; Stagg 1956, 161–166.

6. Quoted in Derry 1957, 127. On the defense of Norway, see Boyesen 1886, 512; Scott 1988, 294; Gjerset 1969, 2:393–395; Stagg 1956, 166.

7. See Stagg 1956, 164; Gjerset 1969, 2:392–396.

8. Quoted in Stomberg 1970, 612. On the Swedish reaction to defeat, see Oakley 1966, 165; Scott 1988, 296–307; Stomberg 1970, 607–615, 627–628.

9. Karl Johan quoted in Gjerset 1969, 2:416. On the treaty between Russia, England, and Sweden, see Boyesen 1886, 514; Scott 1988, 308. On English interest in no single power controlling the entry to the Baltic Sea, see Hobsbawm 1996a, 101; on the importance of the Baltic trade to British hegemony, see Blainey 1968, 3–33. On the Treaty of Kiel, see Gjerset 1969, 2:415–416; Oakley 1966, 167; Stomberg 1970, 630.

10. On the division between Norwegian proponents of union vs. independence and the propaganda laid for union, see Stagg 1956, 178–182; Derry 1957, 130–131; Scott 1988, 316; Stomberg 1970, 610; Boyesen 1886, 518; Gjerset 1969, 2:398–400, 425–428.

11. Quoted in Gjerset 1969, 2:428. On the balance of forces across this period, see Gjerset 1969, 2:434–440; Scott 1988, 312–313; Stomberg 1970, 616, 631.

12. Gjerset 1969, 2:438.

13. On the circumstances favoring a negotiated settlement, see Oakley 1966, 168; Scott 1988, 312. On great power reactions to Scandinavian affairs, see Gjerset 1969, 2:422, 433–434; Stagg 1956, 182–183; Boyesen 1886, 522–523.

14. Karl Johan quoted in Gjerset 1969, 2:442. On Karl Johan's constitutionally ambivalent position, see Derry 1957, 138. On the Norwegian parliament's perceptions and preparations for a resumption of hostilities, see Gjerset 1969, 2:442, 444; Scott 1988, 313.

15. On the agreement for complete formal equality, see Gjerset 1969, 2:445. On the lack of legal consensus, see ibid., 2:536–538. On perceptions of legal supremacy, see ibid., 2:451–452; Nordlund 1905, 72.

16. See Gjerset 1969, 2:455–460; Boyesen 1886, 522–526; Oakley 1966, 187.

17. On the Russian threat in this period, see Gjerset 1969, 2:481, 516–517; Oakley 1966, 188. On the "Ships Crisis," see Scott 1988, 318–319; Oakley 1966, 187–188. South America was not the only liberal cause espoused by Sweden-Norway. The union also borrowed from the U.S. Constitution and its men volunteered on the Northern side in the American Civil War. See Gjerset 1969, 2:418–419, 506n; Stomberg 1970, 579; cf. Arendt 1965, 134–135.

18. On events prior to the Crimean War, see Boyesen 1886, 530; Gjerset 1969, 2:517; Oakley 1966, 198. On events in Schleswig-Holstein and Pan-Scandinavianism, see Gjerset 1969, 2:529; Oakley 1966, 197–216. On the dearth of international events involving Sweden-Norway following 1864, see Scott 1988, 318, 326.

19. Throughout this period, Sweden maintained approximately twice the relative power of Norway. See Hobsbawm 1996b, 311. On the evolution of the Norwegian flag, see Scott 1988, 328; Gjerset 1969, 2:482; Derry 1957, 147; Boyesen 1886, 528. On the failure of attempted

centralization in 1844, see Gjerset 1969, 2:515. On Karl Johan being the first Swedish king to avoid a major war, see Oakley 1966, 192. On the 1848–1859 revaluations of the *Statholder* question, see Gjerset 1969, 2:523–524. On the multiple futile attempts to militarily reorganize, see Gjerset 1969, 2:515, 518, 530, 531–532.

20. Gjerset 1969, 2:560; Boyesen 1886, 535. Boyesen's book is a contribution, curiously enough, to a series of books entitled *The Story of Nations*, which includes, exhaustively: Greece, Rome, Carthage, Spain, Norway, the Jews, and the Saracens. On the escalation of 1882–1886 and the fracture of the liberal party in Norway, see Gjerset 1969, 2:539–544, 556–557; Oakley 1966, 216–217; Stomberg 1970, 747.

21. On the foreign policy of Sweden-Norway, see Nordlund 1905, 64–65; Gjerset 1969, 2:446, 561–562; Stomberg 1970, 747.

22. The Swedish leader quoted is Adolf Hedin in Gjerset 1969, 2:566. The quip is drawn from Stomberg 1970, 712. On Norway's decrepit defenses and conciliation, see ibid., 2:567. For the anecdote about Moltke, see Stomberg 1970, 711–712.

23. On Norway's defensive improvements, see Gjerset 1969, 2:570; Nordlund 1905, 17. On escalation over Norway's "increasingly overwrought sensitiveness" and petitions, see Stagg 1956, 189; Nordlund 1905, 4; Gjerset 1969, 2:571–574. On the growing Russian threat causing the appointment of the commission, see Stomberg 1970, 748. On the large loan floated in case of emergency in 1905, see Scott 1988, 330.

24. On the quasi-unconstitutional preparation and passage on June 6–7, 1905, of measures to dissolve the king's authority, see Derry 1957, 200. Turnout is from Derry 1957, 202; electoral totals are Scott's (1988, 333), though Gjerset (1969, 2:582) arrives at slightly different figures—368,208 to 184—they are nothing worthy of a recount. For military postures during this crisis, see Stomberg 1970, 750, 753; Oakley 1966, 217; Scott 1988, 325; Gjerset 1969, 2:578, 582. For the inverse relationship between Swedish and Norwegian nationalism during this period, see Scott 1988, 326; Stomberg 1970, 746, 755. On the endgame bargaining between Sweden and Norway, see Oakley 1966, 217; Gjerset 1969, 2:578–581; Stomberg 1970, 748–749, 752–753. On the revolutionary action by the Norwegian parliament, see Stomberg 1970, 751. On Norway's solicitation of international sympathy, see Stomberg 1970, 750; Gjerset 1969, 2:576, 579; Nordlund 1905, 54; Scott 1988, 333.

25. See Connor 1994, 172.

26. Quoted in Gjerset 1969, 2:452.

27. On media in Sweden and Norway during the period under consideration, see Hobsbawm 1996a, 266; Hobsbawm 1996b, 85; Nordlund 1905, 54; Oakley 1966, 190; Stagg 1956, 156; Stomberg 1970, 619, 630.

28. See Gjerset 1969, 2:568.

29. For a brief sum of Hroch's main hypotheses, see Hroch in Eley and Suny eds. 1996, 60–68; see also Hobsbawm 1996b, esp. 90, 104. Sweden has past success with changing the nationality of people in territory that it conquered; see Østergård in Eley and Suny eds. 1996, 169–170. On the high congruence between Scandinavian states, see Scott 1988, 327–328.

30. quoted in Gjerset 1969, 2:515.

31. On trade in the Sweden-Norway case, see Nordlund 1905, 12; Gjerset 1969, 2:568.

32. Of course, there is a glaring anomaly to this statement. Nazi Germany did commandeer the country for five years—it is the reason that "Quisling" enters the dictionary as a term of disparagement. Yet it is hard to rationally plan for a Hitler, and Norway put up a longer defense than France did. See Bell 1997, 305, 318–319. On group fragmentation, see Laitin 1998, 20; Posner 2005.

CHAPTER 7

1. Quoted in Masur 1969, 468. Karl Johan's parallel construction is curious. Napoleon also rose through his sword and merit, and he too could claim to be beloved by his people. Perhaps Karl Johan is suggesting that the line between tyrant and liberator is a fine one.

2. Since Thucydides, realism has long mined politics for tragedy (and occasionally, in the case of Machiavelli, comedy). For biographical information on Bolívar, see Karnes 1961, 45–46; Angell 1930; Ducoudray Holstein 1830; Marsland 1954, 134–168; Masur 1969; Parra-Perez 1928; Sherwell 1921. On Bolívar's political thought, see Collier 1983; Fitzgerald 1971. For general historical background on Bolivia, see Riker 1964, 41–42; Barton 1968; Klein 2003; Morales 2003. On Chile, see Cox 1941; Kinsbruner 1973; Loveman 2001; J. Rector 2003; Talbott 1974. On Colombia, see Pearce 1990; Berstein 1964. On Panama, see Howarth 1966. On Peru, see Owens 1963; Rodman 1967. On Venezuela, see Berstein 1964; Fergusson 1939; Jankus and Malloy 1956; Lieuwen 1961; Lott 1972; Marsland 1954.

3. On unrest prior to South American liberation movements, including the conspiracy of the three Antonios, see Morales 2003, 36–37; Pearce 1990, 15; Rodman 1967, 47; Barton 1968, 140–141; Kinsbruner 1973, 34; Lieuwen 1961, 27. On affairs prior to liberation, see Loveman 2001, 99; Cox 1941, 141; Fergusson 1939, 25–26.

4. On events in Europe at this time, see Barton 1968, 147–148; Klein 2003, 93–94; Lott 1972, 56. On elites and the development of South American independence, see Fergusson 1939, 26; Kinsbruner 1973, 44–45; Lieuwen 1961, 27; Loveman 2001, 100.

5. On events in Argentina and Chile during this time, see Loveman 2001, 100–112; Morales 2003, 48; Cox 1941, 159; Kinsbruner 1973, 33–60; Talbott 1974, 21–26; Klein 2003, 94–99; Lieuwen 1961, 31; Morales 2003, 44–47; Rodman 1967, 50–51. Upper Peru/Bolivia was the first to move toward independence, but the movement was strangled in its cradle.

6. See Lieuwen 1961, 28; Lott 1972, 58; Marsland 1954, 118, 130; Berstein 1964, 30–31; Rodman 1967, 48–49. For the Cartagena Manifesto, see Fitzgerald 1971, 10–18.

7. See Marsland 1954, 147–157; Fergusson 1939, 39; Jankus and Malloy 1956, 5; Lieuwen 1961, 30; Berstein 1964, 32; Fitzgerald 1971, 27–44. On the diplomatic history of this period, see Schroeder 1994, 628–636.

8. See Costeloe 1986, 5–6, 52–56, 66–67, 72, 84, 100–101; Rodriguez 1998, chaps. 3–5.

9. Marsland 1954, 159. See also Berstein 1964, 34–35; Collier 1983, 46; Fitzgerald 1971, 45–68; Jankus and Malloy 1956, 6; Masur 1969, 421. On the details and development of Bolívar's thoughts on union over time, see esp. Collier 1983, 50–52, 56; Masur 1969, 416, 411, 413, 417; also Fitzgerald 1971, 19–26, 78, 91. On Bolívar's geopolitical logic behind union, see esp. Fitzgerald 1971, 23, 8, 24–25, 31; also Collier 1983, 44, 58; Klein 2003, 99; Masur 1969, 417; Morales 2003, 48. Bolívar's thoughts on slaves were ahead of their time, but his thoughts on Native Americans were not; see Fitzgerald 1971, 6, 65, 102; Collier 1983, 45.

10. See Lieuwen 1961, 31–32; Marsland 1954, 143, 161–162; Masur 1969, 422–423. Santander and even Sucre were dubious of Bolívar's union schemes early on, see Masur 1969, 417.

11. See Barton 1968, 165–166; Rodman 1967, 55.

12. On the Monroe Doctrine, see Masur 1969, 408–409. On the final battles and Spanish departure, see Jankus and Malloy 1956, 8; Klein 2003, 98; Morales 2003, 47; Owens 1963, 37.

13. On Spanish administrative divisions and South American nationalism, see Fitzgerald 1971, 7; Berstein 1964, 17; Collier 1983, 63; Lieuwen 1961, 33; Masur 1969, 477–478; cf. Slezkine in Eley and Suny eds. 1996, 229. The Soviet Union disintegrated along administrative lines as well. On *uti possidetis*, see Collier 1983, 47; Masur 1969, 385; Talbott 1974, 34.

14. Quoted in Masur 1969, 406. On the tortured history of Upper Peru/Bolivia, see Masur 1969, 385; Morales 2003, 48–51; Klein 2003, 92–100; Barton 1968, 170, 172. On the South American reaction to the American and French Revolutions, see J. Rector 2003, 61.

15. See Masur 1969, 400–401, 406–407, 426, 428.

16. On the border disputes, see Barton 1968, 177. On the Congress of Panama, see Fitzgerald 1971, 75–78; Masur 1969, 413–414. On the suggestion of forming a protectorate, see Parra-Perez 1928, 183; Masur 1969, 413–414; Fitzgerald 1971, 75.

17. Masur 1969, 430. See also ibid., 425, 427. At ibid., 433, Bolívar chastens Páez's officers, "Here there is no other authority and no other power besides mine. Among my companions, I am the sun. If they shine it is because of the light I lend them." On Páez's rebellion, see Marsland 1954, 164–165; Angell 1930, 236. On events in Peru and Bolivia at this time, see Marsland 1954, 165; Masur 1969, 435; Morales 2003, 52.

18. Quoted in Parra-Perez 1928, 166. On the Ocaña Convention, see Lieuwen 1961, 32; Masur 1969, 445–451; Parra-Perez 1928, 197. On New Grenada's revolt, Peru and Bolivia's hostilities, and Dictator Bolívar and his conspirators, see Marsland 1954, 165–166; Masur 1969, 461; Lieuwen 1961, 32; Angell 1930, 253; Parra-Perez 1928, 174, 179.

19. On Bolívar's optimism, see Masur 1969, 471–472. On Bolívar's nadir, see Angell 1930, 259; Masur 1969, 472, 475–476, 482; Lieuwen 1961, 33. On foreign intrigue and Córdoba, see Barton 1968, 178; Masur 1969, 276, 469, 471. On Bolívar's expulsion and outlawry, see Marsland 1954, 166–167; Berstein 1964, 37. Slander was particularly hard on Bolívar since, like Napoleon, Hamilton, and Washington, he had thin skin, see Parra-Perez 1928, 154. On Bolívar's repeated incantation of his solutions to whatever problems a state had, see Parra-Perez 1928, 185; Jankus and Malloy 1956, 11; Fitzgerald 1971, 45–68, 75–77, 93, 136, 138. For Bolívar's repetitive cheap talk that he knew a particular plan would not succeed, see Masur 1969, 415; Fitzgerald 1971, 42.

20. On the Bogotá Convention, see Lieuwen 1961, 33. On the status of Venezuela, see Parra Perez 1928, 177. On the Battle of Tarqui and after, see Rodman 1967, 59–60; Barton 1968, 178; Morales 2003, 53; Masur 1969, 481. On the Caracas Act of Separation, see Angell 1930, 258; Marsland 1954, 166; Masur 1969, 471; Berstein 1964, 36.

21. Bolívar may not have died of tuberculosis. Dr. Paul Auwaerter of the Johns Hopkins School of Medicine suspects arsenicosis and bronchiectasis, essentially a diagnosis of ingesting too much arsenic through medical treatments of the time or accidentally through food or drink. Other physicians suspect a combination of tuberculosis and arsenic poisoning. The point is interesting but immaterial; Bolívar was politically dead regardless.

22. Bolívar in Fitzgerald 1971, 138, 137; the remaining quotes are from Marsland 1954, 168, 134, respectively. The story of union in South America does not entirely end with Bolívar's death. From 1837–1839, Peru and Bolivia formed a union, which was dismantled for geopolitical reasons by Chile and Argentina. However, that is outside the work's purview. On Santa Cruz and the genesis of Peru-Bolivia, see Klein 2003, 114–115; Morales 2003, 54; Barton 1968, 182. On the war to extinguish the Peru-Bolivia union, see Kinsbruner 1973, 66; Klein 2003, 115–116; Morales 2003, 54; Owens 1963, 38.

23. Fitzgerald 1971, 119. On the terrible effects of the colonies' struggle with Spain, see Lott 1972, 57; Marsland 1954, 151.

24. Quoted in Collier 1983, 53. On Anglo-American overtures to charm South America, among which was the Monroe Doctrine, see Barton 1968, 148; Kinsbruner 1973, 74–75; Loveman 2001, 104, 117; Masur 1969, 409; Rodman 1967, 48–49. Hofstadter (1973, 455) makes the point that Great Britain encouraged South American independence from Spain (as well as southeastern European aspirations of independence from the Ottoman Empire) to reap the

geopolitical benefits. The United States would later steal this play from Great Britain to dismantle Britain's empire.

25. Fitzgerald 1971, 77; cf. Collier 1983, 53–54; Masur 1969, chap. 30.

26. On Bolívar's power as the Spanish threat disappeared, see Marsland 1954, 161; Pearce 1990, 16.

27. Fitzgerald 1971, 44.

28. This is Bolívar's Trujillo proclamation, which at more length reads: "Spaniards and Canary Islanders, count on death even though you be neutral, if you do not work actively for American liberty. Americans, count on life even though you be guilty." Quoted in Marsland 1954, 144.

29. See Angell 1930, 245; Barton 1968, 145; Berstein 1964, 37.

30. On the relative power of Páez versus Bolívar, see Berstein 1964, 37; Lieuwen 1961, 32–33; Masur 1969, 430, 471.

31. Quoted in Marsland 1954, 164.

32. Parra-Perez 1928, 139; cf. Masur 1969, 407. See also Parra-Perez 1928, 194; Angell 1930, 258.

33. Both quotes are from Masur 1969, 438 and 425, respectively.

34. However, there were, as always, some identity factors that militated toward dissension. See Fitzgerald 1971, 41; Parra-Perez 1928, 188; Karnes 1961, 7–8. For a constructivist look at South American boundaries, see Parodi 2002. For ideological arguments about nationalism, see Kinsbruner 1973, 34; Klein 2003, 89–90; cf. Collier 1983; Morse in Hartz 1964, 159–169.

35. For evidence that economics played a role in South American liberation, see Barton 1968, 144; J. Rector 2003, 64. On prewar economic conditions, see Berstein 1964, 26; J. Rector 2003, 61, 74; Pearce 1990, 17; Owens 1963, 35; Kinsbruner 1973, 38–39, 42–43, 61; Loveman 2001, 114, 117; Klein 2003, 102–105. On the lack of class struggle, see Loveman 2001, 98–99; Berstein 1964, 27. Although some foreign trade inevitably got scooped up by the British and North Americans, dislocation was substantial because of the end of Spanish monopolies. On Spanish overseas trade shifts from 1792 to 1827, see Costeloe 1986, 150.

36. Angell 1930, 231; Fergusson 1939, 47.

37. See Masur 1969, 418. See also Klein 2003, 107.

38. As a thought experiment, one can push the imagery further. If Bolívar is a Christ-like figure, then the analog of Roman rule is the international system, perhaps with its own ancient constitution but ever-changing statutes. Bolívar had good taste in parallels for his person and project, evoking George Washington and William Tell, see Fitzgerald 1971, 20, 33, 41, 77; cf. Fergusson 1939, 42; Jankus and Malloy 1956, 10; Marsland 1954, 133; Masur 1969, 399–400; Sherwell 1921, 181. But his envy of Washington may have been his undoing. Envy may level people up or down, but Bolívar is a case of upward envy bringing one down. There is much to be said for knowing how to pick the right idol at the right time.

39. The arguments I make above are related to A. O. Hirschman's (1991) futility thesis. On liberty versus greatness, see Parra-Perez 1928, 147, 148, 192; Masur 1969, 477.

CHAPTER 8

1. Chirac quoted in Kupchan 2002, 151; Delors quoted in *Economist* 2005, 52. For similar elite sentiments, see Thatcher 2002, 344, 352; Moravcsik 1998, 390, 472; Cooper 2003, 78–79, 157; G. Morgan 2005, ix, x.

2. The European opinion data may be found in Kennedy and Bouton 2002, 70. The phrase "ever closer union" is from the preamble of the 1957 Treaty of Rome and is reiterated in the constitutional treaty of 2004.

3. On how settlement patterns, ethnicity, and path dependent institutions influence contestation, see Toft 2003; D. Posner 2005; O'Leary 2003.

4. Here I am using the integration benchmarks laid out in the groundwork section of the introductory chapter. The historical section leans most on Lundestad 1997; Nugent 1999; Sidjanski 2000; Lerner and Aron eds. 1957; Trachtenberg 1991, chap. 1; 1999; Mattli 1999; Moravcsik 1998; Milner 1997, chap. 7; Herman, Risse, and Brewer eds. 2004; Rosato 2011.

5. This section relies on Bendix 1980; Hobsbawm 1987; 1995; 1996a; 1996b; Kennedy 1987; Kennan 1979; McNeil 1984; Parker 2001; Schroeder 2004.

6. See Taylor 1977, 392, also xxxii. On integration during World War I, see Kennan 1958, 4, 420–421; McNeill 1984, 344. See also Hooker n.d.

7. Morgenthau and Roosevelt in Trachtenberg 1999, 16. JCS 1067 can be found in United States Department of State 1945. The material on the Morgenthau and Marshall Plans is drawn from McAllister 2002, 17, 28, 51–55, 76–78, 82; Kennan 1967; Milward 1984, 465–466.

8. United States Department of State 1985, 124–125. On the American estrangement with punitive German policy, see McAllister 2002, 90, 108, chap. 4.

9. 1985, 226–227; cf. McAllister 2002.

10. Rosato 2011, chap. 3; Sutton 2007.

11. 1999, 40–41.

12. On the period of the EDC, see McAllister 2002, 193–242; Trachtenberg 1999, 110–125; Aron in Lerner and Aron eds., chap. 1; Rosato 2011, chap. 4.

13. Quoted in Lundestad 1997, 152. As James McAllister (2002, 139) shows, Dulles was loath to coddle the Europeans and did his best to foster quick unification and avoid dependence on an American military presence. On Europe's American pacifier, see Joffe 1984.

14. Acheson 1969, 708.

15. For this period and after, see Aggestam and Hyde-Price 2000; Fransen 2001; Farrell et al. eds. 2001; Gaddis 2005; Haas 1970; S. Jones 2003; Henderson 2005; M. Holmes 2001; Kennan 1967, chaps. 14, 17–19; 1996, 141–151, 169–178; T. Lindberg ed. 2005; L. Lindberg and Scheingold 1970; L. Lindberg and Scheingold eds. 1971; Marks and Steenbergen 2004; McInnes 1992; Menon and Wright eds. 2001; Newman 1996; Sandholtz and Zysman 1989; Sandholtz 1993; Pollack 2003; Winn and Lord 2001; Rosato 2003; Parsons 2003; Watts 2008, chap. 1.

16. Art 1996, esp. 35–39. On events German surrounding reunification, see Zelikow and Rice 1995; Maier 1997; cf. Craig 1982.

17. On what states balance against, see Walt 1987, 22–26; Christensen 1996, 27–28; Levy 2004, 31–45; Wohlforth 1993, 222, 298–299; Kaufman, Little, and Wohlforth eds. 2007, 228–242; Friedberg 1988, chaps. 6–7; Crowe 1907; Schroeder 2004, chap. 10. For vital interests, I use Daryl Press's definition (2005, 26): "Vital interests are those related to a state's survival," specifically "preserving its sovereignty and protecting its citizens." For similar arguments on how security hurts European unity, see Rakove 2003, 39; Posen 2006, 149, 184; Rosato 2011, chap. 6; cf. Walt 1998, 3–11.

18. For realist views on European integration, see Joffe 1984, 64–82; Art 1996, 1–39; Mearsheimer 2001b, 46–61; Grieco 1996, 176–185; Parent 2009b; Sutton 2007, 10–11; Rosato 2011.

19. On European disunity on force deployment, see Tams in Wallander et al. eds. 1999, 81. On America's role in European defense, see Lundestad 2005, 238, 264–266, 281, 285–286. For

survey data on threats to Europe, see Kennedy and Mouton 2002, 70, 72; Ray and Johnston 2007, 86.

20. On current alignments, see Walt 1998; Posen 2006.

21. On the issues blamed for bedeviling the EU, see *Economist* 2007a, 46; *Economist* 2007b, 62.

22. See Machiavelli 1996, 23 [I.6]; Gibbon 1994, 4:121 [chap. 38]. For fine studies in comparative integration efforts, see Goldstein 2001; Zweifel 2002; Menon and Schain eds. 2006; Glencross 2009.

23. On America's British pacifier, see Jensen 1962, 337–343.

24. Rumsfeld's remarks can be found in CNN 2003. On America's long-standing subordination of European unity to American foreign policy goals, see Lundestad 2005, 38, 63, 78, 86–88, 176, 182, 232, 243, 259, 261, 278. On America and divide and rule in Europe, see Layne 2003, 17–29.

25. Eric Hobsbawm 1997, 268; cf. *Economist* 2007c, 44. On the myth of Europe's democratic deficit, see Moravcsik 2008; Zweifel 2002; cf. Hix 2008, chap. 5.

26. For the CIA data, see S. Jones 2007, 15, 222. For EU-U.S. parallels, see Kupchan 2004–2005, 103–120; Marks 1997, 24; Deudney 1995, 193; Rodden 2006, 4.

27. On constructivism and European integration, see Parsons 2003; also Caporaso 1996, 29–52; Fligstein 2009; Deutsch et al. 1957; Kupchan 2010, 216.

28. See Moravcsik 1999.

29. Moravcsik 1998, 18. Previously (Parent 2009b, 520), I attributed to Moravcsik the view that "the most important cause of integration is economic interest." Subsequently, Moravcsik has most courteously informed me that he does not hold that view, and that he instead believes that foreign policy cooperation "is driven by security considerations." (personal correspondence October 8, 2009). I apologize for misrepresenting his beliefs. See also Moravcsik 1997; Moravcsik and Schimmelfennig 2009; Moravcsik 2009.

30. For binding arguments in Europe, see S. Jones 2003; 2007; Deudney 2007, chap. 5.

31. Art 1996, 25.

32. Rosato 2011, chap. 6; Moravcsik 2009.

33. See also Howorth and Keeler eds. 2003; Howorth 2007; Foradori, Rosa, and Scartezzini eds. 2007.

34. In theory, Russia could stir up unions on its eastern or western flanks, and occasionally there are noises made in this direction. But as William Wohlforth shows, presently Russia is too large to balance for its immediate Eurasian neighbors. See Wohlforth in Paul, Wirtz, and Fortmann eds. 2004, 226.

35. On the obsolescence of great power war and the decreasing relevance of territory, see Mueller 2004, 1–5; Spruyt 2005, 4; Kaysen 1990, 42–64.

36. On the rise of China, see Brown et al. eds. 2000; Ross and Feng eds. 2008; Dreyer 2004.

37. One could wonder why we ought to honor the authors of the Marshall Plan when they acted under duress; these are, after all, the same gentlemen who behaved callously toward Western Europe a short time before. But without knowing the incentive structure, praise and blame are impossible. Hindsight should not obscure that these men had multiple options to deal with the Soviet threat. All is vanity, but few forms of selfishness help build anything comparable to a stable, prosperous Europe. How many humanitarian policies have achieved the humanitarian results of the self-serving Marshall Plan?

38. Central America and ASEAN have, to varying degrees, patterned themselves after Europe's integrative model. Because of American hegemony and geography, neither has advanced far, though that may change with relative power shifts. On ASEAN, see Antolik

1990; Beeson ed. 2004; Bessho 1999; Gill 1997; Henderson 1999; Leifer 1989; Mahapatra 1990; Scalapino and Wanandi 1982; Taylor ed. 1996. See also Katzenstein 2005, chap. 4. On Central American union see Karnes 1961.

39. Taylor 1977, xxi; cf. Carr, 1964, 22–40; Cooper 2003, 171–172; Rifkin 2004, 7–8.

40. See Madison in Hamilton et al. 1987, 163–164 [no. 18]; cf. Waltz 1979, 127; Polybius 2000, 6:77 [XXIX.20].

CHAPTER 9

1. Renan in Eley and Suny eds. 1996, 45; cf. Stigler 1982, 111.

2. On high versus low politics, see Keohane and Nye 1989, 27–29; Milner 1997, 181. For sanguine accounts of political integration's prospects, see Haas 1964; 1968; L. Lindberg and Scheingold 1970; L. Lindberg and Scheingold eds. 1971; Scheingold 1970; Nye ed. 1968; Stone Sweet, Sandholtz, and Fligstein eds. 2001.

3. Keohane in Keohane ed. 1986, 198; also Wendt 2003; Rodrik 1999; Deudney 2007. Realists have inclined toward similar positions for similar reasons, see Kennan 1954, 105–107; Lippmann 1963, 77.

4. The prevailing culprit for the demise of the USSR is domestic factors; see Dobrynin 2001, 612; Beissinger 2002; Roeder 1991, 196, 232; Solnick 1998, 242–245, 253. However, some accounts do give a starring role to external factors, see Kennan 1967, chaps. 11, 15; 1984, part II; Deudney and Ikenberry 1991/1992.

5. Abramowitz et al. 2006, 89; cf. Toner and Rutenberg 2006; Parent and Bafumi 2009.

6. For analyses that align with mine, see Montesquieu 1965, 93–95, 169 [chaps. 9, 18]; Gibbon 1993, 1:65–66 [chap. 2]; 1993, 4:119–121 [chap. 38]; Polybius 2000, 6:437 [XXXVIII.21]; Hintze 1975, 161–162, 181–185; Simmel 1964, 98–99. There remains much dispute about the causes of Rome's fall, see Kagan ed. 1962; Tainter 2005, 148–152; Mackay 2004, 351–353; Heather 2006.

7. See Gaddis 1994; Juvenal 1967, 137 [VI.290–291]; Amar 2005, 299; Livy 1971, 34 [I.1]; Herodotus 1987 [I.32]; Tolstoy 1996, 608 [book 10]; Smith 1984, 158; Tainter 2005, 201–202; Knight 1997, chaps. 1–2. On American primacy, see Brooks and Wohlforth 2002; Jervis 2005, 92–93.

8. 1954, 82; cf. Kennan 1967, 7; 1996, 306; Chekhov 1979, 59 [*At Home*].

APPENDIX

1. Gilbert 1939, 483; cf. Carr 1964, 89; Viroli 1995, 36–37. All chapter references are to *The Prince* unless otherwise stated.

2. Letter 179, of 17 May 1521. See Machiavelli 1961, 200.

3. Machiavelli 1996, 38 [I.12]; cf. Machiavelli 2003a, [VII.247]. Since this passage is from the *Discourses*, we cannot assume a reader of *The Prince* would be familiar with it. Yet there is enough anti-Church sentiment and praise of lone unifiers in *The Prince* for a reader to understand that reorganizing the Church aids the liberation of Italy. See Sullivan 1996, chaps. 1–2; Machiavelli 1998, chap. 11.

4. Machiavelli 1998, 47 [chap. 11]; cf. Machiavelli 1988, I.9. Full disclosure: the author is Catholic.

5. On political autonomy, fear of relative gains, and balancing in Italy, see Machiavelli 1996 chaps. 11 and 20. A counterargument to this point is that Machiavelli desired a temporary

military alliance to drive out the foreigners instead of a true unification. While Machiavelli advocates expedient balancing behavior, such a quick fix is anathema to his doctrine of self-help through expansion. To be competitive in the system, Italy would have to ape England and France, and Machiavelli says as much in *The Prince*, chap. 3 (cf. *Discourses* II.4; Waltz 1979, 127). Such temporary coalitions are the statecraft equivalent of drug addiction; they are attempts to maximize short-run utility that destroy long-run utility. On this point, see Machiavelli letters 131 and 134 to Vettori 10 August 1513 and 26 August 1513 in Machiavelli 1961, 128–129, 136–137.

6. Machiavelli 1998, 102. Whitfield sees a parallel construction between chapters 6 and 26 in the four epithets "powerful, secure, honored, and happy" at the end of chapter 6 with "beaten, despoiled, torn, and pillaged" in chapter 26. See Whitfield 1969, 27.

7. Machiavelli 1998, 22. On how strongly Machiavelli encourages imitation, see 1998, chaps. 6, 14, 21, 26; cf. Olschki 1945, 43–44; Gilbert 1984, 238–239. A secondary omission in *The Prince* is Numa Pompilius, Rome's second king. In the *Discourses* Machiavelli gives credit to the founding of Rome to Romulus as well as Numa, see *Discourses* I.11. Ultimately, Machiavelli prefers Romulus to Numa (*Discourses* I.19.4) but his warm praise for Numa in the *Discourses* contrasts starkly with his stony silence toward him in *The Prince*.

8. On the importance of founders and the example of Rome, see Machiavelli 1996, I.6, II.2; Villari 1968, 2:134.

9. See Machiavelli 2003b, 3; cf. Macfarland 1999; Lefort 1972, 336, 362, 422. Likewise, one could read Machiavelli's pregnant silence in chapter 26 as a literary strategy of all-or-nothing tough love. Machiavelli plants the seed of the idea but then abandons it in rough soil.

10. Moses excepted. Lorenzo de' Medici is also very young—and perhaps malleable—when he becomes duke of Urbino. This is consistent with Machiavelli's assertion that fortune favors the young, but that should not obscure a profound tension in *The Prince*. Machiavelli's work is founded on the belief that a correct understanding of politics is indispensable to successful action. Yet, who knows less than the young? It appears as though there is a trade-off between learning and audacity that must be optimized. See Whitfield 1969, 103–104; Kontos 1972.

11. I use Herodotus's account for chapter 6 because Machiavelli goes out of his way twice to refer to the Cyrus "by Xenophon" in chapter 14. By implication, some other Cyrus (historical Cyrus? The effectual truth of Cyrus? Herodotus's Cyrus?) is meant in the other three chapters in which Cyrus appears. I speculate on meager evidence that it is Herodotus's Cyrus. Xenophon tells a tale of a death more peaceful and deliberate for Cyrus than Herodotus relates. On Machiavelli's ambivalence toward and differentiation from Xenophon, see Newell 1988; cf. Nadon 1996.

12. Machiavelli is sensitive about moving from generalities to particulars, see his *Prince*, chap. 20.1, *Discourses* II.33.

13. This story is drawn from Titus Livy 1971, 39 [I.6]. Livy also suggests that Romulus's victory over Remus was not random. Earlier, only Remus fell into a trap laid for both of them. Machiavelli blames Tatius's death on Romulus, but excuses him carte blanche in *Discourses* I.9. And if one is to believe Plutarch, Romulus is also responsible for slaying two of his foster fathers. If we are to lay responsibility on Romulus on a grander scale, it was not long before Rome swallowed Alba. See Plutarch 1992, 1:32.

14. Machiavelli 1996, III.30.1; cf. ibid., I.9.3.

15. Machiavelli uses this terminology in chapter 3, where he discusses how Louis XII could have conquered Italy, highlighting mistakes a succeeding conqueror could avoid. See Tarcov 2000. Cesare Borgia and *The Life of Castruccio Castracani* also illustrate traps for an Italian unifier to avoid.

16. On Machiavelli's criticism of destroyers of religion, see *Discourses* I.10.1. On morals in *The Prince*, see Berlin 1998, 269–325; Scott and Sullivan 1994, 890–891. With regard to Numa's absence from *The Prince*, Numa may be excluded because sixteenth-century Italy, a land with more religion than military virtue, was ripe for a new Romulus, not a new Numa.

17. Machiavelli 1998, 61 [chap. 15], see also 102 [chap. 26]. The Medici were not the only family so situated. Shortly we will turn to the Borgias, but here I should note that Machiavelli has positive things to say about Francesco Maria della Rovere, the militant *nepote* of Pope Julius II. See Machiavelli 1996, II.10.1, II.24.4.

18. For background, see Reinhard 1935; Najemy 1982. On the initial tensions among the Medici, see Butters 1985, 240; Devonshire Jones 1972, 111; Ridolfi 1963, 176; Stephens 1983, 80. On Lorenzo's role as scapegoat, see Butters 1985, 234. On Lorenzo's spending and debt problems, see Stephens 1983, 100; Butters 1985, 235. On the issues of Lorenzo's quest for and securing of a marital match, see Butters 1985, 237, 269, 299; Stephens 1983, 97, 100, 106. On Lorenzo's offensive political self-assertion, see Devonshire Jones 1972, 119, 136; Butters 1985, 240, 269, 300; Stephens 1983, 98–100, 102, 107. On the speedy undoing of Lorenzo's rule in Florence and the lack of lamentation at his death, see Ridolfi 1963, 176; Devonshire Jones 1972, 138–139; Stephens 1983, 108.

19. Najemy 1993, 147.

20. Machiavelli 1996, II.13; 1988, I.27; 1998, chap. 8. Although the greatest examples do not illustrate the practice, Machiavelli discusses the reverse in other prominent examples. That is, he highlights uncles killing nephews to found a new principality. Machiavelli may merely want to catalyze fear of such duplicity in Lorenzo to stoke a security dilemma and provoke preemption. See Machiavelli 1998, 35, 37, 47, 67, 79. For glory as supreme motive and particularly necessary in the state-building enterprise in Machiavelli, see Price 1977, 595, 618; de Grazia 1989, 259, 375; Strauss 1978, chap. 4; Villari 1968, 2:chaps. 2–3; Machiavelli 1996, 31 [I.10].

21. Machiavelli 1996, 64 [I.27].

22. Machiavelli 1961, 180. The passage is drawn from letter 155, of 20 December 1514.

23. Burckhardt 1990, 88; cf. Machiavelli 1998, 102; Machiavelli 2003a, 12 [I.43].

24. See Machiavelli 1998, 29, 30, and 65.

25. Machiavelli 1998, 33. Scott and Sullivan (1994, 888, 895) have made these interpretations of chapters 7 and 8 before.

26. Machiavelli 1988, 264. Keeping with a motif, Machiavelli once again posits Petrarch as the poetic inspiration of Italian unification.

27. Guicciardini 1984, 244. See also Machiavelli 1996, II.16.2, II.17.1, II.17.4, II.24.3, III.41.2–44.3.

28. Machiavelli 1996, 149; cf. Machiavelli 2003a, 159 [VII.178]; Mansfield 1979, 216.

29. Livy 1976, 209 [XXXV.14].

30. Machiavelli's thoughts on surprise are more complicated than usually thought (e.g., Handel 1992, 3–4) and, because it would impede the argument, as presented here. On how the diplomatic use of ambiguity can elicit desired outcomes, see Jervis 1989, chap. 5; cf. Callieres 1963, 14, 31–32.

31. Machiavelli 1996, 156 [II.13]. See also ibid., II.1.2, III.40.

32. On Machiavelli's caution about circulating his work or giving it to its dedicatee, see Baron 1991, 88–89; de Grazia 1989, 40. There is a story—perhaps apocryphal—that Machiavelli did give his little work to Lorenzo de' Medici, who was uninterested in it and more taken by some hounds he had received as a gift. See Chabod 1958, 17–18, 106; Ridolfi 1963, 164. Contra Baron, I interpret this hesitance not as uncertainty about the conclusion but as the

prudent floating of a trial balloon on a work that could endanger the author's life. On agenda setting, concealment, and complicity, see Strauss 1987, 312. See also Machiavelli 2003a, 152, 154 [VII.99, VII.124]; Machiavelli 1996, I.25, I.39, III.48. In the present case it is a second-order conspiracy: Machiavelli conspires to get Lorenzo to conspire.

33. See Strauss 1978, 63–69. This pacific façade was not complete fraud. In the expansions of the Roman Republic (510 BC to 121 BC), Rome went to war on average about once every twenty years. Keeley 1997, 33. Lorenzo was no stranger to the balance of power; his grandfather is credited in one of the earliest formulations of it, see Guicciardini 1984, book 1.

34. For this reason, I initially refused to write this piece. Stefan Pedatella, my longtime roommate and gifted Italianist, good naturedly wagered me: if I could show him who did it first, dinner on him at the establishment of my choice. If I could not, I had to write it up.

35. Chabod 1958, 69.

36. See Meinecke 1998, 41, 166, 293, 359; Whitfield 1969, 27, 123, 157, 158, 161, 204; Strauss 1978, 69, 308, n34–35, 309; cf. Lefort 1972, 446–447.

37. See also Machiavelli 1988, VIII.1. As Rousseau noticed (1987, 183), "Under the pretext of teaching kings, he has taught important lessons to the peoples. Machiavelli's *The Prince* is the book of republicans." When Machiavelli tells princes how to avoid conspiracies, he is simultaneously announcing to conspirators where princes are most vulnerable to conspiracies. Guicciardini famously criticizes Machiavelli for his fetish with Rome, see Guicciardini 1965; 1972, 69–70.

38. There may be an additional listing, though it leaves the analysis unchanged. After case one, Machiavelli discourses about the divinity of Moses and whether he is comparable to the others. Machiavelli then remarks (1998, 22): "But let us consider Cyrus and the others . . ." (the ellipsis bars breaking the prior pattern). Once the first two names are given in sequence, it is logically impossible for any subsequent permutation to alter the Moses, Cyrus, Theseus relationship.

39. The math is $(1) \times (1/6) \times (1/6) \times (1/6) = 0.46$ percent. If there are 5 listings instead of 4 (see previous note), the formula is $(1) \times (1/6) \times (1/6) \times (1/6) \times (1/6) = 0.08$ percent. There are 24, or 4 factorial, permutations of the names, only 4 of which can maintain any 3 names in the same order. The first draw is a given, but after that each draw has a 4 in 24 chance (i.e., 1/6) of mantaining the pattern. My thanks to Ryan Parks for his supererogatory help on this point.

40. It is curious that Felix Gilbert sees no preparatory groundwork laid for chapter 26, and believes the chapter to be decorative. Gilbert is Meinecke's student and Gilbert appears not to have learned what his teacher knew. Plus, Gilbert dismisses the last chapter as ornament in a work that states upfront "I have not ornamented this work" (Machiavelli 1998, 4). See also Whifield 1969, 27.

41. Baron 1991, 101–102.

42. See Tarcov 1982. See note 5 above.

43. "Lets herself be won" is from Machiavelli 1998, 101 [chap. 25].

44. Machiavelli 1998, 103 [chap. 26]. The founders listed in chapter 6 are of highly dubious paternity; Machiavelli supposes them to "have had such humble fathers that, feeling ashamed of them, they have made themselves out to be sons of Jupiter or some other god." (Machiavelli 2003b, 3). See also Strauss 1978, 75; Pitkin 1984, 260.

45. Machiavelli 1998, 102 [chap. 26], see also 61 [chap. 15].

46. For Baron's claim and the text on which he bases it, see his 1991, 95–96; Machiavelli 1998, 47.

47. For the reference of which I speak, see Machiavelli 1998, 35, 37, 47, 67, 79. On cruelty well used, see also the Remirro de Orco and Severus narratives in ibid., 30, 65, 78.

48. De Grazia 1989, 53. Gennaro Sasso also makes this point, albeit tentatively. See Sasso 1987, 2:340–341.

49. Machiavelli 1998, 22–23.

50. Martelli 1999, 135–137. On Machiavelli's method and empirics, see Butterfield 1967; Gilbert 1984, chap. 6; 1986; Olschki 1945.

51. To keep my accounting transparent, what follows are the cases, where they can be found in the *Florentine Histories*, and whether the target was hated and the conspiracy strategically (as opposed to tactically) successful. The cases are: Walter, Duke of Athens (II.36–38) [hated, successful], Ciompi (II.13–16) [not hated, successful], Maso Degli Albizzi (III.27) [hated—NM calls the people "malcontent," unsuccessful], Florentine Revolution (III.28) [unclear—hence this case is dropped, unsuccessful], Pagolo (IV.25) [hated—NM calls him a "tyrant," successful], Cosimo de' Medici (IV.27–29) [not hated, a qualified success], Rinaldo Peruzzi (IV.32–33) [hated, a qualified success], Erasmo (V.6–7) [hated, successful], Annibale Bentivoglio (VI.10) [not hated, unsuccessful], the pope (VI.29) [hated, not successful], Piero de Medici (VII.10–17) [hated for collecting debts mercilessly, unsuccessful], Cesare Petrucci (VII.26–27) [not hated, unsuccessful], Duke of Milan/Galeazzo (VII.33–34) [hated, unsuccessful], Pazzi (VIII.2) [not hated, unsuccessful], Girolamo Riario (VIII.34) [hated, not successful], Galeatto Manfredi (VIII.35) [not hated, successful]. I code hatred based on Machiavelli's favorable or unfavorable references to conspiracy targets in the passage. By strategic success I mean gaining and maintaining power for more than one year.

52. Contra Baron, Strauss believes (1978, 48, 52) that 26 was the original number of chapters intended for *The Prince*. This is in keeping with his numerological interpretation of Machiavelli. Twenty-six is, says Strauss (1987, 311), 2 times 13, which signifies fortune, or it could be the alphanumeric sum of the Hebrew God. Perhaps, perhaps not, though this last interpretation strikes me as far-fetched. If one is to read Machiavelli numerologically, I offer an alternative. Twenty-six could be a calendrical reference. There are 26 weeks in a half-year, suggesting the Machiavellian theme of cycles and nature's variability. See Machiavelli 1961, 185. Why 26 as opposed to 52 or some other multiple of 13 is a larger issue, but it could relate to middle ways, half-truths, and the *Discourses*. English readers should not suspect that 26 refers to the alphabet; sixteenth-century Italian did not have 26 letters.

53. I owe to John Langton (1987, 1281) the insight that Machiavelli praises absolute leaders with popular armies such as Tullus, Pelopidas, Epaminondas, and the king of England. This view concurs with the Cambridge School's idea that a prince, or princely power, is necessary in founding. See, for example, Bock, Skinner, and Viroli eds. 1990; cf. McCormick 2003; Femia 2004.

REFERENCES

Abbott, Andrew. 2001. *Chaos of Disciplines*. Chicago: University of Chicago Press.

Abramowitz, Alan, et al. 2006. Don't Blame Redistricting for Uncompetitive Elections. *Political Science & Politics* 39: 87–90.

Acharya, Amitav, and Alastair Iain Johnston, eds. 2007. *Crafting Cooperation: Regional International Institutions in Comparative Perspective*. New York: Cambridge University Press.

Acheson, Dean. 1969. *Present at the Creation: My Years in the State Department*. New York: Norton.

Ackerman, Bruce. 1993. *We the People: Foundations*. Cambridge: Harvard University Press.

Ackerman, Bruce. 1998. *We the People: Transformations*. Cambridge: Harvard University Press.

Adams, Charles Francis. 1911. *Studies Military and Diplomatic, 1775–1865*. New York: Macmillan.

Adams, Henry. 1986a. *History of the United States of America during the Administrations of Thomas Jefferson*. New York: Library of America.

Adams, Henry. 1986b. *History of the United States of America during the Administrations of James Madison*. New York: Library of America.

Adams, Henry. 1990. *The Education of Henry Adams*. New York: Liberty Fund.

Adamthwaite, Anthony. 1985. Britain and the World, 1945–9: The View from the Foreign Office. *International Affairs* 61: 223–235

Addo, Ebenezer O. 1997. *Kwame Nkrumah: A Case Study of Religion and Politics in Ghana*. New York: University Press of America.

Adler, Emanuel, and Michael Barnett, eds. 1998. *Security Communities*. New York: Cambridge University Press.

Aggestam, Lisbeth, and Adrian Hyde-Price. 2000. *Security and Identity in Europe: Exploring the New Agenda*. New York: St. Martin's Press.

Agyeman, Opoku. 1992. *Nkrumah's Ghana and East Africa: Pan-Africanism and African Interstate Relations*. Teaneck: Fairleigh Dickinson University Press.

Akerlof, George. 1970. The Market for Lemons: Quality Uncertainty and the Market Mechanism. *Quarterly Journal of Economics* 54: 488–500.

Alesina, Alberto, and Enrico Spolaore. 1997. On the Number and Size of Nations. *Quarterly Journal of Economics* 112: 1027–1056.

Alesina, Alberto, and Enrico Spolaore. 2003. *The Size of Nations*. Cambridge: MIT Press.

Alesina, Alberto, et al. 2000. Economic Integration and Political Disintegration. *American Economic Review* 90: 1276–1296.

Allcock, John. 2000. *Explaining Yugoslavia*. New York: Columbia University Press.

Allison, Graham, and Philip Zelikow. 1999. *Essence of Decision: Explaining the Cuban Missile Crisis*. New York: Addison Wesley Longman.

Amar, Akhil Reed. 2005. *America's Constitution: A Biography*. New York: Random House.

American Antiquarian Society. 2010. "A New Nation Votes" database. Available at: http://elections.lib.tufts.edu/aas_portal/index.xq. Accessed April 11, 2010.

American Historical Review. 1897. Documents Relating to the Shays Rebellion, 1787. *American Historical Review* 2: 693–699.

American Historical Review. 1931. Documents: Shays's Rebellion. *American Historical Review* 36: 776–778.

Anderson, Benedict. 1991. *Imagined Communities*. New York: Verso.

Anderson, Kym, and Richard Blackhurst, eds. 1993. *Regional Integration and the Global Trading System*. New York: Harvester Wheatsheaf.

Anderson, Thornton. 1993. *Creating the Constitution*. University Park: Pennsylvania State University Press.

Angell, Hildegarde. 1930. *Simon Bolivar, South American Liberator*. New York: W.W. Norton.

Angell, Norman. 1933. *The Great Illusion*. New York: G. P. Putnam's Sons.

Antolik, Michael. 1990. *ASEAN and the Diplomacy of Accommodation*. New York: M. E. Sharp.

Appian. 1996. *The Civil Wars*. John Carter trans. New York: Penguin Books.

Apter, David E. 1972. *Ghana in Transition*. 2nd ed. Princeton: Princeton University Press.

Arendt, Hannah. 1965. *On Revolution*. New York: Penguin Books.

Arendt, Hannah. 1989. *The Human Condition*. Chicago: University of Chicago Press.

Arendt, Hannah. 1994. *The Origins of Totalitarianism*. New York: Harcourt Books.

Aristotle. 1958. *The Politics of Aristotle*. Ernest Barker trans. New York: Oxford University Press.

Aron, Raymond. 1966. *Peace and War: A Theory of International Relations*. Richard Howard and Annette Baker Fox trans. New York: Doubleday.

Art, Robert. 1996. Why Western Europe Needs the United States and NATO. *Political Science Quarterly* 111: 1–39.

Asante, K. B. 1997. *Foreign Policy Making in Ghana: Options for the 21st Century*. Accra: Friedrich Ebert Foundation.

Axelrod, Robert. 1984. *The Evolution of Cooperation*. New York: Basic Books.

Bachrach, Peter, and Morton S. Baratz. 1962. Two Faces of Power. *American Political Science Review* 56: 947–952.

Bagehot, Walter. 1999. *Physics and Politics*. Chicago: Ivan R. Dee.

Bailyn, Bernard. 1990. *The Ideological Origins of the American Revolution*. Cambridge: Harvard University Press.

Bailyn, Bernard. 2003. *To Begin the World Anew: The Genius and Ambiguities of the American Founders*. New York: Alfred A. Knopf.

Bailyn, Bernard, ed. 1993. *The Debate on the Constitution*. 2 vols. New York: Library of America.

Baldwin, David A. 1985. *Economic Statecraft*. Princeton: Princeton University Press.

Baldwin, David A., ed. 1993. *Neorealism and Neoliberalism: the Contemporary Debate.* New York: Columbia University Press.

Baldwin, David A. 1998. Correspondence: Evaluating Economic Sanctions. *International Security* 23: 189–198.

Baldwin, Leland D. 1939. *Whiskey Rebels: The Story of a Frontier Uprising.* Pittsburgh: University of Pittsburgh Press.

Barnett, Michael N. 1998. *Dialogues in Arab Politics.* New York: Columbia University Press.

Barnett, Michael, and Raymond Duvall eds. 2005. *Power in Global Governance.* New York: Cambridge University Press.

Barnhart, Michael A. 1996. *Japan Prepares for Total War: The Search for Economic Security, 1919–1941.* Ithaca: Cornell University Press.

Barnum, P. T. 2000. *The Life of P. T. Barnum Written by Himself.* Chicago: University of Illinois Press.

Baron, Joshua. 2005. A World Newly Ordered. Ph.D. diss.: Columbia University.

Baron, Hans. 1961. Machiavelli: The Republican Citizen and the Author of *The Prince. English Historical Review* 76: 217–253.

Baron, Hans. 1991. The *Principe* and the Puzzle of the Date of Chapter 26. *Journal of Medieval and Renaissance Studies* 21: 83–102.

Barton, Robert. 1968. *A Short History of the Republic of Bolivia.* La Paz: Werner Guttentag.

Barzun, Jacques. 2001. *From Dawn to Decadence: 500 Years of Western Cultural Life, 1500 to the Present.* New York: Perennial.

Beard, Charles A. 1941. *An Economic Interpretation of the Constitution of the United States.* New York: Free Press.

Beard, Charles, and Mary Beard. 1933. *The Rise of American Civilization.* New York: Macmillan.

Beauvoir, Simone. 1989. *The Second Sex.* H. M. Parshley, trans. and ed. New York: Vintage Books.

Beeman, Richard. 2010. *Plain, Honest Men: The Making of the American Constitution.* New York: Random House.

Beeson, Mark, ed. 2004. *Contemporary Southeast Asia: Regional Dynamics, National Differences.* New York: Palgrave Macmillan.

Beissinger, Mark R. 2002. *Nationalist Mobilization and the Collapse of the Soviet State.* New York: Cambridge University Press.

Bell, Duncan, and Paul K. MacDonald. 2001. Correspondence: Start the Evolution without Us. *International Security* 26: 187–198.

Bell, P. M. H. 1997. *The Origins of the Second World War in Europe.* 2nd ed. New York: Longman.

Bemis, Samuel F. 1926. *Pinckney's Treaty: A Study of America's Advantage from Europe's Distress, 1783–1800.* Baltimore: The Johns Hopkins Press.

Bemis, Samuel F. 1950. *John Quincy Adams and the Foundations of American Foreign Policy.* New York: Knopf.

Bendix, Reinhard. 1980. *Kings or People: Power and the Mandate to Rule.* Berkeley: University of California Press.

Berlin, Isaiah. 1998. The Originality of Machiavelli. In Henry Hardy and Roger Hausheer, eds. *The Proper Study of Mankind.* New York: Farrar, Straus and Giroux.

Berstein, Harry. 1964. *Venezuela and Colombia.* New Jersey: Prentice Hall.

Bessho, Koro. 1999. *Identities and Security in East Asia: Adelphi Paper 325.* New York: Oxford University Press.

Betts, Richard K. 1999. Must War Find a Way? A Review Essay. *International Security* 24: 166–198.

Biddle, Stephen. 2004. *Military Power: Explaining Victory and Defeat in Modern Battle.* Princeton: Princeton University Press.

Blackstone, William. 1979. *Commentaries on the Laws of England*. 4 vols. Chicago: University of Chicago Press.

Blainey, Geoffrey. 1968. *The Tyranny of Distance: How Distance Shaped Australia's History*. New York: St. Martin's Press.

Blainey, Geoffrey. 1988. *The Causes of War*. New York: Free Press.

Bleier, Ruth. 1984. *Science and Gender: A Critique of Biology and Its Theories on Women*. New York: Pergamon Press.

Blundell, Mary Whitlock. 1991. *Helping Friends and Harming Enemies: A Study in Sophocles and Greek Ethics*. New York: Cambridge University Press.

Bock, Gisela, Quentin Skinner, and Maurizio Viroli, eds. 1990. *Machiavelli and Republicanism*. New York: Cambridge University Press.

Bodin, Jean. 1996. *On Sovereignty*. Julian Franklin, trans. New York: Cambridge University Press.

Bonjour, E. et al. 1952. *A Short History of Switzerland*. New York: Oxford University Press.

Bora, Bijit, and Christopher Findlay, eds. 1996. *Regional Integration and the Asia-Pacific*. New York: Oxford University Press.

Boulding, Kenneth E. 1962. *Conflict and Defense: A General Theory*. New York: Harper.

Boyd, Steven R., ed. 1985. *The Whiskey Rebellion: Past and Present Perspectives*. Westport, CT: Greenwood Press.

Boyesen, Hjalmar. 1886. *The Story of Norway*. New York: Putnam's Sons.

Brackenridge, H. M. 1859. *History of the Western Insurrection in Western Pennsylvania, Commonly Called the Whiskey Insurrection, 1794*. Pittsburgh: W. S. Haven.

Breuilly, John. 1994. *Nationalism and the State*. 2nd ed. Chicago: University of Chicago Press.

British Information Services. 1961. *Tanganyika: The Making of a Nation*. New York: Cox & Sharland Ltd.

Brooks, Stephen, and William Wohlforth. 2000/2001. Power, Globalization, and the End of the Cold War. *International Security* 25: 5–53.

Brooks, Stephen, and William Wohlforth. 2002. American Primacy in Perspective. *Foreign Affairs* 81: 20–33.

Brown, Michael, et al., eds. 1993. *Debating the Democratic Peace*. Cambridge: MIT Press.

Brown, Michael, et al., eds. 1995. *The Perils of Anarchy: Contemporary Realism and International Security*. Cambridge: MIT Press.

Brown, Michael, et al., eds. 1996–1997. *Nationalism and Ethnic Conflict*. Cambridge: MIT Press.

Brown, Michael, et al., eds. 2000. *The Rise of China*. Cambridge: MIT Press.

Brown, Richard D. 1983. Shays's Rebellion and Its Aftermath: The View from Springfield, Massachusetts, 1787. *William and Mary Quarterly* 40: 598–615.

Brynner, Rock. 1993. Fire Beneath our Feet: Shays' Rebellion and Its Constitutional Impact. Ph.D. diss., Columbia University.

Bueno de Mesquita, Bruce, James D. Morrow, Randolph Siverson, and Alastair Smith. 1999. An Institutional Explanation of the Democratic Peace. *American Political Science Review* 93: 791–807.

Bukovansky, Mlada. 1994. Revolutionary States and the International System: Socialization and Structural Change. Ph.D. diss.: Columbia University.

Bukovansky, Mlada. 1997. American Identity and Neutral Rights from Independence to the War of 1812. *International Organization* 51: 209–243.

Bull, Hedley. 1995. *The Anarchical Society: A Study of Order in World Politics*. New York: Columbia University Press.

Burckhardt, Jacob. 1979. *Reflections on History*. M. D. Hottinger, trans. Indianapolis: Liberty Fund.

Burckhardt, Jacob. 1990. *The Civilization of the Renaissance in Italy*. S. G. C. Middlemore, trans. New York: Penguin Books.

Burckhardt, Jacob. 1998. *The Greeks and Greek Civilization*. Sheila Stern, trans. Oswyn Murray, ed. New York: St. Martin's Press.

Burckhardt, Jacob. 1999. *Judgments on History and Historians*. Harry Zohn, trans. Indianapolis: Liberty Fund.

Bureau of African Affairs. 1963. *Historical Facts about the Zanzibar (Unguja) National Struggle*. Accra, Ghana: Bureau of African Affairs.

Burke, Edmund. 1963. *Edmund Burke: Selected Writings and Speeches*. Peter Stanlis, ed. Washington DC: Gateway Editions.

Burke, Edmund. 1999. *Select Works of Edmund Burke*. 3 vols. Indianapolis: Liberty Fund.

Butterfield, Herbert. 1967. *The Statecraft of Machiavelli*. New York: Collier.

Butters, Humphrey C. 1985. *Governors and Government in Early Sixteenth-Century Florence, 1502–1519*. New York: Oxford University Press.

Buzan, Barry. 1993. From International System to International Society: Structural Realism and Regime Theory Meet the English School. *International Organization* 47: 327–352.

Buzan, Barry. 2007. *People, States, and Fear: An Agenda for International Security Studies in the Post-Cold War Era*. 2nd ed. Colchester, UK: ECPR Press.

Callieres, Francois de. 1963. *On the Manner of Negotiating with Princes*. A. F. White, trans. Notre Dame: University of Notre Dame Press.

Campanella, Tommaso. 1981. *The City of the Sun: A Poetical Dialogue*. Daniel J. Donno, trans. Berkeley: University of California Press.

Caporaso, James A. 1995. Research Design, Falsification, and the Qualitative-Quantitative Divide. *American Political Science Review* 89: 457–460.

Caporaso, James A. 1996. The European Union and Forms of State: Westphalian, Regulatory, or Post-Modern? *Journal of Common Market Studies* 34: 29–52.

Carr, E. H. 1945. *Nationalism and After*. London: Macmillan.

Carr, E. H. 1961. *What is History?* New York: Vintage Books.

Carr, E. H. 1964. *The Twenty Years Crisis, 1919–1939*. New York: Harper & Row.

Carr, E. H. 1979. *The Russian Revolution: From Lenin to Stalin*. New York: Free Press.

Carr, E. H. 1985. *The Bolshevik Revolution, 1917–1923*. Vol. 3. New York: W. W. Norton.

Carr, Fergus, and Theresa Callan. 2002. *Managing Conflict in the New Europe: The Role of International Institutions*. New York: Palgrave Macmillan.

Cederman, Lars-Erik. 2003. Modeling the Size of Wars: From Billiard Balls to Sandpiles. *American Political Science Review* 97: 135–150.

Cha, Victor D. 1994. Alignment Despite Antagonism: Japan and Korea as Quasi-Allies. Ph.D. diss.: Columbia University.

Cha, Victor D. 1999. *Alignment Despite Antagonism: The US-Korea-Japan Security Triangle*. Stanford: Stanford University Press.

Chabod, Federico. 1958. *Machiavelli and the Renaissance*. David Moore, trans. London: Bowes & Bowes.

Chekhov, Anton. 1979. *Anton Chekhov's Short Stories*. Ralph E. Matlaw, trans. New York: W. W. Norton.

Chernow, Ron. 1998. *Titan: The Life of John D. Rockefeller, Sr.* New York: Vintage.

Chomsky, Noam. 2002. *Understanding Power: The Indispensable Chomsky*. Peter Mitchell and John Schoeffel, eds. New York: New Press.

Christensen, Thomas J. 1996. *Useful Adversaries: Grand Strategy, Domestic Mobilization, and Sino-American Conflict, 1947–1958*. Princeton: Princeton University Press.

CIA World Factbook. 2008. Available at: https://www.cia.gov/library/publications/the-world-factbook/. Accessed March 5, 2008.

Clausewitz, Carl. 1976. *On War*. Michael Howard and Peter Paret, eds., Princeton: Princeton University Press.

Clausewitz, Carl. 1980. *Vom Kriege: Hinterlassenes Werk*. Bonn: Ferd. Dummlers Verlag.

Clayton, Anthony. 1981. *The Zanzibar Revolution and Its Aftermath*. Hamden, CT: Archon Books.

CNN. January 23, 2003. Rumsfeld: France, Germany Are "Problems" in Iraqi Conflict. Available at: http://www.cnn.com/2003/WORLD/meast/01/22/sprj.irq.wrap/. Accessed August 1, 2010.

Coase, R. H. 1990. *The Firm, the Market, and the Law*. Chicago: University of Chicago Press.

Coase, R. H. 1995. *Essays on Economics and Economists*. Chicago: University of Chicago Press.

Coke, Edward. 2004. *The Selected Writings of Sir Edward Coke*. 3 vols. Steve Sheppard, ed. Indianapolis: Liberty Fund.

Collier, David. 1995. Translating Quantitative Methods for Qualitative Researchers: The Case of Selection Bias. *American Political Science Review* 89: 461–466.

Collier, Simon. 1983. Nationality, Nationalism, and Supranationalism in the Writings of Simon Bolivar. *Hispanic American Historical Review* 63: 37–64.

Colton, Julia M. 1897. *Annals of Switzerland*. New York: A. S. Barnes.

Comte, Auguste. 1988. *Introduction to Positive Philosophy*. Frederick Ferré, ed. and trans. Indianapolis: Hackett Publishing.

Conley, Patrick T., and John Kaminski, eds. 1988. *The Constitution and the States: The Role of the Original Thirteen in the Framing and Adoption of the Federal Constitution*. Madison: Madison House.

Conley, Patrick T., and John Kaminski, eds. 1992. *The Bill of Rights and the States: The Colonial and Revolutionary Origins of American Liberties*. Madison: Madison House.

Connor, Walker. 1994. *Ethnonationalism*. Princeton: Princeton University Press.

Cooley, Alexander. 2005. *Logics of Hierarchy: The Organization of Empires, States, and Military Occupations*. Ithaca: Cornell University Press.

Cooley, Alexander, and Hendrik Spruyt. 2009. *Contracting States: Sovereign Transfers in International Relations*. Princeton: Princeton University Press.

Cooper, Robert. 2003. *The Breaking of Nations: Order and Chaos in the Twenty-first Century*. London: Atlantic Books.

Coser, Lewis. 1964. *The Functions of Social Conflict*. New York: The Free Press.

Costeloe, Michael P. 1986. *Response to Revolution: Imperial Spain and the Spanish American Revolutions, 1810–1840*. New York: Cambridge University Press.

Craig, Campbell. 2003. *Glimmer of a New Leviathan*. New York: Columbia University Press.

Craig, Gordon A. 1978. *The Politics of the Prussian Army, 1640–1945*. New York: Oxford University Press.

Craig, Gordon A. 1980. *Germany, 1866–1945*. New York: Oxford University Press.

Craig, Gordon A. 1982. *The Germans*. New York: Putnam.

Croce, Benedetto. 2000. *History as the Story of Liberty*. Sylvia Sprigge, trans. Indianapolis: Liberty Fund.

Cronin, Bruce L. 1994. Defining a *Raison d'être*: The Politics of Identity and Purpose in the Nineteenth Century New World Order. Ph.D. diss.: Columbia University.

Cronin, Bruce L. 1999. *Community under Anarchy: Transnational Identity and the Evolution of Cooperation*. New York: Columbia University Press.

Crow, Jeffrey J. 1980. Slave Rebelliousness and Social Conflict in North Carolina, 1775 to 1802. *William and Mary Quarterly* 37: 79–102.

Crowe, Eyre. 1907. "Memorandum on the Present State of British Relations with France and Germany" in G. P. Gooch and Harold Temperley, eds. *British Documents on the Origins of the War, 1898–1914*, vol. 3. London: HMSO, pp. 397–420.

Cruz, Consuelo. 2000. Identity and Persuasion: How Nations Remember Their Pasts and Make Their Futures. *World Politics* 52: 275–312.

David, Jean-Michel. 1996. *The Roman Conquest of Italy*. Antonia Nevill, trans. Cambridge, MA: Blackwell Publishers.

Davis, W. W. H. 1899. *The Fries' Rebellion, 1798–99*. Doylestown, PA: Doylestown Publishing.

DeConde, Alexander. 1966. *The Quasi-War: The Politics and Diplomacy of the Undeclared War with France, 1797–1801*. New York: Charles Scribner's Sons.

de Grazia, Sebastian. 1989. *Machiavelli in Hell*. Princeton: Princeton University Press.

Dehousse, Renaud. "We the States": Why the Anti-Federalists Won. In Nicolas Jabko and Craig Parsons, eds. *With US or Against US? European Trends in American Perspective*. New York: Oxford University Press.

Derry, T. K. 1957. *A Short History of Norway*. London: Allen & Unwin.

DeSalis, J-R. 1971. *Switzerland and Europe*. Alexander and Elizabeth Henderson, trans. Alabama: University of Alabama Press.

Deudney, Daniel, and G. J. Ikenberry. 1991/1992. The International Sources of Soviet Change. *International Security* 16: 74–113.

Deudney, Daniel H. 1995. The Philadelphia System: Sovereignty, Arms Control, and Balance of Power in the American States-Union, Circa 1787–1861. *International Organization* 49: 191–228.

Deudney, Daniel H. 2007. *Bounding Power: Republican Security Theory from the Polis to the Global Village*. Princeton: Princeton University Press.

Deutsch, Karl, et al. 1957. *Political Community and the North Atlantic Area: International Organization in the Light of Historical Experience*. Westport, CT: Greenwood Press.

Deutsch, Karl. 1963. *The Nerves of Government: Models of Political Communication and Control*. New York: Macmillan.

Deutsch, Karl, and William Foltz, eds. 1963. *Nation-Building*. New York: Prentice Hall.

Deutsch, Karl, Lewis Edinger, Roy Macridis, and Richard Merritt. 1967. *France, Germany, and the Western Alliance: A Study of Elite Attitudes on European Integration and World Politics*. New York: Charles Scribner's Sons.

Deutsch, Karl. 1976. *Die Schweiz als ein paradigmatischer Fall politischer Integration*. Bern: Verlag Paul Haupt.

Devonshire Jones, Rosemary. 1972. *Francesco Vettori: Florentine Citizen and Medici Servant*. New York: Athlone Press.

Dewey, John. 1985. *Democracy and Education*. Carbondale: Southern Illinois University Press.

Dewey, John. 1988. *The Later Works, 1925–1953*. Vol. 2. Jo Ann Boydston, ed. Carbondale: Southern Illinois University Press.

Diamond, Jared. 2006. *Collapse: How Societies Choose to Fail or Succeed*. New York: Penguin.

Dietz, Mary. 1986. Trapping the Prince: Machiavelli and the Politics of Deception. *American Political Science Review* 80: 777–799.

Dikshit, Ramesh Dutta. 1975. *The Political Geography of Federalism: An Inquiry into Origins and Stability*. Delhi: Macmillan Company of India.

Dimmig, Jeffrey S. 2001. Palatine Liberty: Pennsylvania German Opposition to the Direct Tax of 1798. *American Journal of Legal History* 45: 371–390.

Dinkin, Robert J. 1977. *Voting in Provincial America: A Study of Elections in the Thirteen Colonies, 1689–1776*. London: Greenwood Press.

Dinkin, Robert J. 1982. *Voting in Revolutionary America: A Study of Elections in the Original Thirteen States, 1776–1789*. London: Greenwood Press.

Dio, Cassius. 1987. *The Roman History: the Reign of Augustus*. Ian Scott-Kilvert trans. New York: Penguin Books.

Dobrynin, Anatoly. 1995. *In Confidence: Moscow's Ambassador to America's Six Cold War Presidents*. Seattle: University of Washington Press.

Dougherty, Keith L. 2001. *Collective Action under the Articles of Confederation*. New York: Cambridge University Press.

Dover, K. J. 1974. *Greek Popular Morality in the Time of Plato and Aristotle*. Indianapolis: Hackett Publishing.

Dreyer, June Teufel. 2004. The Limits to China's Growth. *Orbis* 48: 233–246.

Ducoudray Holstein, H. L. V. 1830. *Memoirs of Simon Bolivar*. 2 vols. London: Colburn and Bentley.

Dugatkin, Lee. 1999. *Cheating Monkeys and Citizen Bees: The Nature of Cooperation in Animals and Humans*. Cambridge: Harvard University Press.

Durkheim, Emile. 1965. *The Elementary Forms of the Religious Life*. Joseph Swain, trans. New York: The Free Press.

Durkheim, Emile. 1979. *Suicide: A Study in Sociology*. John Spaulding and George Simpson, trans. New York: The Free Press.

Durkheim, Emile. 1984. *The Division of Labor in Society*. W. D. Halls, trans. New York: The Free Press.

Durkheim, Emile. 2001. *The Elementary Forms of Religious Life*. Carol Cosman, trans. New York: Oxford.

Dyson, Michael Eric. 2001. *I May Not Get There With You: The True Martin Luther King, Jr.* New York: Touchstone Books.

Earle, Edward Mead. 1986. Adam Smith, Alexander Hamilton, Friedrich List: The Economic Foundations of Military Power. In Paret, ed. *The Makers of Modern Strategy*. Princeton: Princeton University Press.

Eaton, Clement. 1975. *A History of the Old South*. 3rd ed. New York: Macmillan Publishing Co.

Economist. 2005. Charlemagne: Crisis, What Crisis? September 8: 52.

Economist. 2007a. Charlemagne: A Monster Lives Again. January 6: 46

Economist. 2007b. Charlemagne: Existential Dreaming. March 24: 62.

Economist. 2007c. Charlemagne: For Your Eyes Only. August 11: 44.

Edelstein, David. 2002. Managing Uncertainties: Beliefs about Intentions and the Rise of Great Powers. *Security Studies* 12: 1–40.

Eley, Geoff, and R. G. Suny, eds. 1996. *Becoming National: A Reader*. New York: Oxford University Press.

Elkins, Stanley, and Eric McKitrick. 1993. *The Age of Federalism*. New York: Oxford University Press.

Ellickson, Robert C. 1991. *Order Without Law: How Neighbors Settle Disputes*. Cambridge: Harvard University Press.

Ellis, Joseph J. 2002. *Founding Brothers: The Revolutionary Generation*. New York: Vintage Books.

Elster, Jon. 1979. *Ulysses and the Sirens: Studies in Rationality and Irrationality.* New York: Cambridge University Press.

Elster, Jon. 1983. *Sour Grapes: Studies in the Subversion of Rationality.* New York: Cambridge University Press.

Elster, Jon. 2000. *Ulysses Unbound.* New York: Cambridge University Press.

Elster, Jon, ed. 1999b. *Deliberative Democracy.* New York: Cambridge University Press.

Epstein, Richard A. 1997. *Simple Rules for a Complex World.* Cambridge: Harvard University Press.

Erasmus, Desiderius. 1989. *The Praise of Folly and Other Writings.* Robert Adams, trans. New York: Norton.

Ericksen, Karen Paige, and Heather Horton. 1992. "Blood Feuds": Cross-Cultural Variations in Kin Group Vengeance. *Behavior Science Research* 26: 57–85.

Erikson, Emily, and Joseph M. Parent. 2007. Central Authority and Order. *Sociological Theory* 25: 244–267.

Etzioni, Amitai. 1965. *Political Unification: A Comparative Study of Leaders and Forces.* New York: Holt, Rinehart, Winston.

Etzioni, Amitai. 2001. *Political Unification Revisited: On Building Supranational Communities.* Lanham: Lexington Books.

Evangelista, Matthew. 1999. *Unarmed Force: The Transnational Movements to End the Cold War.* Ithaca: Cornell University Press.

Falk, Richard, et al., eds. 1985. *International Law: A Contemporary Perspective.* Boulder: Westview Press.

Farnham, Barbara. 1990. Political Cognition in Decision-making. *Political Psychology* 11: 83–111.

Farnham, Barbara. 1997. *Roosevelt and the Munich Crisis: A Study of Political Decision-Making.* Princeton: Princeton University Press.

Farrand, Max. 1966. *Records of the Federal Convention of 1787.* 4 vols. New Haven: Yale University Press.

Farrand, Max. 1968. *The Framing of the Constitution of the United States.* New Haven: Yale University Press.

Farrell, Joseph, and Matthew Rabin. 1996. Cheap Talk. *Journal of Economic Perspectives* 10: 103–118.

Farrell, Mary Stefano Fella, and Michael Newman, eds. 2001. *European Integration in the 21st Century.* London: Sage Publications.

Fausto-Sterling, Anne. 1985. *Myths of Gender: Biological Theories about Women and Men.* 2nd ed. New York: Basic Books.

Fazal, Tanisha. 2002. Rocks and Hard Places: Why Only Some States Fight for Survival. Paper presented at 2002 APSA Convention: Boston, Massachusetts.

Fazal, Tanisha. 2004. State Death in the International System. *International Organization* 58: 311–344.

Fearon, James D. 1993. Ethnic War as a Commitment Problem. Unpublished Manuscript: University of Chicago.

Fearon, James D. 1995. Rationalist Explanations for War. *International Organization* 49: 379–414.

Fearon, James D. 1997a. Signaling Foreign Policy Interests: Tying Hands and Sinking Costs. *Journal of Conflict Resolution* 41: 68–90.

Fearon, James D. 1997b. The Offense-Defense Balance and War since 1648. Unpublished Manuscript: University of Chicago.

Fearon, James D., and David D. Laitin. 1996. Explaining Interethnic Cooperation. *American Political Science Review* 90: 715–735.

Fearon, James D., and David D. Laitin. 2000. Violence and the Social Construction of Ethnic Identity. *International Organization* 54: 845–877.

Fearon, James D., and David D. Laitin. 2004. Neotrusteeship and the Problem of Weak States. *International Security* 28: 5–43.

Fearon, James, and Alexander Wendt. 2002. Rationalism v. Constructivism: A Skeptical View. In Walter Carlsnaes, Thomas Risse, and Beth Simmons, eds. *A Handbook of International Relations*. London: Sage Publications.

Feer, Robert A. 1969. Shays's Rebellion and the Constitution: A Study in Causation. *New England Quarterly* 42: 388–410.

Femia, Joseph. 2004. Machiavelli and Italian Fascism. *History of Political Thought* 25: 1–15.

Ferejohn, John, et al., eds. 2001. *Constitutional Culture and Democratic Rule*. New York: Cambridge University Press.

Ferguson, Adam. 1995. *An Essay on the History of Civil Society*. Fania Oz-Salzberger, ed. New York: Cambridge University Press.

Fergusson, Erna. 1939. *Venezuela*. New York: Alfred A. Knopf.

de Figueiredo, R. J. P., Jr., and Barry R. Weingast. 1999. The Rationality of Fear: Political Opportunism and Ethnic Conflict. In Barbara F. Walter and Jack Snyder, eds. *Civil Wars, Insecurity, and Intervention*. New York: Columbia University Press.

Finnemore, Martha. 1996. *National Interest in International Society*. Ithaca: Cornell University Press.

Finnemore, Martha, and Kathryn Sikkink. 1998. International Norm Dynamics and Political Change. *International Organization* 52: 887–917.

Fitzgerald, Gerald E. 1971. *The Political Thought of Bolivar*. The Hague: Martinus Nijhoff.

Fligstein, Neil. 2009. Who Are the Europeans and How Does This Matter for Politics? In Jeffrey Checkel and Peter Katzenstein, eds. *European Identity*. New York Cambridge University Press.

Foradori, Paolo, Paolo Rosa, and Riccardo Scartezzeni, eds. 2007. *Managing a Multilevel Foreign Policy: The EU in International Affairs*. New York: Lexington Books.

Forsyth, Murray. 1981. *Unions of States: The Theory and Practice of Confederation*. New York: Holmes and Meier Publishers.

Fortna, V. Page. 2004. *Peace Time: Cease-Fire Agreements and the Durability of Peace*. Princeton: Princeton University Press.

Foucault, Michel. 1972. *The Archaeology of Knowledge and the Discourse on Language*. A. M. Sheridan Smith, trans. New York: Pantheon Books

Foucault, Michel. 1990. *The History of Sexuality: An Introduction*. New York: Vintage Books.

Foucault, Michel. 1995. *Discipline and Punish: The Birth of the Prison*. Alan Sheridan, trans. New York: Vintage Books.

Fox, William T. R., ed. 1959. *Theoretical Aspects of International Relations*. Notre Dame: University of Notre Dame Press.

Franklin, Benjamin. 1987. *Writings*. J. A. Leo Lemay, ed. New York: Library of America.

Fransen, Frederic J. 2001. *The Supranational Politics of Jean Monnet: Ideas and Origins of the European Community*. Westport, CT: Greenwood Press.

Freeman, Joanne. 2001. *Affairs of Honor: National Politics in the New Republic*. New Haven: Yale University Press.

Friedberg, Aaron. 1988. *The Weary Titan*. Princeton: Princeton University Press.

Friedman, David. 1977. A Theory of the Size and Shape of Nations. *Journal of Political Economy* 85: 59–77.

Friedman, Milton. 1953. The Methodology of Positivist Economics. In *Essays in Positive Economics*. Chicago: University of Chicago Press.

Fukuyama, Francis. 2004. *State-Building: Governance and World Order in the 21st Century*. Ithaca: Cornell University Press.

Gaddis, John Lewis. 1994. The Long Peace: Elements of Stability in the Postwar International System. In Lynn-Jones and Miller, eds. *The Cold War and After*. Cambridge: MIT Press.

Gaddis, John Lewis. 2005. *Strategies of Containment: A Critical Appraisal of American National Security Policy during the Cold War*. New York: Oxford University Press.

Galdames, Luis. 1941. *A History of Chile*. Isaac Joslin Cox, trans. Chapel Hill: University of North Carolina Press.

Gambari, Ibrahim A. 1991. *Political and Comparative Dimensions of Regional Integration: The Case of ECOWAS*. New Jersey: Humanities Press.

Gartzke, Erik, and Kristian Skrede Gleditsch. 2006. Identity and Conflict: Ties That Bind and Differences That Divide. *European Journal of International Relations* 12: 53–87.

Gaubatz, Kurt T. 1996. Democratic States and Commitment in International Relations. *International Organization* 50: 109–139.

Geertz, Clifford. 1973. *The Interpretation of Cultures*. New York: Basic Books.

Gellner, Ernest. 1983. *Nations and Nationalism*. Ithaca: Cornell University Press.

Gerring, John. 2007. *Case Study Research: Principles and Practices*. New York: Cambridge University Press.

Gerschenkron, Alexander. 1966. *Economic Backwardness in Historical Perspective*. Cambridge: Harvard University Press.

Gibbon, Edward. 1994. *The Decline and Fall of the Roman Empire*. 6 vols. New York: Everyman.

Gilbert, Felix. 1939. The Humanist Concept of the Prince and *The Prince* of Machiavelli. *The Journal of Modern History* 11: 449–483.

Gilbert, Felix. 1961. *To the Farewell Address*. Princeton: Princeton University Press.

Gilbert, Felix. 1984. *Machiavelli and Guicciardini: Politics and History in 16th Century Florence*. New York: Norton.

Gilbert, Felix. 1986. Machiavelli: The Renaissance of the Art of War. In Peter Paret, ed. *Makers of Modern Strategy*. Princeton: Princeton University Press.

Gill, Ranjit. 1997. *ASEAN: Towards the 21st Century*. London: ASEAN Academic Press.

Gillespie, Michael Allen, and Michael Lienesch, eds. 1989. *Ratifying the Constitution*. Lawrence, KS: University of Kansas Press.

Gillham, Nicholas W. 2001. *A Life of Sir Francis Galton*. New York: Oxford University Press.

Gilliard, Charles. 1955. *A History of Switzerland*. D. L. B. Hartley, trans. London: Allen & Unwin.

Gilligan, Carol. 1993. *In a Different Voice: Psychological Theory and Women's Development*. Cambridge: Harvard University Press.

Gilpin, Robert. 1981. *War and Change in World Politics*. New York: Cambridge University Press.

Gilpin, Robert. 1986. The Richness of the Tradition of Political Realism. In Robert Keohane, ed., *Neorealism and Its Critics*. New York: Columbia University Press.

Gjerset, Knut. 1969. *History of the Norwegian People*. New York: AMS Press.

Glaser, Charles. 1996. Realists as Optimists: Cooperation as Self-Help. *Security Studies* 5: 122–163.

Glencross, Andrew. 2009. *What Makes the EU Viable? European Integration in the Light of the Antebellum US Experience*. New York: Palgrave Macmillan.

Goddard, Stacie E. 2003. "Uncommon Ground: The Making of Indivisible Issues." Ph.D. diss., Columbia University.

Goddard, Stacie E. 2006. Uncommon Ground: Indivisible Territory and the Politics of Legitimacy. *International Organization* 60: 35–68.

Goemans, Hein. 2001. *War and Punishment: The Causes of War Termination and the First World War*. Princeton: Princeton University Press.

Goertz, Gary, and Paul Diehl. 1991. *Territorial Changes and International Conflict*. New York: Routledge.

Goertz, Gary. 2006. *Social Science Concepts: A User's Guide*. Princeton: Princeton University Press.

Goffman, Erving. 1959. *The Presentation of Self in Everyday Life*. New York: Anchor Books.

Goffman, Erving. 1961. *Asylums*. New York: Anchor Books.

Goldstein, Judith, and Robert Keohane, eds. 1993. *Ideas and Foreign Policy: Beliefs, Institutions, and Political Change*. Ithaca: Cornell University Press.

Goldstein, Leslie F. 2001. *Constituting Federal Sovereignty: The European Union in Comparative Context*. Baltimore: Johns Hopkins University Press.

Goodin, Robert E., and Geoffrey Brennan. 2001. Bargaining over Beliefs. *Ethics* 111: 256–277.

Gould, Roger V. 1996. Patron-Client Ties, State Centralization, and the Whiskey Rebellion. *American Journal of Sociology* 102: 400–429.

Gowa, Joanne. 1986. Anarchy, Egoism, and Third Images: *The Evolution of Cooperation* and International Relations. *International Organization* 40: 167–186.

Gowa, Joanne. 1994. *Allies, Adversaries, and International Trade*. Princeton: Princeton University Press.

Grampp, William. 2000. What Did Smith Mean by the Invisible Hand? *Journal of Political Economy* 108: 441–465.

Gramsci, Antonio. 1999. *Selections from the Prison Notebooks*. New York: International Publishers.

Grant, U. S. 1999. *Personal Memoirs*. New York: Modern Library.

Greenberg, Kenneth S. 1996. *Honor and Slavery*. Princeton: Princeton University Press.

Greene, Jack P. 1976. *All Men Are Created Equal: Some Reflections on the Character of the American Revolution*. Oxford: Clarendon Press.

Greene, Jack P. 1993. *The Intellectual Construction of America: Exceptionalism and Identity from 1492 to 1800*. Chapel Hill: University of North Carolina Press.

Greene, Jack P., ed. 1987. *The American Revolution: Its Character and Limits*. New York: New York University Press.

Greenfeld, Liah. 1992. *Nationalism: Five Roads to Modernity*. Cambridge: Harvard University Press.

Grieco, Joseph. 1996. State Interests and Institutional Rule Trajectories: A Neorealist Interpretation of the Maastricht Treaty and European Economic and Monetary Union. *Security Studies* 5: 176–185.

Grofman, Bernard, and Donald Wittman, eds. 1989. *The Federalist Papers and the New Institutionalism*. New York: Agathon Press.

Grotius, Hugo. 1949. *The Law of War and Peace*. Louise R. Loomis, trans. New York: Walter J. Black.

Grotius, Hugo. 2004. *The Free Sea*. Richard Hakluyt, trans. Indianapolis: Liberty Fund.

Grotius, Hugo. 2005. *The Rights of War and Peace*. 3 vols. Jean Barbeyrac, trans. Indianapolis: Liberty Fund.

Gruber, Lloyd. 2000. *Ruling the World: Power Politics and the Rise of Supranational Institutions*. Princeton: Princeton University Press.

Guicciardini, Francesco. 1965. *Selected Writings*. Cecil Grayson, ed. Margaret Grayson, trans. New York: Oxford University Press.

Guicciardini, Francesco. 1972. *Ricordi*. Mario Domandi, trans. Philadelphia: University of Pennsylvania Press.

Guicciardini, Francesco. 1984. *The History of Italy*. Sidney Alexander, trans. Princeton: Princeton University Press.

Gurr, Ted Robert, ed. 2000. *Peoples versus States*. Washington, DC: United States Institute of Peace Press.

Haas, Ernst B. 1956. Regionalism, Functionalism, and Universal International Organization. *World Politics* 8: 238–263.

Haas, Ernst B. 1958. The Challenge of Regionalism. *International Organization* 12: 440–458.

Haas, Ernst B. 1964. *Beyond the Nation-State: Functionalism and International Organization*. Stanford: Stanford University Press.

Haas, Ernst B. 1968. *The Uniting of Europe: Political, Social, and Economic Forces, 1950–1957*. Stanford: Stanford University Press.

Haas, Ernst B. 1970. The Study of Regional Integration: Reflections on the Joy and Anguish of Pretheorizing. *International Organization* 24: 607–646.

Haas, Ernst B. 1975. *The Obsolescence of Regional Integration Theory*. Berkeley: Institute for International Studies, University of California, Berkeley.

Haas, Ernst B., Mary Pat Williams, and Don Babai. 1977. *Scientists and World Order: The Uses of Technical Knowledge in International Organizations*. Berkeley: University of California Press.

Haas, Ernst B. 1990. *When Knowledge Is Power: Three Models of Change in International Organizations*. Berkeley: University of California Press.

Habermas, Juergen. 1984. *The Theory of Communicative Action*. 2 vols. Thomas McCarthy, trans. Boston: Beacon Press.

Habermas, Juergen. 1989. *The Structural Transformation of the Public Sphere*. Cambridge: MIT Press.

Hadjor, Kofi B. 1988. *Nkrumah and Ghana: The Dilemma of Post-Colonial Power*. New York: Kegan Paul International.

Hale, Henry. 2004. Divided We Stand: Institutional Sources of Ethnofederal State Survival and Collapse. *World Politics* 56: 165–193.

Hall, Kermit L., ed. 1987. *The Formation and Ratification of the Constitution: Major Historical Interpretations*. New York: Garland Publishing.

Hamilton, Alexander. 1985. *Selected Writings and Speeches of Alexander Hamilton*. Morton J. Frisch, ed. Washington DC: American Enterprise Institute.

Hamilton, Alexander. 2001. *Writings*. Joanne Freeman, ed. New York: Library of America.

Hamilton, Alexander, John Jay, and James Madison. 1987. *The Federalist Papers*. New York: Penguin.

Handel, Michael. 1992. *Masters of War: Classical Strategic Thought*. 2nd ed. London: Frank Cass.

Hansen, Mogens Herman. 1999. *The Athenian Democracy in the Age of Demosthenes*. Norman: University of Oklahoma Press.

Hardin, Russell. 1995. *One for All: The Logic of Group Conflict*. Princeton: Princeton University Press.

Harrington, James. 2001. *The Commonwealth of Oceana and a System of Politics*. J. G. A. Pocock, ed. New York: Cambridge University Press.

Hartz, Louis. 1964. *The Founding of New Societies*. New York: Harcourt Brace Jovanovich.

Hartz, Louis. 1991. *The Liberal Tradition in America*. New York: Harcourt Brace.

Haslam, Jonathan. 2000. *The Vices of Integrity: E. H. Carr, 1892–1982*. New York: Verso.

Haslam, Jonathan. 2002. *No Virtue Like Necessity: Realist Thought in International Relations since Machiavelli*. New Haven: Yale University Press.

Hatch, John. 1972. *Tanzania: A Profile*. New York: Praeger.

Hayek, Friedrich A. 1978. *The Constitution of Liberty*. Chicago: University of Chicago Press.

Hayek, Friedrich A. 1983. *Law, Legislation, and Liberty*. 3 Vols. Chicago: University of Chicago Press.

Hayek, Friedrich A. 1994. *The Road to Serfdom*. Chicago: University of Chicago Press.

Heather, Peter. 2006. *The Fall of the Roman Empire: A History of Rome and the Barbarians*. New York: Oxford University Press.

Henderson, Dwight. 1970. Treason, Sedition, and Fries' Rebellion. *American Journal of Legal History* 14: 308–318.

Henderson, Jeannie. 1999. *Reassessing ASEAN: Adelphi Paper 328*. New York: Oxford University Press.

Henderson, Karen. 2005. *The Area of Freedom, Security and Justice in the Enlarged Europe*. New York: Palgrave Macmillan.

Hendrickson, David C. 2003. *Peace Pact: The Lost World of the American Founding*. Lawrence: University of Kansas Press.

Herbst, Jeffrey. 2000. *States and Power in Africa: Comparative Lessons in Authority and Control*. Princeton: Princeton University Press.

Herodotus. 1987. *The History*. David Grene, trans. Chicago: University of Chicago Press.

Herodotus. 1992. *The Histories*. Walter Blanco, trans. New York: W. W. Norton.

Herold, J. Christopher. 1948. *The Swiss Without Halos*. New York: Columbia University Press.

Herrmann, Richard, Thomas Risse, and Marilynn Brewer, eds. 2004. *Transnational Identities: Becoming European in the EU*. New York: Rowman and Littlefield Publishers.

Herwig, Holger. 1991. Clio Deceived: Patriotic Self-Censorship in Germany after the Great War. In Steven Miller et al., eds. *Military Strategy and the Origins of the First World War*. 2nd ed. Princeton: Princeton University Press.

Herz, John. 1963. *International Politics in the Atomic Age*. New York: Columbia University Press.

Hintze, Otto. 1975. *The Historical Essays of Otto Hintze*. Felix Gilbert, ed. New York: Oxford University Press.

Hirschleifer, Jack. 2001. *The Dark Side of the Force: Economic Foundations of Conflict Theory*. New York: Cambridge University Press.

Hirschleifer, Jack, and John G. Riley. 1992. *The Analytics of Uncertainty and Information*. New York: Cambridge University Press.

Hirschman, Albert O. 1970. *Exit, Voice, and Loyalty: Responses to Decline in Firms, Organizations, and States*. Cambridge: Harvard University Press.

Hirschman, Albert O. 1977. *The Passions and the Interests*. Princeton: Princeton University Press.

Hirschman, Albert O. 1991. *The Rhetoric of Reaction*. Cambridge: Harvard University Press.

Hix, Simon. 2008. *What's Wrong with the European Union and How to Fix It*. Malden, MA: Polity Press.

Hobbes, Thomas. 1985. *Leviathan*. New York; Penguin.

Hobbes, Thomas. 1993. *Man and Citizen*. Charles T. Wood, T. S. K. Craig-Scott, and Bernard Gert, trans. Indianapolis: Hackett Publishing.

Hobsbawm, E. J. 1987. *The Age of Empire, 1875–1914*. New York: Vintage Books.

Hobsbawm, E. J. 1995. *The Age of Extremes: A History of the World, 1914–1991*. New York: Vintage Books.

Hobsbawm, E. J. 1996a. *The Age of Revolution, 1789–1848*. New York: Vintage Books.

Hobsbawm, E. J. 1996b. *The Age of Capital, 1848–1875*. New York: Vintage Books.

Hobsbawm, E. J. 1997. An Afterword: European Integration at the End of the Century. In Jytte Klausen and Louise Tilly, eds. *European Integration in Social and Historical Perspective: 1850 to the Present*. New York: Rowman and Littlefield.

Hobsbawm, E. J. 2000. *Nations and Nationalism since 1780: Programme, Myth, Reality*. 2nd ed. New York: Cambridge University Press.

Hobson, J. A. 1965. *Imperialism*. Ann Arbor: University of Michigan Press.

Hodd, Michael, ed. 1988. *Tanzania After Nyerere*. New York: Pinter Publishers.

Hoff Sommers, Christina. May 2000. "The War Against Boys." *The Atlantic Monthly*: 59–74.

Hoffman, Bruce. 1999. Terrorism Trends and Prospects. In *Countering the New* Terrorism. California: RAND, chapter 2.

Hoffman, Ronald. 1993. *A Spirit of Dissension: Economics, Politics, and the Revolution in Maryland*. Baltimore: The Johns Hopkins University Press.

Hofstadter, Richard. 1950. Beard and the Constitution: The History of an Idea. *American Quarterly* 2: 195–213.

Hofstadter, Richard. 1973. *The American Political Tradition and the Men Who Made It*. New York: Vintage.

Holsti, Kalevi J. 1998. *Peace and War: Armed Conflicts and International Order 1648–1989*. New York: Cambridge University Press.

Holsti, Ole, Terence Hopmann, and John Sullivan. 1973. *Unity and Disintegration in International Alliances: Comparative Studies*. New York: John Wiley and Sons.

Holmes, Martin. 2001. *European Integration: Scope and Limits*. New York: Palgrave.

Hooker, Richard J. n.d. The Background of Federal Union: Community and Conflict in the Thirteen States. In *Common Cause: A Monthly Report* Document no. 139.

Horkheimer, Max and Theodor Adorno. 1972. *Dialectic of Enlightenment*. John Cumming, trans. New York: Continuum.

Horsman, Reginald. 1985. *The Diplomacy of the New Republic, 1776–1815*. Arlington Heights, IL: Harlan Davidson.

Howarth, David. 1966. *Panama: Four Hundred Years of Dreams and Cruelty*. New York: McGraw Hill.

Howorth, Jolyon. 2007. *Security and Defence Policy in the European Union*. New York: Palgrave Macmillan.

Howorth, Jolyon, and John T. S. Keeler, eds. 2003. *Defending Europe: The EU, NATO and the Quest for European Autonomy*. New York: Palgrave Macmillan.

Hume, David. 1987. *Essays Moral, Political, and Literary*. Eugene Miller, ed. Indianapolis: Liberty Fund.

Hume, David. 1998. *Political Essays*. Knud Haakonssen, ed. New York: Cambridge University Press.

Hyneman, Charles S., and Donald Lutz, eds. 1983. *American Political Writings during the Founding Era, 1760–1805*. 2 vols. Indianapolis: Liberty Fund.

Ienaga, Saburo. 1996. The Glorification of War in Japanese Education. In Michael Brown et al., eds. *East Asian Security*. Cambridge: MIT Press.

Ikenberry, G. John. 2001. *After Victory: Institutions, Strategic Restraint, and the Rebuilding of Order after Major Wars*. Princeton: Princeton University Press.

Ikenberry, G. John, ed. 2002. *America Unrivaled: The Future of the Balance of Power*. Ithaca: Cornell University Press.

Iliffe, John. 1979. *A Modern History of Tanganyika*. New York: Cambridge University Press.

International Institute for Strategic Studies. 2007. *The Military Balance 2007*. London: Routledge.

Iriye, Akira. 1993. *The Origins of the Second World War in Asia and the Pacific*. New York: Longman.

Jefferson, Thomas. 1975. *The Portable Thomas Jefferson*. Merrill Peterson, ed. New York: Penguin Books.

Jefferson, Thomas. 1984. *Writings*. Merrill D. Peterson, ed. New York: Library of America.

Jeffreys-Jones, Rhodri, and Bruce Collins, eds. 1983. *The Growth of Federal Power in American History*. DeKalb: Northern Illinois University Press.

Jankus, Alfred P., and Neil M. Malloy. 1956. *Venezuela: Land of Opportunity*. New York: Pageant Press.

Jensen, Merrill. 1962. *The New Nation: A History of the United States During the Confederation, 1781–1789*. New York: Knopf.

Jervis, Robert. 1976. *Perception and Misperception in International Politics*. Princeton: Princeton University Press.

Jervis, Robert. 1978. Cooperation under the Security Dilemma. *World Politics* 30: 168–214.

Jervis, Robert. 1989. *The Logic of Images in International Relations*. New York: Columbia University Press.

Jervis, Robert. 1997. *System Effects: Complexity in Political and Social Life*. Princeton: Princeton University Press.

Jervis, Robert. 1999. Realism, Neoliberalism, and Cooperation: Understanding the Debate. *International Security* 24: 42–63.

Jervis, Robert. 2005. *American Foreign Policy in a New Era*. New York: Routledge.

Joffe, Josef. 1984. Europe's American Pacifier. *Foreign Policy* 54: 64–82.

Joffe, Josef. 2002. Defying History and Theory: The United States as the "Last Remaining Superpower." In G. John Ikenberry, ed. *America Unrivaled: The Future of the Balance of Power*. Ithaca: Cornell University Press.

Joll, James. 1992. *The Origins of the First World War*. 2nd ed. New York: Longman.

Jones, Howard. 2010. *Blue and Gray Diplomacy: A History of the Union and Confederate Foreign Relations*. Chapel Hill: University of North Carolina Press.

Jones, Seth. 2003. The European Union and the Security Dilemma. *Security Studies* 12: 114–156.

Jones, Seth. 2007. *The Rise of European Security Cooperation*. New York: Cambridge University Press.

Jupille, Joseph. 2004. *Procedural Politics: Issues, Influence, and Institutional Choice in the European Union*. New York: Cambridge University Press.

Juvenal. 1967. *The Sixteen Satires*. Peter Green, trans. New York: Penguin.

Kagan, Donald. 1962. *The Decline and Fall of the Roman Empire: Why Did It Collapse?* Boston: Heath.

Kagan, Donald. 1995. *On the Origins of War and the Preservation of Peace*. New York: Doubleday.

Kahl, Colin. 2006. *States, Scarcity, and Civil Strife in the Developing World*. Princeton: Princeton University Press.

Kalvoda, Josef. 1989. The Origins of Czechoslovakia. In Norman Stone and Eduard Strouhal, eds. *Czechoslovakia: Crossroads and Crises, 1918–1988*. New York: St. Martin's.

Kant, Immanuel. 1995. *Political Writings*. H. B. Nisbet, trans. New York: Cambridge University Press.

Kaplan, Irving, ed. 1978. *Tanzania: A Country Study*. Washington, DC: American University.

Karnes, Thomas. 1961. *The Failure of Union: Central America, 1824–1960*. Chapel Hill: University of North Carolina Press.

Katzenstein, Peter, ed. 1996. *The Culture of National Security*. New York: Columbia University Press.

Katzenstein, Peter, ed. 2005. *A World of Regions: Asia and Europe in the American Imperium*. Ithaca: Cornell University Press.

Katznelson, Ira, and Martin Shefter, eds. 2002. *Shaped by War and Trade: International Influences on American Political Development*. Princeton: Princeton University Press.

Kaufman, Stuart J., Richard Little, and William C. Wohlforth, eds. 2007. *The Balance of Power in World History*. New York: Palgrave.

Kaufmann, Chaim. 1996. Possible and Impossible Solutions to Ethnic War. In Michael Brown et al., eds. *Nationalism and Ethnic Conflict*. Cambridge: MIT Press.

Kaufmann, Chaim. 1999. When All Else Fails: Evaluating Populations Transfers and Partition as Solutions to Ethnic Conflict. In Barbara F. Walter and Jack Snyder, eds. *Civil Wars, Insecurity, and Intervention*. New York: Columbia University Press.

Kaufmann, Chaim, and Robert Pape. 1999. Explaining Costly International Moral Action: Britain's Sixty Year Campaign against the Atlantic Slave Trade. *International Organization* 53: 631–668.

Kaysen, Carl. 1990. Is War Obsolete? A Review Essay. *International Security* 14: 42–64.

Keck, Margaret, and Kathryn Sikkink. 1998. *Activists Beyond Borders: Advocacy Networks in International Politics*. Ithaca: Cornell University Press.

Keeley, Lawrence. 1997. *War Before Civilization: The Myth of the Peaceful Savage*. New York: Oxford University Press.

Keilhan, Wilhelm. 1944. *Norway in World History*. London: MacDonald.

Kennan, George Frost. 1954. *Realities of American Foreign Policy*. Princeton: Princeton University Press.

Kennan, George Frost. 1956. *Soviet-American Relations, 1917–1920: Volume I, Russia Leaves the War*. Princeton: Princeton University Press.

Kennan, George Frost. 1958. *Soviet-American Relations, 1917–1920: Volume 2, The Decision to Intervene*. Princeton: Princeton University Press.

Kennan, George Frost. 1967. *Memoirs, 1925–1950*. New York: Pantheon.

Kennan, George Frost. 1979. *The Decline of Bismarck's European Order: Franco-Russian Relations 1875–1890*. Princeton: Princeton University Press.

Kennan, George Frost. 1984. *American Diplomacy: Expanded Edition*. Chicago: University of Chicago Press.

Kennan, George Frost. 1993. *Around the Cragged Hill: A Personal and Political Philosophy*. New York: W.W. Norton.

Kennan, George Frost. 1996. *At a Century's Ending: Reflections 1982–1995*. New York: Norton.

Kennedy, Paul. 1987. *The Rise and Fall of the Great Powers*. New York: Vintage Books.

Kennedy, Craig, and Marshall Bouton. 2002. The Real Trans-Atlantic Gap. *Foreign Policy* 133: 70.

Keohane, Robert O. 1984. *After Hegemony*. Princeton: Princeton University Press.

Keohane, Robert O. 1986. *Neorealism and Its Critics*. New York: Columbia University Press.

Keohane, Robert, and Lisa Martin. 1998. The Promise of Institutionalist Theory. In Michael Brown et al., eds. *Theories of War and Peace*. Cambridge: MIT Press.

Keohane, Robert, and Joseph Nye. 1989. 2nd ed. *Power and Interdependence*. New York: Addison Wesley Longman.

Khoo, Kay Kim. 1987. *30 Years of Nationhood*. Kuala Lampur: Persatuan Muzium Malaysia.

King, Gary, Robert Keohane, and Sidney Verba. 1994. *Designing Social Inquiry: Scientific Inference in Qualitative Research*. Princeton: Princeton University Press.

Kinsbruner, Jay. 1973. *Chile: A Historical Interpretation*. New York: Harper and Row.

Kissinger, Henry. 1995. *Diplomacy*. New York: Touchstone Books.

Klein, Herbert S. 2003. *A Concise History of Bolivia*. New York: Cambridge University Press.

Knight, Frank H. 1982. *Freedom and Reform*. Indianapolis: Liberty Fund.

Knight, Frank H. 1997. *The Ethics of Competition*. New Brunswick: Transaction Publishers.

Kohn, Hans. 1953. *Pan-Slavism: Its History and Ideology*. Notre Dame: University of Notre Dame Press.

Kohn, Richard H. 1972. The Washington Administration's Decision to Crush the Whiskey Rebellion. *Journal of American History* 59: 567–584.

Kontos, Alkis. 1972. Success and Knowledge in Machiavelli. In Anthony Parel, ed. *The Political Calculus: Essays on Machiavelli's Philosophy*. Toronto: University of Toronto Press.

Krasner, Stephen. 1978. *Defending the National Interest: Raw Materials Investments and U.S. Foreign Policy*. Princeton: Princeton University Press.

Krasner, Stephen. 1999. *Sovereignty: Organized Hypocrisy*. Princeton: Princeton University Press.

Krasner, Stephen, ed. 1995. *International Regimes*. Ithaca: Cornell University Press.

Krasner, Stephen. 2004. Sharing Sovereignty: New Institutions for Collapsed and Failing States. *International Security* 29: 85–120.

Kumar, Radha. 1997. The Troubled History of Partition. *Foreign Affairs* 76: 22–34.

Kupchan, Charles A. 2002. *The End of the American Era: U.S. Foreign Policy and the Geopolitics of the Twenty-first Century*. New York: Knopf.

Kupchan, Charles A. 2004–2005. The Travails of Union: The American Experience and its Implications for Europe. *Survival* 46: 103–120.

Kupchan, Charles A. 2010. *How Enemies Become Friends: The Sources of Stable Peace*. Princeton: Princeton University Press.

Kuran, Timur. 1997. *Private Truths, Public Lies: The Social Consequences of Preference Falsification*. Cambridge: Harvard University Press.

Kurland, Philip B., and Ralph Lerner. 1987. *The Founder's Constitution*. 5 vols. Indianapolis: Liberty Fund.

Kydd, Andrew. 2000. Trust, Reassurance, and Cooperation. *International Organization* 54: 325–357.

Kydd, Andrew. 2005. *Trust and Mistrust in International Relations*. Princeton: Princeton University Press.

LaFeber, Walter. 1998. *The New Empire: An Interpretation of American Expansion, 1860–1898*. Ithaca: Cornell University Press.

Laibson, David. 1997. Golden Eggs and Hyperbolic Discounting. *Quarterly Journal of Economics* 112: 443–477.

Laitin, David D. 1995. Disciplining Political Science. *American Political Science Review* 89: 454–456.

Laitin, David D. 1998. *Identity in Formation: The Russian-Speaking Populations in the Near Abroad*. Ithaca: Cornell University Press.

Lake, David A. 1996. Anarchy, Hierarchy, and the Variety of International Relations. *International Organization* 50: 1–33.

Lake, David A. 1997. The Rise, Fall, and Future of the Russian Empire: A Theoretical Interpretation. In Karen Dawisha and Bruce Parrott, eds. *The End of Empire? The Transformation of the USSR in Comparative Perspective*. New York: M. E. Sharpe.

Lake, David A. 1999. *Entangling Relations*. Princeton: Princeton University Press.

Lake, David A. 2003. The New Sovereignty in International Relations. *International Studies Review* 5: 303–323.

Lake, David A. 2004. Hierarchy in International Relations: Authority, Sovereignty, and the New Structure of World Politics. Paper presented at the American Political Science Association Meeting, Chicago, September 2004.

Lake, David A.2009. *Hierarchy in International Relations*. Ithaca: Cornell University Press.

Langer, William L. 1928. Russia, the Straits Question and the Origins of the Balkan League, 1908–1912. *Political Science Quarterly* 43: 321–363.

Langton, John, and Mary Dietz. 1987. Machiavelli's Paradox: Trapping or Teaching the Prince. *American Political Science Review* 81: 1277–1288.

Laslovich, Michael J. 1993. The American Tradition: Federalism in the United States. In Michael Burgess and Alain-G. Gagnon. *Comparative Federalism and Federation: Competing Traditions and Future Directions.* New York: Harvester Wheatsheaf, chap. 11.

Lau, Albert. 1991. *The Malayan Union Controversy, 1942–1948.* New York: Oxford University Press.

Layne, Christopher. 2003. America as European Hegemon. *National Interest* 72: 17–29.

Layne, Christopher. 2005. The War on Terrorism and the Balance of Power: The Paradoxes of American Hegemony. In T. V. Paul, James Wirtz, and Michel Fortmann, eds. *Balance of Power: Theory and Practice in the Twenty-first Century.* Stanford: Stanford University Press.

Lee, Tommy, et al. 2002. *The Dirt.* New York: Harper Collins.

Leff, Carol Skalnik. 1988. *National Conflict in Czechoslovakia: The Making and Remaking of a State, 1918–1987.* Princeton: Princeton University Press.

Leff, Carol Skalnik. 1997. *The Czech and Solvak Republics: Nation Versus State.* Boulder, CO: Westview Press.

Lefort, Claude. 1972. *Le travail de l'oeuvre Machiavel.* Paris: Gallimard.

Legro, Jeffrey W. 2005. *Rethinking the World: Great Power Strategies and International Orders.* Ithaca: Cornell University Press.

Leifer, Michael. 1989. *ASEAN and the Security of South-East Asia.* New York: Routledge.

Lenin, V. I. 1989. *Imperialism: The Highest Stage of Capitalism.* New York: International Publishers.

Lerner, Daniel, and Raymond Aron, eds. 1957. *France Defeats the EDC.* New York: Praeger.

Levy, Jack. 1992a. An Introduction to Prospect Theory. *Political Psychology* 13: 171 186.

Levy, Jack. 1992b. Prospect Theory and International Relations: Theoretical Applications and Analytical Problems. *Political Psychology* 13: 283–310.

Levy, Jack. 1994. Learning and Foreign Policy: Sweeping a Conceptual Minefield. *International Organization* 48: 279–312.

Levy, Jack. 2004. What Do Great Powers Balance Against and When? In T. V. Paul, James Wirtz, and Michel Fortmann, eds. *Balance of Power: Theory and Practice in the Twenty-first Century.* Stanford: Stanford University Press.

Levy, Leonard W., ed. 1987. *Essays on the Making of the Constitution.* New York: Oxford University Press.

Liberman, Peter. 1996. *Does Conquest Pay?* Princeton: Princeton University Press.

Lieuwen, Edwin. 1961. *Venezuela.* New York: Oxford University Press.

Lincoln, Abraham. 1992. *Selected Speeches and Writings.* New York: Library of America.

Lindberg, Leon, and Stuart Scheingold. 1970. *Europe's Would-Be Polity: Patterns of Change in the European Community.* Englewood Cliffs, NJ: Prentice Hall.

Lindberg, Leon, and Stuart Scheingold, eds. 1971. *Regional Integration: Theory and Research.* Cambridge: Harvard University Press.

Lindberg, Tod ed. 2005. *Beyond Paradise and Power: Europe, America, and the Future of a Troubled Partnership.* New York: Routledge.

Linz, Juan, and Alfred Stepan. 1996. *Problems of Democratic Transition and Consolidation.* Baltimore, MD: Johns Hopkins University Press.

Lippmann, Walter. 1963. *The Essential Walter Lippmann: A Political Philosophy for Liberal Democracy.* Clinton Rossiter and James Lare, eds. New York: Random House.

Lippmann, Walter. 1997. *Public Opinion.* New York: Free Press.

Lippmann, Walter. 1999. *The Phantom Public.* New Brunswick: Transactions Publishers.

Listowel, Judith. 1965. *The Making of Tanganyika.* New York: London House & Maxwell.

Livy, Titus. 1971. *The Early History of Rome.* Aubrey de Selincourt, trans. New York: Penguin Books.

Livy, Titus. 1982. *Rome and Italy.* Betty Radice, trans. New York: Penguin Books.

Livy, Titus. 1972. *The War with Hannibal.* Aubrey de Selincourt, trans. New York: Penguin Books.

Livy, Titus. 1976. *Rome and the Mediterranean.* Henry Bettenson, trans. New York: Penguin Books.

Lofchie, Michael F. 1965. *Zanzibar: Background to Revolution.* Princeton: Princeton University Press.

Lott, Leo B. 1972. *Venezuela and Paraguay: Political Modernity and Tradition in Conflict.* New York: Holt, Rinehart, and Winston.

Loveman, Brian. 2001. *Chile: The Legacy of Hispanic Capitalism.* 3rd ed. New York: Oxford University Press.

Luard, Evan. 1987. *War in International Society.* New Haven: Yale University Press.

Lucan. 1999. *Civil War.* Susan Braund, trans. New York: Oxford University Press.

Lundestad, Geir. 1998. *"Empire" by Integration: The United States and European Integration, 1945–1997.* New York: Oxford University Press.

Lundestad, Geir. 2005. *The United States and Western Europe since 1945.* New York: Oxford University Press.

Lunn, Arnold. 1952. *The Cradle of Switzerland.* London: Hollis and Carter.

Luxemburg, Rosa. 1977. *The Russian Revolution and Leninism or Marxism?* Bertram D. Wolfe, ed. Ann Arbor: University of Michigan Press.

Lynn-Jones, Sean M. 1995. Offense-Defense Theory and Its Critics. *Security Studies* 4: 660–691.

MacDonald, Alexander. 1966. *Tanzania: Young Nation in a Hurry.* New York: Hawthorn Publishers.

MacDonald, Paul K. 2003. Useful Fiction or Miracle Maker: The Competing Epistemological Foundations of Rational Choice Theory. *American Political Science Review* 97: 551–563.

MacDonald, Paul K., and David Lake. 2008. Correspondence: The Role of Hierarchy in International Politics. *International Security* 32: 171–180.

Macfarland, Joseph C. 1999. Machiavelli's Imagination of Excellent Men: An Appraisal of the Lives of Cosimo de' Medici and Castruccio Castracani. *American Political Science Review* 93: 133–146.

MacFarlane, Alan. 1979. *The Origins of English Individualism.* New York: Cambridge University Press.

Mackay, Christopher S. 2004. *Ancient Rome: A Military and Political History.* New York: Cambridge University Press.

Mackinder, Halford J. 1904. The Geographical Pivot of History. *The Geographical Journal* 23: 421–437.

Machiavelli, Niccolo. 1961. *The Letters of Machiavelli*. Allen Gilbert, ed. New York: Capricorn.

Machiavelli, Niccolo. 1988. *Florentine Histories*. Laura Banfield and Harvey Mansfield, trans. Princeton: Princeton University Press.

Machiavelli, Niccolo. 1996. *Discourses on Livy*. Harvey Mansfield and Nathan Tarcov, trans. Chicago: University of Chicago Press.

Machiavelli, Niccolo. 1998. *The Prince*. Harvey Mansfield, trans. Chicago: University of Chicago Press.

Machiavelli, Niccolo. 2003a. *Art of War*. Christopher Lynch, trans. Chicago: University of Chicago Press.

Machiavelli, Niccolo. 2003b. *The Life of Castruccio Castracani*. Andrew Brown, trans. London: Hesperus.

MacKenzie, Harriet D. S. 1899. *Switzerland*. New York: Werner Company.

Madison, James, Jr. 1999. *Writings*. Jack Rakove, ed. New York: Library of America.

Mahan, A. T. 1987. *The Influence of Sea Power Upon History, 1660–1783*. New York: Dover Publications.

Mahapatra, Chintamani. 1990. *The American Role in the Origin and Growth of ASEAN*. New Delhi: ABC Publishing House.

Maier, Charles S. 1997. *Dissolution: The Crisis of Communism and the End of East Germany*. Princeton: Princeton University Press.

Main, Jackson Turner. 1964. *The Antifederalists: Critics of the Constitution, 1781–1788*. Chicago: Quadrangle Books.

Main, Jackson Turner. 1965. *The Social Structure of Revolutionary America*. Princeton: Princeton University Press.

Mametey, Victor S., and Radomir Luza, eds. 1973. *The History of the Czechoslovak Republic*. Princeton: Princeton University Press.

Manin, Bernard. 1997. *The Principles of Representative Government*. New York: Cambridge University Press.

Mansfield, Edward D., and Helen Milner, eds. 1997. *The Political Economy of Regionalism*. New York: Columbia University Press.

Mansfield, Edward D., and Brian M. Pollins, eds. 2003. *Economic Interdependence and International Conflict: New Perspectives on an Enduring Debate*. Ann Arbor: University of Michigan Press.

Mansfield, Harvey C. 1979. *Machiavelli's New Modes and Orders*. Chicago: University of Chicago Press.

Marks, Frederick W., III. 1973. *Independence on Trial: Foreign Affairs and the Making of the Constitution*. Baton Rouge: Louisiana State University Press.

Marks, Gary. 1997. A Third Lens: Comparing European Integration and State Building. In Jytte Klausen and Louise Tilly, eds. *European Integration in Social and Historical Perspective: 1850 to the Present*. New York: Rowman and Littlefield.

Marks, Gary, and Marco Steenbergen, eds. 2004. *European Integration and Political Conflict*. New York: Cambridge University Press.

Marshall, John. 2000. *The Life of George Washington*. Robert Faulkner and Paul Carrese, eds. Indianapolis: Liberty Fund.

Marsland, Amy L., and William D. Marsland. 1954. *Venezuela Through Its History*. New York: Thomas Crowell Co.

Martelli, Mario. 1999. *Saggio Sul Principe*. Rome: Salerno Editrice.

Martin, William. 1931. *A History of Switzerland*. London: Grant Richards.

Marx, Anthony W. 1998. *Making Race and Nation*. New York: Cambridge University Press.

Marx, Karl. 1978. *The Marx-Engels Reader*. 2nd ed. Robert C. Tucker, ed. New York: Norton.

Masur, Gerhard. 1969. *Simon Bolivar*. Albuquerque: University of New Mexico Press.

Mattli, Walter. 1999. *The Logic of Regional Integration: Europe and Beyond*. New York: Cambridge University Press.

McCormick, John P. 2003. Machiavelli Against Republicanism: On the Cambridge School's "Guicciardinian Moments." *Political Theory* 31: 615–643.

McCrackan, W. D. 1901. *The Rise of the Swiss Republic*. 2nd ed. New York: Holt.

McCullough, David. 2002. *John Adams*. New York: Touchstone Books.

McDonald, Forrest. 1979. *E Pluribus Unum: The Formation of the American Republic, 1776–1790*. Indianapolis: Liberty Fund.

McDougall, Walter A. 2004. *Freedom Just Around the Corner: A New American History, 1585–1828*. New York: Harper Collins.

McDougall, Walter A. 2008. *Throes of Democracy: The American Civil War Era, 1829–1877*. New York: Harper Collins.

McInnes, Colin, ed. 1992. *Security and Strategy in the New Europe*. New York: Routledge.

McNeill, William. 1984. *The Pursuit of Power*. Chicago: University of Chicago Press.

Mead, Walter R. 2001. *Special Providence: American Foreign Policy and How It Changed the World*. New York: Knopf.

Mearsheimer, John J. 1998a. Back to the Future: Instability in Europe After the Cold War. In Michael Brown et al., eds. *Theories of War and Peace*. Cambridge: MIT Press.

Mearsheimer, John J. 1998b. The False Promise of International Institutions. In Michael Brown et al., eds. *Theories of War and Peace*. Cambridge: MIT Press.

Mearsheimer, John J. 2001a. *The Tragedy of Great Power Politics*. New York: W.W. Norton.

Mearsheimer, John J. 2001b. The Future of the American Pacifier. *Foreign Affairs* 80: 46–61.

Mearsheimer, John J. 2004. E.H. Carr vs. Idealism: The Battle Rages On. E. H. Carr Memorial Lecture, presented at Aberystwyth, England.

Meinecke, Friedrich. 1967. *The German Catastrophe: The Social and Historical Influences Which Led to the Rise and Ruin of Hitler and Germany*. Sidney Fay, trans. Boston: Beacon Press.

Meinecke, Friedrich. 1970. *Cosmopolitanism and the National State*. Robert Kimber, trans. Princeton: Princeton University Press.

Meinecke, Friedrich. 1977. *The Age of German Liberation, 1795–1815*. Peter Paret and Helmuth Fischer, trans. Berkeley: University of California Press.

Meinecke, Friedrich. 1998. *Machiavellism: The Doctrine of Raison D'état and Its Place in Modern History*. Douglas Scott, trans. New Brunswick: Transaction Publishers.

Menon, Anand, and Vincent Wright, eds. 2001. *From the Nation-State to Europe? Essays in Honor of Jack Hayward*. New York: Oxford University Press.

Menon, Anand, and Martin Shain. 2006. *Comparative Federalism: The European Union and the United States in Comparative Perspective*. New York: Oxford University Press.

Mercer, Jonathan. 1995. Anarchy and Identity. *International Organization* 49: 229–252.

Mercer, Jonathan. 1996. *Reputation and International Politics*. Ithaca: Cornell University Press.

Merrill, Dennis, and Thomas Paterson, eds. 2005. *Major Problems in American Foreign Relations: Volume 1: to 1920*. 6th ed. New York: Houghton Mifflin.

Merritt, Richard L. 1966. *Symbols of American Community, 1735–1775*. New Haven: Yale University Press.

Merritt, Richard L., and Bruce Russett, eds. 1981. *From National Development to Global Community: Essays in Honor of Karl Deutsch*. London: Allen & Unwin.

Micklethwait, John, and Adrian Wooldridge. 2003. *The Company: A Short History of a Revolutionary Idea*. New York: Modern Library.

Middlekauff, Robert. 1982. *The Glorious Cause: The American Revolution, 1763–1789*. New York: Oxford University Press.

Middleton, Richard. 1994. *Colonial America: A History, 1585–1776*. Second ed. Cambridge: Blackwell Publishers.

Middleton, John, and Jane Campbell. 1965. *Zanzibar: Its Society and Politics*. New York: Oxford University Press.

Migdal, Joel. 1988. *Strong Societies, Weak States*. Princeton: Princeton University Press.

Mill, John Stuart. 1991. *Considerations on Representative Government*. Amherst, NY: Prometheus Books.

Milner, Helen V. 1993. The Assumption of Anarchy in International Relations Theory: A Critique. In David Baldwin, ed. *Neorealism and Neoliberalism: The Contemporary Debate*. New York, Columbia University Press: 143–169.

Milner, Helen V. 1997. *Interests, Institutions, and Information: Domestic Politics and International Relations*. Princeton: Princeton University Press.

Miller, Harry. 1965. *The Story of Malaysia*. London: Faber and Faber.

Milward, Alan S. 1984. *The Reconstruction of Western Europe, 1945–51*. Los Angeles: University of California Press.

Ministry of Information, United Republic of Tanzania. 1968. *Tanzania Today*. Nairobi, Kenya: United Press of Africa.

Minot, George R. 1970. *The History of the Insurrections in Massachusetts in the Year Seventeen Hundred and Eighty Six and the Rebellion Consequent Thereon*. 2nd ed. Freeport, NY: Books for Libraries Press.

Mitrany, David. 1948. The Functional Approach to World Organization. *International Affairs* 24: 350–363.

Mitrany, David. 1966. *A Working Peace System*. Hans J. Morgenthau, introduction. Chicago: Quadrangle Books.

Mitrany, David. 1971. The Functional Approach in Historical Perspective. *International Affairs* 47: 532–543.

Mitrany, David. 1975. *The Functional Theory of Politics*. New York: St. Martin's Press.

Mommsen, Wolfgang. 1982. *Theories of Imperialism*. P. S. Falla, trans. Chicago: University of Chicago Press.

Montaigne. 1991. *The Complete Essays*. M. A. Screech, trans. New York: Penguin.

Monten, Jonathan. 2006. Thucydides and Modern Realism. *International Studies Quarterly* 50: 3–25.

Montesquieu, Charles de Secondat, Baron de. 1965. *Considerations on the Causes of the Greatness of the Romans and Their Decline*. David Lowenthal, trans. Indianapolis: Hackett Publishing.

Montesquieu, Charles de Secondat, Baron de. 1993. *The Persian Letters*. C. J. Betts, trans. New York: Penguin Books.

Montesquieu, Charles de Secondat, Baron de. 1995. *The Spirit of the Laws*. Anne Cohler, Basia Miller, and Harold Stone, trans. New York: Cambridge University Press.

Moore, Barrington. 1993. *Social Origins of Dictatorship and Democracy: Lord and Peasant in the Making of the Modern World*. Boston: Beacon Press.

Moore, William E., and Melvin M. Tumin. 1949. Some Social Functions of Ignorance. *American Sociological Review* 14: 787–795.

Morales, Waltraud Q. 2003. *A Brief History of Bolivia*. New York: Facts on File.

Moravcsik, Andrew. 1997. Taking Preferences Seriously: A Liberal Theory of International Politics. *International Organization* 51: 513–553.

Moravcsik, Andrew. 1998. *The Choice for Europe: Social Purpose and State Power from Messina to Maastricht*. Ithaca: Cornell University Press.

Moravcsik, Andrew. 1999. A New Statecraft? Entrepreneurs and International Cooperation. *International Organization* 53: 267–306.

Moravcsik, Andrew. 2008. The Myth of Europe's Democratic Deficit. *Intereconomics: Journal of European Public Policy* (Nov./Dec.): 331–340.

Moravcsik, Andrew. 1 August 2009. Europe Defies the Skeptics: How Crisis Will Make the EU Stronger. *Newsweek*. Available at: http://www.newsweek.com/2009/07/31/europe-defies-the-skeptics.html. Accessed May 15, 2010.

Moravcsik, Andrew, and Frank Schimmelpfennig. 2009. Liberal Intergovernmentalism. In Antje Wiener and Thomas Diez, eds. *European Integration Theory*. New York: Oxford University Press.

Morgan, Edmund. 1956. *The Birth of the Republic, 1763–89*. Chicago: University of Chicago Press.

Morgan, Edmund. 1989. *Inventing the People: The Rise of Popular Sovereignty in England and America*. New York: W. W. Norton.

Morgan, Glyn. 2005. *The Idea of a European Superstate: Public Justification and European Integration*. Princeton: Princeton University Press.

Morgenthau, Hans J. 1993. *Politics among Nations: The Struggle for Power and Peace*. New York: McGraw Hill.

Mueller, John. 2004. *The Remnants of War*. Ithaca: Cornell University Press.

Mueller, John. 2006. *Overblown*. New York: Free Press.

Nadel, S. F. 1965. *The Theory of Social Structure*. London: Cohen and West.

Nadon, Christopher. 1996. From Republic to Empire: Political Revolution and the Common Good in Xenophon's *Education of Cyrus*. *American Political Science Review* 90: 361–374.

Najemy, John. 1982. Machiavelli and the Medici: The Lessons of Florentine History. *Renaissance Quarterly* 35: 551–576.

Najemy, John. 1993. *Between Friends: Discourses of Power and Desire in the Machiavelli-Vettori Letters of 1513–1515*. Princeton: Princeton University Press.

Najemy, John. 1996. Baron's Machiavelli and Renaissance Republicanism. *American Historical Review* 101: 119–129.

Nevins, Allan. 1927. *The American States: During and After the Revolution, 1775–1789*. New York: Macmillan.

Newell, W. R. 1988. Machiavelli and Xenophon on Princely Rule: A Double-Edged Encounter. *Journal of Politics* 50: 108–130.

Newman, Michael. 1996. *Democracy, Sovereignty, and the European Union*. New York: St. Martin's Press.

Newman, Paul D. 2004. *Fries' Rebellion: The Enduring Struggle for the American Revolution*. Philadelphia: University of Pennsylvania Press.

Niebuhr, Reinhold. 1959. *The Structure of Nations and Empires*. New York: Charles Scribner's Sons.

Niebuhr, Reinhold. 1972. *The Children of Light and the Children of Darkness*. New York: Charles Scribner's Sons.

Niebuhr, Reinhold. 1986. *The Essential Reinhold Niebuhr: Selected Essays and Addresses*. Robert Brown, ed. New Haven: Yale University Press.

Niebuhr, Reinhold. 2001. *Moral Man and Immoral Society*. Louisville: Westminster John Knox Press.

Nietzsche, Friedrich. 1980. *On the Advantage and Disadvantage of History for Life*. Peter Preuss, trans. Indianapolis: Hackett Publishing.

Nietzsche, Friedrich. 1989a. *Beyond Good and Evil: Prelude to a Philosophy of the Future*. Walter Kaufmann, trans. New York: Vintage Books.

Nietzsche, Friedrich. 1989b. *On the Genealogy of Morals and Ecce Homo*. Walter Kaufmann, trans. New York: Vintage Books.

Niou, Emerson, and Peter Ordeshook. 1998. Alliances Versus Federations: An Extension of Riker's Analysis of Federal Formation. *Constitutional Political Economy* 9: 271–288.

Nkrumah, Kwame. 1963. *Africa Must Unite*. New York: Frederick A. Praeger.

Nkrumah, Kwame. 1973. *Autobiography of Kwame Nkrumah*. London: Panaf Books.

Nordland, K. 1905. *The Swedish-Norwegian Union Crisis*. Stockholm: Almquist & Wiksell.

North, Douglass C. 1961. *The Economic Growth of the United States, 1790–1860*. Englewood Cliffs, NJ: Prentice-Hall, Inc.

North, Douglass C. 1999. *Institutions, Institutional Change and Economic Performance*. New York: Cambridge University Press.

Nugent, Neill. 1999. *The Government and Politics of the European Union*. 4th ed. Durham: Duke University Press.

Nussbaum, Martha C. 1999. *Sex and Social Justice*. New York: Oxford University Press.

Nye, Joseph S., Jr. 1965. *Pan Africanism and East African Integration*. Cambridge: Harvard University Press.

Nye, Joseph S., Jr., ed. 1968. *International Regionalism: Readings*. Boston: Little, Brown.

Nyerere, Julius. 1967. *Freedom and Unity*. New York: Oxford University Press.

Nyerere, Julius. 1978. *Crusade for Liberation*. New York: Oxford University Press.

Nyong'o, Anyang.' 1990. *Regional Integration in Africa: Unfinished Agenda*. Kenya: Academy Science Publishers.

Oakley, Stewart. 1966. *A Short History of Sweden*. New York: Frederick Praeger.

Ober, Josiah. 1989. *Mass and Elite in Democratic Athens*. Princeton: Princeton University Press.

Ober, Josiah. 1998. *Political Dissent in Democratic Athens: Intellectual Critics of Popular Rule*. Princeton: Princeton University Press

Okello, John. 1973. *Revolution in Zanzibar*. Nairobi, Kenya: Afropress.

O'Leary, Brendan. 2003. What States Can Do with Nations: An Iron Law of Nationalism and Federation? In T. V. Paul, G. John Ikenberry, and John Hall, eds. *The Nation-State in Question*. Princeton: Princeton University Press.

Olschki, Leonardo. 1945. *Machiavelli the Scientist*. Berkeley, CA: Gillick Press.

Olson, Mancur. 1965. *The Logic of Collective Action*. Cambridge: Harvard University Press.

Olson, Mancur, and Richard Zeckhauser. 1966. An Economic Theory of Alliances. *The Review of Economics and Statistics* 48: 266–279.

Oneal, John. 1990. Theory of Collective Action and Burden Sharing in NATO. *International Organization* 44: 379–402.

Ongkili, James P. 1985. *Nation-building in Malaysia, 1946–1974*. New York: Oxford University Press.

O'Niell, Barry. 2001. *Honor, Symbols, and War*. Ann Arbor: Michigan University Press.

Onuf, Nicholas G. 1998. *The Republican Legacy in International Thought*. New York: Cambridge University Press.

Onuf, Peter. 1983. *The Origins of the Federal Republic: Jurisdictional Controversies in the United States 1775–1787*. Philadelphia: University of Pennsylvania Press.

Onuf, Peter, and Nicholas Onuf. 1993. *Federal Union, Modern World: The Law of Nations in an Age of Revolutions, 1776–1814*. Madison: Madison House.

Osterweis, Rollin G. 1949. *Romanticism and Nationalism in the Old South*. New Haven: Yale University Press.

Ostrom, Elinor. 1999. *Governing the Commons: The Evolution of Institutions for Collective Action*. New York: Cambridge University Press.

Ostrom, Vincent. 1991. *The Meaning of American Federalism: Constituting a Self-Governing Society*. San Francisco: Institute for Contemporary Studies Press.

Owens, R. J. 1963. *Peru*. New York: Oxford University Press.

Oye, Kenneth A., ed. 1986. *Cooperation Under Anarchy*. Princeton: Princeton University Press.

Page, Benjamin, and Robert Y. Shapiro. 1992. *The Rational Public*. Chicago: University of Chicago Press.

Paine, Thomas. 1985. *Rights of Man*. New York: Penguin Books.

Paine, Thomas. 1986. *Common Sense*. New York: Penguin Books.

Pape, Robert A. 1996. *Bombing to Win: Air Power and Coercion in War*. Ithaca: Cornell University Press.

Pape, Robert A. 1997. Why Economic Sanctions Do Not Work. *International Organization* 22: 90–136.

Parra-Perez, Caracciolo. 1928. *Bolivar: A Contribution to the Study of His Political Ideas*. Nels Andrew Nelson Cleven, trans. Paris: Editions Excelsior

Parent, Joseph M. 2005. Machiavelli's Missing Romulus and the Murderous Intent of *The Prince*. *History of Political Thought* 26: 625–645.

Parent, Joseph M. 2007. Institutions Identity and Unity: The Anomaly of Australian Nationalism. *Studies in Ethnicity and Nationalism* 7: 2–28.

Parent, Joseph M. 2009a. Duelling and the Abolition of War. *Cambridge Review of International Affairs* 22: 281–300.

Parent, Joseph M. 2009b. Europe's Structural Idol: An American Federalist Republic? *Political Science Quarterly* 124: 513–535.

Parent, Joseph M. 2010. Publius's Guile and the Paranoid Style. *Public Integrity* 12: 219–237.

Parent, Joseph M., and Joseph Bafumi. 2008. Correspondence: Of Polarity and Polarization. *International Security* 33: 170–172.

Parent, Joseph M., and Emily Erikson. 2009. Anarchy, Hierarchy and Order. *Cambridge Review of International Affairs* 22: 129–145.

Parker, Geoffrey. 2001. *The Military Revolution: Military Innovation and the Rise of the West 1500–1800*. New York: Cambridge University Press.

Parodi, Carlos. 2002. *The Politics of South American Boundaries*. London: Praeger.

Parsons, Craig. 2003. *A Certain Idea of Europe*. Ithaca: Cornell University Press.

Pearce, Jennifer. 1990. *Colombia: Inside the Labyrinth*. Nottingham, England: Latin America Bureau.

Peirce, Charles S. 1998. *The Essential Writings*. Edward C. Moore, ed. New York: Prometheus Books.

Pencak, William. 1989. Samuel Adams and Shays's Rebellion. *New England Quarterly* 62: 63–74.

Pencak, William, Matthew Dennis, and Simon P. Newman, eds. 2002. *Riot and Revelry in Early America*. University Park: Pennsylvania State University Press.

Perkins, Bradford. 1961. *Prologue to War*. Berkeley: University of California Press.

Pincus, Steve. 2009. *1688: The First Modern Revolution*. New Haven: Yale University Press.

Pitkin, Hanna. 1984. *Fortune Is a Woman: Gender and Politics in the Thought of Niccolo Machiavelli*. Berkeley: University of California Press.

Planta, Joseph. 1807. *The History of the Helvetic Confederacy*. 2nd ed. 2 vols. London: John Stockdale.

Plato. 1991. *The Republic*. Allan Bloom, trans. Chicago: University of Chicago Press.

Plutarch. 1992. *The Lives of the Noble Grecians and Romans*. 2 vols. Dryden trans. New York: Modern Library.

Pocock, J. G. A. 2003. *The Machiavellian Moment: Florentine Political Thought and the Atlantic Republican Tradition*. Princeton: Princeton University Press.

Pocock, J. G. A., ed. 1980. *Three British Revolutions: 1641, 1688, 1776*. Princeton: Princeton University Press.

Poe, D. Z. 2003. *Kwame Nkrumah's Contribution to Pan-Africanism: An Afrocentric Analysis*. New York: Routledge.

Pois, Robert. 1972. *Friedrich Meinecke and German Politics in the Twentieth Century*. Berkeley: University of California Press.

Pollack, Mark A. 2003. *The Engines of European Integration: Delegation, Agency, and Agenda Setting in the EU*. New York: Oxford University Press.

Polybius. 1922. *The Histories*. Vol. I. W. R. Paton, trans. Cambridge: Harvard University Press.

Polybius. 1979. *The Rise of the Roman Empire*. Ian Scott-Kilvert, trans. New York: Penguin Books.

Polybius. 2000. *The Histories*. Vol. VI. W. R. Paton, trans. Cambridge: Harvard University Press.

Porter, Bruce D. 1994. *War and the Rise of the State: The Military Foundations of Modern Politics*. New York: Free Press.

Posen, Barry. 1984. *The Sources of Military Doctrine*. Ithaca: Cornell University Press.

Posen, Barry. 1993a. Nationalism, the Mass Army, and Military Power. *International Security* 18: 80–124.

Posen, Barry. 1993b. The Security Dilemma and Ethnic Conflict. *Survival* 35: 27–47.

Posen, Barry. 2006. European Union Security and Defense Policy: Response to Unipolarity? *Security Studies* 15: 149–186.

Posner, Daniel N. 2005. *Institutions and Ethnic Politics in Africa*. New York: Cambridge University Press.

Posner, Eric A. 2002. *Law and Social Norms*. Cambridge: Harvard University Press.

Posner, Richard A. 1983. *The Economics of Justice*. Cambridge: Harvard University Press.

Posner, Richard A. 1996. *Overcoming Law*. Cambridge: Harvard University Press.

Posner, Richard A. 1999. *The Problematics of Moral and Legal Theory*. Cambridge: Harvard University Press.

Posner, Richard A. 2001. *Public Intellectuals: A Study of Decline*. Cambridge: Harvard University Press.

Postrel, Virginia. 30 December 2004. The Consequences of the 1960's Race Riots Come into View. *New York Times*, C2.

Powell, Robert. 1996a. Stability and the Distribution of Power. *World Politics* 48: 239–267.

Powell, Robert. 1996b. Uncertainty, Shifting Power, and Appeasement. *American Political Science Review* 90: 749–764.

Powell, Robert. 2004. The Inefficient Use of Power: Costly Conflict with Complete Information. *American Political Science Review* 98: 231–241.

Press, Daryl. 2005. *Calculating Credibility: How Leaders Assess Military Threats*. Ithaca: Cornell University Press.

Price, Russell. 1977. The Theme of *Gloria* in Machiavelli. *Renaissance Quarterly* 30: 588–631.

Pufendorf, Samuel. 1998. *On the Duty of Man and Citizen*. Michael Silverthorne, trans. New York: Cambridge University Press.

Pufendorf, Samuel. 2002. *The Divine Feudal Law: Or, Covenants with Mankind, Represented*. Theophilus Dorrington, trans. Simone Zarbuchen, ed. Indianapolis: Liberty Fund.

Putnam, Robert. 1988. Diplomacy and Domestic Politics: The Logic of Two-Level Games. *International Organization* 42: 427–460.

Purcell, Victor. 1965. *Malaysia*. London: Thames and Hudson.

Quester, George. 1988. Crises and the Unexpected. In Robert Rotberg and Theodore Rabb, eds. *The Origin and Prevention of Major Wars*. New York: Cambridge University Press.

Rakove, Jack. 1996. *Original Meanings*. New York: Vintage Books.

Rakove, Jack. 2003. Europe's Floundering Fathers. *Foreign Policy* 138: 28–38.

Ray, Leonard and Gregory Johnston. 2007. European Anti-Americanism and Choices for a European Defense Policy. *Political Science and Politics* 40: 86.

Rector, Chad. 2003. Federations in International Politics. Ph.D. diss.: University of California San Diego.

Rector, Chad. 2009. *Federations: The Political Dynamics of Cooperation*. Ithaca: Cornell University Press.

Rector, John. 2003. *The History of Chile*. Westport, CT: Greenwood Press.

Reinhard, Hilde. 1935. *Lorenzo von Medici, Herzog von Urbino*. Freiburg im Breisgau.

Richards, Leonard L. 2002. *Shays's Rebellion: The American Revolution's Final Battle*. Philadelphia: University of Pennsylvania Press.

Ridley, Jasper. 2001. *The Freemasons*. New York: Arcade Publishing.

Ridolfi, Roberto. 1963. *The Life of Niccolo Machiavelli*. Cecil Grayson, trans. Chicago: University of Chicago Press.

Rifkin, Jeremy. 2004. *The European Dream: How's Europe's Vision of the Future Is Quietly Eclipsing the American Dream*. New York: Tarcher/Penguin.

Riker, William. 1964. *Federalism: Origin, Operation, Significance*. Boston: Little, Brown.

Riker, William. 1975. *The Theory of Political Coalitions*. New Haven: Yale University Press.

Riker, William. 1987. *The Development of American Federalism*. Boston: Kluwer Academic Publishers.

Riker, William. 1996. *The Strategy of Rhetoric: Campaigning for the American Constitution*. New Haven: Yale University Press

Risjord, Norman K. 1978. *Chesapeake Politics, 1781–1800*. New York: Columbia University Press.

Risse-Kappen, Thomas. 1994. Ideas Do Not Float Freely: Transnational Coalitions, Domestic Structures, and the End of the Cold War. *International Organization* 48: 185–214.

Ritcheson, Charles R. 1969. *Aftermath of Revolution: British Policy Towards the United States, 1783–1795*. Dallas: Southern Methodist University Press.

Robertson, David Brian. 2005. Madison's Opponents and Constitutional Design. *American Political Science Review* 99: 225–243.

Rodman, Selden. 1967. *The Peru Traveler: A Concise History and Guide*. New York: Meredith Press.

Rodden, Jonathan, and Erik Wibbels. 2002. Beyond Fiction of Federalism: Macroeconomic Management in Multitiered Systems. *World Politics* 54: 494–531.

Rodden, Jonathan. 2006. *Hamilton's Paradox*. New York: Cambridge University Press.

Rodriguez O., Jaime E. 1998. *The Independence of Spanish America*. New York: Cambridge University Press.

Rodrik, Dani. How Far Will International Economic Integration Go? *The Journal of Economic Perspectives* 14: 177–186.

Roeder, Phillip G. 1991. Soviet Federalism and Ethnic Mobilization. *World Politics* 43: 196–232.

Rogowski, Ronald. 1995. The Role of Theory and Anomaly in Social-Scientific Inference. *American Political Science Review* 89: 467–470.

Rosato, Sebastian. 2003. The Flawed Logic of the Democratic Peace Theory. *American Political Science Review* 97: 585–602.

Rosato, Sebastian. 2011. *Europe United: Power Politics and the Making of the European Community*. Ithaca: Cornell University Press.

Rosecrance, Richard, and Arthur Stein eds. 1993. *The Domestic Bases of Grand Strategy*. Ithaca: Cornell University Press.

Rosen, Stephen Peter. 1991. Net Assessment as an Analytical Concept. In Andrew Marshall, J. J. Martin, and Henry Rowen, eds. *On Not Confusing Ourselves: Essays in Honor of Albert and Roberta Wohlstetter*. Boulder: Westview Press.

Ross, Robert, and Zhu Feng eds. 2008. *China's Ascent: Power, Security, and the Future of International Politics*. Ithaca: Cornell University Press.

Rotberg, Robert I., ed. 2004. *When States Fail: Causes and Consequences*. Princeton: Princeton University Press.

Rousseau, Jean Jacques. 1987. *The Basic Political Writings*. Donald Cress, trans. Indianapolis: Hackett.

Royster, Charles. 1981. *Light-Horse Harry Lee and the Legacy of the American Revolution*. New York: Knopf.

Russett, Bruce. 1993. *Grasping the Democratic Peace: Principles for a Post-Cold War World*. Princeton: Princeton University Press.

Ryan, N. J. 1967. *The Making of Modern Malaysia*. New York: Oxford University Press.

Ryan, N. J. 1976. *A History of Malaysia and Singapore*. New York: Oxford University Press.

Said, Edward. 1996. *Representations of the Intellectual*. New York: Vintage.

Sandholtz, Wayne. 1993. Choosing Union: Monetary Politics and Maastricht. *International Organization* 47: 1–39.

Santayana, George. 1954. *The Life of Reason, or The Phases of Human Progress*. Rev. ed. Daniel Cory, ed. New York: Charles Scribner's Sons.

Sasso, Gennaro. 1987. *Machiavelli e gli antichi e altri saggi*. 3 vols. Milan: Ricciardi.

Saxon, A. H. 1989. *P. T. Barnum: The Legend and the Man*. New York: Columbia University Press.

Scalapino, Robert, and Jusuf Wanandi, eds. 1982. *Economic, Political, and Security Issues in Southeast Asia in the 1980s*. Berkeley: Institute of East Asian Studies, University of California.

Scheingold, Stuart A. 1970. Domestic and International Consequences of Regional Integration. *International Organization* 24: 978–1002.

Schelling, Thomas C. 1960. *The Strategy of Conflict*. Cambridge: Harvard University Press.

Schelling, Thomas C. 1964. Strategy and Conscience. *American Economic Review* 54: 1082–1088.

Schelling, Thomas C. 1966. *Arms and Influence*. New Haven: Yale University Press.

Schelling, Thomas C. 1978a. *Micromotives and Macrobehavior*. New York: W. W. Norton.

Schelling, Thomas C. 1978b. Egonomics, or the Art of Self-Management. *American Economic Review* 68: 290–294.

Schelling, Thomas C. 1984a. *Choice and Consequence*. Cambridge: Harvard University Press.

Schelling, Thomas C. 1984b. Self-Command in Practice, in Policy, and in a Theory of Rational Choice. *American Economic Review* 74: 1–11.

Schelling, Thomas C. 1985. Enforcing Rules on Oneself. *Journal of Law, Economics, and Organization* 1: 357–383.

Schlesinger, Arthur M., Jr. 1999. *The Cycles of American History*. New York: Mariner Books.

Schmitt, Carl. 1996. *The Concept of the Political*. George Schwab, trans. Chicago: University of Chicago Press.

Schneider, Louis. 1962. The Role of Category and Ignorance in Sociological Theory: An Exploratory Statement. *American Sociological Review* 27: 492–508.

Schroeder, Paul W. 1994. *The Trasformation of European Politics, 1763–1848*. New York: Oxford University Press.

Schroeder, Paul W. 2004. *Systems, Stability, and Statecraft: Essays on the International History of Modern Europe*. New York: Palgrave.

Schultz, Kenneth A. 1998. Domestic Opposition and Signaling in International Crises. *American Political Science Review* 92: 829–843.

Schultz, Kenneth A. 1999. Do Democratic Institutions Constrain or Inform? Contrasting Two Institutional Perspectives on Democracy and War. *International Organization* 53: 233–266.

Schumpeter, Joseph A. 1976. *Capitalism, Socialism and Democracy*. New York: Harper & Row.

Schweller, Randall. 1995. Bandwagoning for Profit: Bringing the Revisionist State Back In. In Michael Brown et al., eds. *The Perils of Anarchy: Contemporary Realism and International Security*. Cambridge: MIT Press.

Schweller, Randall. 2004. Unanswered Threats: A Neoclassical Realist Theory of Underbalancing. *International Security* 29: 159–201.

Schwoerer, Lois G. 1974. *"No Standing Armies!" The Antiarmy Ideology in Seventeenth-Century England*. Baltimore: The Johns Hopkins University Press.

Scott, Franklin D. 1988. *Sweden: The Nation's History*. Enlarged ed. Carbondale: Southern Illinois University Press.

Scott, John. 1992. *Social Network Analysis: A Handbook*. New York: Sage.

Scott, John T., and Vickie B. Sullivan. 1994. Patricide and the Plot of *The Prince*: Cesare Borgia and Machiavelli's Italy. *American Political Science Review* 88: 887–900.

Sealey, Raphael. 1976. *A History of the Greek City States, 700–338 B.C.* Berkeley: University of California Press.

Shapiro, Ian, and Grant Reeher. 1988. *Power, Inequality, and Democratic Politics: Essays in Honor of Robert A. Dahl*. Boulder: Westview Press.

Sherwell, Guillermo. 1921. *Simon Bolivar: Patriot, Warrior, Statesman, Father of Five Nations*. Washington, DC: Byron Adams Press.

Sidjanski, Dusan. 2000. *The Federal Future of Europe: From the European Community to the European Union*. Ann Arbor: University of Michigan Press.

Sidney, Algernon. 1996. *Discourses Concerning Government*. Thomas West, ed. Indianapolis: Liberty Fund.

Sidwick, Henry. 1981. *The Methods of Ethics*. 7th ed. Indianapolis: Hackett Publishing.

Simmel, Georg. 1955. *Conflict and the Web of Group-Affiliations*. New York: Free Press.

Simmel, Georg. 1971. *On Individuality and Social Forms*. Donald Levine, ed. Chicago: University of Chicago Press.

Skocpol, Theda. 1979. *States and Social Revolutions*. New York: Cambridge University Press.

Slaughter, Thomas P. 1986. *The Whiskey Rebellion: Frontier Epilogue to the American Revolution*. New York: Oxford University Press.

Sleeper, R. W. 2001. *The Necessity of Pragmatism: John Dewey's Conception of Philosophy*. Chicago: University of Illinois Press.

Smith, Adam. 1976. *An Inquiry into the Nature and Causes of the Wealth of Nations*. Edwin Cannan ed. Chicago: University of Chicago Press.

Smith, Adam. 1980. The History of Astronomy. In W. Wightman, ed. *Essays on Philosophical Subjects*. Indianapolis: Liberty Fund.

Smith, Adam. 1982. *Lectures on Jurisprudence*. R. L. Meek, D. D. Raphael, and P. G. Stein, eds. Indianapolis: Liberty Fund.

Smith, Adam. 1984. *The Theory of Moral Sentiments*. D. D. Raphael and A. L. Macfie, eds. Indianapolis: Liberty Fund.

Smith, Jonathan. 1948. The Depression of 1785 and Daniel Shays' Rebellion. *William and Mary Quarterly* 5: 77–94.

Smith, Roy C. 2004. *Adam Smith and the Origins of American Enterprise*. New York: Truman Talley Books St. Martin's Griffin.

Smith, W. Roy. 1909. Sectionalism in Pennsylvania During the Revolution. *Political Science Quarterly* 24: 208–235.

Snyder, Jack. 1984. *The Ideology of the Offensive*. Ithaca: Cornell University Press.

Snyder, Jack. 1991a. *Myths of Empire: Domestic Politics and International Ambition*. Ithaca: Cornell University Press.

Snyder, Jack. 1991b. Civil Military Relations and the Cult of the Offensive, 1914 and 1984. In Steven Miller et al., eds. *Military Strategy and the Origins of the First World War*. Princeton: Princeton University Press, pp. 20–58.

Snyder, Jack. 2000. *From Voting to Violence: Democratization and Nationalist Conflict*. New York: W. W. Norton.

Snyder, Jack. 2002. Anarchy and Culture: Insights from the Anthropology of War. *International Organization* 56: 7–45.

Snyder, Jack, and Robert Jervis. 1999. Civil War and the Security Dilemma. In Barbara F. Walter and Jack Snyder, eds. *Civil Wars, Insecurity, and Intervention*. New York: Columbia University Press.

Solnick, Steven L. 1998. *Stealing the State: Control and Collapse in Soviet Institutions*. Cambridge: Harvard University Press.

Sprout, Harold, and Margaret Sprout. 1965. *The Ecological Perspective on Human Affairs*. Princeton: Princeton University Press.

Spruyt, Hendrik. 1994a. *The Sovereign State and Its Competitors*. Princeton: Princeton University Press.

Spruyt, Hendrik. 1994b. Institutional Selection in International Relations: State Anarchy as Order. *International Organization* 48: 527–557.

Spruyt, Hendrik. 2002. The Origins, Development, and Possible Decline of the Modern State. *Annual Review of Political Science* 5: 127–149.

Spruyt, Hendrik. 2005. *Ending Empire: Contested Sovereignty and Territorial Partition*. Ithaca: Cornell University Press.

Spykman, Nicholas J. 1965 [1925]. *The Social Theory of Georg Simmel*. New York: Atherton Press.

Stagg, Frank Noel. 1956. *East Norway and Its Frontier*. London: Allen & Unwin.

Stein, Arthur A. 1976. Conflict and Cohesion: A Review of the Literature. *Journal of Conflict Resolution* 20: 143–172.

Stein, Arthur A. 1983. Coordination and Collaboration: Regimes in an Anarchic World. In Steven Krasner, ed. *International Regimes* Ithaca: Cornell University Press.

Stein, Eric. 1997. *Czecho/Slovakia: Ethnic Conflict, Constitutional Fissure, Negotiated Breakup*. Ann Arbor: University of Michigan Press.

Steinberg, Jonathan. 1976. *Why Switzerland?* New York: Cambridge University Press.

Stephens, John N. 1983. *The Fall of the Florentine Republic, 1512–1530*. New York: Oxford University Press.

Stern, Fritz. 1987. *Dreams and Delusions: The Drama of German History*. New York: Knopf.

Stevens, Richard G. 1997. *The American Constitution and Its Provenance*. New York: Rowman and Littlefield Publishers.

Stigler, George. 1982. *The Economist as Preacher, and Other Essays*. Chicago: University of Chicago Press.

Stomberg, Andrew A. 1970. *A History of Sweden*. New York: AMS Press.

Stone Sweet, Alec, Wayne Sandholtz, and Neil Fligstein, eds. 2001. *The Institutionalization of Europe*. New York: Oxford University Press.

Strauss, Leo. 1978. *Thoughts on Machiavelli*. Chicago: University of Chicago Press.

Strauss, Leo. 1987. Machiavelli. In Leo Strauss and Joseph Cropsey, eds. *History of Political Philosophy*. 3rd ed. Chicago: University of Chicago Press.

Strotz, R. H. 1955. Myopia and Inconsistency in Dynamic Utility Maximization. *Review of Economic Studies* 23: 165–180.

Sullivan, Vickie B. 1996. *Machiavelli's Three Romes: Religion, Human Liberty, and Politics Reformed*. De Kalb: Northern Illinois University Press.

Sumner, William Graham. 1992. *On Liberty, Society, and Politics: The Essential Essays of William Graham Sumner*. Robert C. Bannister, ed. Indianapolis: Liberty Fund.

Sumner, William Graham. 1995. *What Social Classes Owe to Each Other*. Idaho: The Caxton Printers.

Sumner, William Graham. 2002. *Folkways: A Study of Mores, Manners, Customs, and Morals*. New York: Dover.

Sunstein, Cass R. 1993. *The Partial Constitution*. Cambridge: Harvard University Press.

Sunstein, Cass R. 1997. *Free Markets and Social Justice*. New York: Oxford University Press.

Sunstein, Cass R. ed. 2000. *Behavioral Law and Economics*. New York: Cambridge University Press.

Sutton, Michael. 2007. *France and the Construction of Europe, 1944–2007*. New York: Berghahn Books.

Swidler, Ann. 1986. Culture in Action: Symbols and Strategies. *American Sociological Review* 51: 273–286.

Swift, Jonathan. 1957. *Gulliver's Travels*. New York: Fine Editions Press.

Szatmary, David P. 1980. *Shays' Rebellion: The Making of an Agrarian Insurrection*. Amherst: University of Massachusetts Press.

Tacitus. 1942. *Complete Works of Tacitus*. Church and Brodripp, trans., Moses Hadas, ed. New York: The Modern Library.

Tajfel, Henri. 1981. *Human Groups and Social Categories*. New York: Cambridge University Press.

Talbott, Robert D. 1973. *A History of the Chilean Boundaries*. Ames: Iowa State University Press.

Tarcov, Nathan. 1982. Quentin Skinner's Method and Machiavelli's *Prince*. *Ethics* 92: 692–709.

Tarcov, Nathan. 2000. Machiavelli and the Foundations of Modernity: A Reading of Chapter 3 of *The Prince*. In Mark Blitz and William Kristol, eds. *Educating the Prince: Essays in Honor of Harvey Mansfield*. New York: Rowman and Littlefield.

Taylor, A. J. P. 1977. *The Struggle for Mastery in Europe 1848–1918*. New York: Oxford University Press.

Taylor, A. J. P. 1996. *The Origins of the Second World War*. New York: Touchstone.

Taylor, A. J. P. 2003. *Bismarck: The Man and the Statesman*. Glouchestershire: Sutton Publishing.

Taylor, R. H., ed. 1996. *The Politics of Elections in Southeast Asia*. New York: Cambridge Unviersity Press.

Thaden, Edward C. 1965. *Russia and the Balkan Alliance of 1912*. University Park: Pennsylvania State University Press.

Thaler, Richard H. 1994. *Quasi-Rational Economics*. New York: Russell Sage.

Thatcher, Margaret. 2002. *Statecraft: Strategies for a Changing World*. New York: Harper Perennial.

Thayer, Bradley. 2000. Bringing in Darwin: Evolutionary Theory, Realism, and International Politics. *International Security* 25: 124–151.

Thompson, W. Scott. 1969. *Ghana's Foreign Policy, 1957–1966*. Princeton: Princeton University Press.

Thucydides. 1982. *The Peloponnesian War*. Richard Crawley, trans. New York: the Modern Library.

Thucydides. 1998. *The Peloponnesian War*. Walter Blanco, trans. New York: W. W. Norton & Co.

Thürer, Georg. 1971. *Free and Swiss*. Coral Gables: University of Miami Press.

Tilly, Charles. 1984. *Big Structures, Large Processes, Huge Comparisons*. New York: Russell Sage Foundation.

Tilly, Charles. 1993. *Coercion, Capital, and European States, AD 990–1992*. Cambridge: Blackwell.

Tilly, Charles. 2003. *The Politics of Collective Violence*. New York: Cambridge University Press.

Timmons, Heather, and Eric Pfanner. August 17, 2006. Europe Says It Will Unify Effort in Fight on Terrorism. *New York Times*: A15.

Timothy, Bankole. 1981. *Kwame Nkrumah from Cradle to Grave*. Dorset: The Gavin Press.

de Tocqueville, Alexis. 1983. *The Old Regime and the French Revolution*. Stuart Gilbert, trans. New York: Anchor Books.

de Tocqueville, Alexis. 1988. *Democracy in America*. George Lawrence trans., J. P. Mayer, ed. New York: Harper & Row.

Toft, Monica Duffy. 2003. *Geography of Ethnic Violence*. Princeton: Princeton University Press.

Toner, Robin, and Jim Rutenberg. July 30, 2006. Partisan Divide on Iraq Exceeds Split on Vietnam. *New York Times* 155. A1.

Trachtenberg, Marc. 1991a. The Meaning of Mobilization in 1914. In Steven Miller et al., eds. *Military Strategy and the Origins of the First World War*. Princeton: Princeton University Press, pp. 195–225.

Trachtenberg, Marc. 1991b. *History and Strategy*. Princeton: Princeton University Press.

Trachtenberg, Marc. 1999. *A Constructed Peace: The Making of European Settlement, 1945–1963*. Princeton: Princeton University Press.

Trachtenberg, Marc. 2005. Preventive War and U.S. Foreign Policy. Manuscript: University of California, Los Angeles.

Treisman, Daniel. 2007. *The Architecture of Government: Rethinking Political Decentralization*. New York: Cambridge University Press.

Tuck, Richard. 2001. *The Rights of War and Peace: Political Thought and the International Order from Grotius to Kant*. New York: Oxford University Press.

Turnbull, C. Mary. 1989. *A History of Malaysia, Singapore, and Brunei*. London: Allen & Unwin.

Turner, Frederick Jackson. 1996. *The Frontier in American History*. New York: Dover.

Tyler, Mason W. 1917. The Balkan League. *American Journal of International Law* 11: 739–744.

United States Department of State. 1945. JCS 1067: Directive to Commander-in-Chief of United States Forces of Occupation Regarding the Military Government of Germany. Accessed June 1, 2010, at: usa.usembassy.de/etexts/ga3-450426.pdf.

United States Department of State. 1985 [1947]. JCS 1779. *Documents on Germany, 1944–1985.* Washington, DC: Government Printing Office.

Van Alstyne, Richard W. 1965. *Empire and Independence: The International History of the American Revolution.* New York: John Wiley and Sons.

Van Evera, Stephen. 1991. The Cult of the Offensive and the Origins of the First World War. In Steven Miller et al., eds. *Military Strategy and the Origins of the First World War.* Princeton: Princeton University Press, pp. 59–108.

Van Evera, Stephen. 1999. *Causes of War.* Ithaca: Cornell University Press.

Villari, Pasquale. 1968. *The Life and Times of Niccolo Machiavelli.* 3 vols. Linda Villari, trans. New York: Unwin.

Viroli, Maurizio. 1995. *For Love of Country.* New York: Oxford University Press.

Viroli, Maurizio. 2000. *Niccolo's Smile: A Biography of Machiavelli.* Anthony Shugaar, trans. New York: Farrar, Straus and Giroux.

Voltaire. 1990. Candide. In Roger Pearson, trans. *Candide and Other Stories.* New York: Oxford University Press.

Wallander, Celeste, Helga Haftendorn, and Robert Keohane, eds. 1999. *Imperfect Unions: Security Institutions over Time and Space.* New York: Oxford University Press.

Walt, Stephen M. 1987. *Origins of Alliances.* Ithaca: Cornell University Press.

Walt, Stephen M. 1996. *Revolution and War.* Ithaca: Cornell University Press.

Walt, Stephen M. 1998. The Ties that Fray: Why Europe and America Are Drifting Apart. *National Interest* 54: 3–11.

Walt, Stephen M. 1999. Rigor or Rigor Mortis? *International Security* 23: 5–48.

Walter, Barbara F. 1997. The Critical Barrier to Civil War Settlement. *International Organization* 51: 335–364.

Walter, Barbara F. 1999. Designing Transitions from Civil War. In Barbara F. Walter and Jack Snyder, eds. *Civil Wars, Insecurity, and Intervention.* New York: Columbia University Press.

Waltz, Kenneth N. 1959. *Man, the State and War.* New York: Columbia University Press.

Waltz, Kenneth N. 1970. The Myth of National Interdependence. In Charles P. Kindleberger, ed. *The International Corporation: A Symposium.* Cambridge: MIT Press.

Waltz, Kenneth N. 1979. *Theory of International Politics.* New York: McGraw Hill.

Waltz, Kenneth N. 1990. Realist Thought and Neorealist Theory. *Journal of International Affairs* 44: 21–37.

Walzer, Michael. 1992. *Just and Unjust Wars: A Moral Argument with Historical Illustrations.* 2nd ed. New York: Basic Books.

Ward, W. E. F. 1967. *A History of Ghana.* London: Allen and Unwin.

Warren, Joseph P. 1905. The Confederation and the Shays Rebellion. *American Historical Review* 11: 42–67.

Washington, George. 1997. *Writings.* John Rhodehamel, ed. New York: Library of America.

Watts, Duncan. 2008. *The European Union.* Edinburgh: Edinburgh University Press.

Weber, Katja. 1997. Hierarchy Amidst Anarchy: A Transaction Cost Approach to International Security Cooperation. *International Studies Quarterly* 41: 324–340.

Weber, Max. 1958. *From Max Weber: Essays in Sociology.* Gerth and Mills, trans. and ed. New York: Oxford University Press.

Weber, Max. 1964. *The Theory of Social and Economic Organization.* A. M. Henderson and Talcott Parsons, trans. New York: The Free Press.

Weber, Max. 1993. *The Sociology of Religion.* Ephraim Fischoff, trans. Boston: Beacon Press.

Weitsman, Patricia. 1997. Intimate Enemies: The Politics of Peacetime Alliances. *Security Studies* 7: 156–192.

Wendt, Alexander. 1999. *Social Theory of International Politics.* New York: Cambridge University Press.

Wendt, Alexander. 2003. Why a World State Is Inevitable. *European Journal of International Relations* 9: 491–542.

Whitaker, Arthur P. 1927. *The Spanish-American Frontier: 1783–1795, The Westward Movement and the Spanish Retreat in the Mississippi Valley.* Lincoln: University of Nebraska Press.

Whitfield, J. H. 1969. *Discourses on Machiavelli.* Cambridge: W. Heffer and Sons.

Williamson, Oliver E. 1983. *Markets and Hierarchies: Analysis and Antitrust Implications.* New York: Free Press.

Williamson, Oliver E. 1985. *The Economic Institutions of Capitalism.* New York: Free Press.

Williamson, Oliver E. 2000. The New Institutional Economics: Taking Stock, Looking Ahead. *Journal of Economics Literature* 38: 595–613.

Williamson, Oliver, and Sidney Winter, eds. 1991. *The Nature of the Firm: Origins, Evolution, and Development.* New York: Oxford University Press.

Winn, Neil, and Christopher Lord. 2001. *EU Foreign Policy beyond the Nation-State: Joint Actions and Institutional Analysis of the Common Foreign and Security Policy.* New York: Palgrave.

Wohlforth, William. 1993. *The Elusive Balance: Power and Perceptions during the Cold War.* Ithaca: Cornell University Press.

Wolfers, Arnold. 1991. *Discord and Collaboration: Essays on International Politics.* Baltimore: Johns Hopkins University Press.

Wood, Gordon. 1993. *The Radicalism of the American Revolution.* New York: Vintage.

Wood, Gordon. 1998. *The Creation of the American Republic, 1776–1787.* Chapel Hill: University of North Carolina Press.

Wood, Gordon. 2009. *Empire of Liberty: A History of the Early Republic, 1789–1815.* New York: Oxford University Press.

Wright, J. Leitch, Jr. 1975. *Britain and the American Frontier, 1783–1815.* Athens: University of Georgia Press.

Xenophon. 1972. *The Persian Expedition.* Rex Warner, trans. New York: Penguin Books.

Xenophon. 1979. *A History of My Times.* Rex Warner, trans. New York: Penguin Books.

Xenophon. 2001. *The Education of Cyrus.* Wayne Ambler, trans. Ithaca: Cornell University Press.

Yaeger, Roger. 1989. *Tanzania: An African Experiment.* 2nd ed. Boulder, CO: Westview Press.

Young, Oran. 1989. *International Cooperation: Building Regimes for Natural Resources and the Environment.* Ithaca: Cornell University Press.

Zakaria, Fareed. 1998. *From Wealth to Power: The Unusual Origins of America's World Role.* Princeton: Princeton University Press.

Zelikow, Philip, and Condoleezza Rice. 1995. *Germany Unified and Europe Transformed: A Study of Statecraft.* Cambridge: Harvard University Press.

Ziblatt, Daniel. 2004. Rethinking the Origins of Federalism: Puzzle, Theory, and Evidence from Nineteenth Century Europe. *World Politics* 57: 70–98.

Zweifel, Thomas D. 2002. *Democratic Deficit? Institutions and Regulation in the European Union, Switzerland, and the United States.* New York: Lexington Books.

INDEX